GW00599415

ROOFS AND ROOTS

Roofs and Roots

The Care of Separated Children in the Developing World

David Tolfree

Save the Children Ϯ

arena

Copyright © The Save the Children Fund 1995

All rights reserved. No part of this publication may be reproduced, stored in a retrieval system, or transmitted in any form or by any means, electronic, mechanical, photocopying, recording or otherwise, without the prior permission of the publisher.

Published by
Arena
Ashgate Publishing Limited
Gower House
Croft Road
Aldershot
Hants GU11 3HR
England

Ashgate Publishing Company
Old Post Road
Brookfield
Vermont 05036
USA

British Library Cataloguing in Publication Data

Tolfree, David
  Roofs and Roots: Care of
  Separated Children in the
  Developing World
  I. Title
  362.73
ISBN 1 85742 277 5

Library of Congress Catalog Card Number: 94–80263

Typeset in Great Britain by Bournemouth Colour Press, Parkstone, Dorset and printed by Biddles Ltd, Guildford.

Contents

Part III: Substitute family care

List of boxes

Foreword

Throughout the developing world, the vast majority of children unable to live with their own families are cared for within extended family or community networks. But most of the agencies which provide care for separated children concentrate their energies and resources on developing institutional forms of care. Not only is this extremely expensive, but in most cases it also fails to provide children with the environment they need to grow up into healthy and well-adjusted adults. At a conservative estimate, between 6 and 8 million children worldwide currently live in some form of residential care. This is not a very large proportion of children living in 'especially difficult circumstances' due to poverty, exploitation, war or famine, but children in institutions are especially disadvantaged, and their situation is especially depressing because very few actually *need* to be there – most could be cared for much more effectively by extended family or community networks, or in some form of substitute family care.

It was against this background that, in 1991, Save the Children (SCF) decided to launch a three-year research programme, Residential Care and Alternative Approaches in Developing Countries, under the direction of David Tolfree. The aim of this programme was to document and analyse the experience of SCF and others in the field of residential and alternative forms of care for separated children in 'developing countries'. *Roofs and Roots* represents the fruit of field visits to almost twenty countries, fourteen specially commissioned case studies, a comprehensive review of the literature, and the accumulated experience of one of the largest organisations concerned with children's development in the world. This book represents the first and so far the only overview of current practice in this important field. Its conclusions need to be read and taken to heart by all those involved with children's development. The focus of the book is, and was intended to be, current agency practice toward children separated from their families;

some readers may feel that this focus underestimates the enormous daily contribution of ordinary people around the world towards the care of children who may not be theirs by birth. Necessarily, the book is also grounded in Western social work theory and practice, as this is the framework within which most agencies which are active in the field operate. The dangers of cross-cultural generalisation, and the role played by ordinary people, are fully acknowledged in the book, but its focus remains on agency practice.

Save the Children is not arguing that all residential care is bad in principle, but current practice is certainly deficient, and in most cases it fails to respond to the full range of children's needs. The book's overall message is that more emphasis needs to be placed on children's basic need – and right – to be loved and cared about; to feel a sense of belonging, and to develop a strong personal identity. In other words, a shift in emphasis from *roofs* to *roots*.

M J Aaronson, Director, Overseas Department

Acknowledgements

This book is the result of the ideas and experiences of many people within and beyond Save the Children. As part of SCF's research programme, a number of case studies were commissioned, and these were compiled by: Shalini Bharat, Helen Charnley, Quok Chi-Sum, Leith Dunn, James Kaboggaza, Sam Kasule, Josefa Langa, Miguel Mausse, John Parry-Williams, William Potter, Chris Roys, Joana Simão, Monica Sitoi, Marrolin Taylor and Supaporn Tharincharoen. These case studies have provided many thought-provoking insights and have provided a wealth of material for this book. The material on family tracing in Chapter 11 owes a great deal to Lucy Bonnerjea, who compiled *Family Tracing: A Good Practice Guide* (1994) as part of SCF's overall research programme.

Particular gratitude is expressed to the many colleagues within SCF – too many to mention them all by name – who have not only made their programmes available for critical examination but have also contributed freely of their own ideas and expertise. The contributions of Maggie Brown and Barbara Gray were especially valuable. Other organisations have also allowed access to their experience: in particular, thanks are due to Redd Barna, Rädda Barnen, the Indian Association for the Promotion of Adoption, the Guild of Service (Central), Child Workers in Nepal, Save the Children (Lesotho), the Community Aid and Sponsorship Programme, and to the governments of the various countries included in the research.

Valuable comments on early drafts of various parts of the book were received from Eva Lloyd and Helen Charnley, and Jean La Fontaine's anthropological guidance was especially appreciated.

Mike Edwards and Hugo Slim have provided a supportive environment which has greatly facilitated the research and writing, and Mike's editorial work is particularly acknowledged. Catherine Williams laboured long and hard to prepare the final manuscript.

Last but not least, Patsy, Stephen, Jo and Robert have made it possible for me both to travel widely and to work quietly at home: this book is dedicated to them.

Introduction

Recent years have seen unprecedented media coverage of the plight of children in institutional care – in Romania, in Bosnia and most recently in Rwanda. Television pictures of children living in appalling physical environments, often denied many of life's necessities, and visibly deprived of love and affection, have had an immense impact on public opinion in the West. Events in Eastern and Central Europe have created a particularly strong impression on people who, though partially immune from the horrors of war, famine and deprivation in Africa, have been shocked by pictures of children for whom the State has been acting as parent in countries so close to their own.

The dispatch of truck-loads of material goods to institutions in countries such as Romania and Bosnia has reflected, on the one hand, a real humanitarian concern for such children, and on the other, a complete misunderstanding of their real needs and the complexity of achieving sustainable change in the systems which have created such appalling provision for parentless children. Consignments of unsolicited toys and sweets for children in institutions are no substitute for a careful appraisal of the situation of vulnerable children and families and the responses which are required if their needs are to be met and their rights respected. Material aid alone will not address the issues which cause children to be separated from their families in the first place; neither will it help to challenge the assumption that an institutional response is the only practicable way of assisting separated children.

Throughout the developing world, the vast majority of children unable to live with their own families are absorbed – often unquestioningly – within their extended families, or within wider community networks. But the majority of agencies (governments and non-governmental organisations) providing care for separated children have concentrated their energies and

1

resources on developing institutional (or residential) forms of care. All too often, institutional care is uncritically accepted as 'the answer', without a thorough examination of the problems facing the individual child, or an active searching for alternatives. Such alternatives include support to enable children to remain with their families, and various forms of substitute family care. Moreover, it is rare to find systematic work undertaken to address the causes of family breakdown and child separation, and to promote preventive programmes which help to avoid the need to provide substitute care in the first place.

Why is the subject of separated children important?

Children in institutions are frequently referred to by UNICEF as one category of 'children in especially difficult circumstances'. In a very real sense, most children in institutional care face a triple disadvantage:

1 Through the experiences which have made it impossible for them to be cared for in their own family and community setting, whether on account of the loss of their parent(s), separation in the course of armed conflict, abandonment, rejection, child abuse, destitution or breakdown in relationships.

2 In the vast majority of cases, such children have the added disadvantage of being cared for in an institutional environment which often not only fails to meet the 'ordinary' physical, social and psychological needs of children, but also proves inadequate in enabling the child to come to terms with separation from parents and the circumstances surrounding that separation. At worst, children in institutions may experience gross violations of their rights, and be subjected to neglect, physical ill-treatment and sexual abuse.

3 Institutionalised children are likely to face an uncertain future as young adults. Frequently denied opportunities for learning about the roles and skills needed for adult life, and deprived of the emotional experiences which are necessary for healthy social adjustment, they face the uncertainty of a future without the support which families traditionally provide to their young adult offspring. Parentless, rootless and often ill-prepared for adult life, it is no surprise to find that many of these young people are unable to cope successfully in society and may even seek refuge in dependency-creating environments such as prisons or psychiatric hospitals.

This book paints a very depressing picture of institutional care, since the substantial majority of residential homes reviewed during SCF's research fall far short of meeting the complete range of children's needs. However, some exceptions to this conclusion are to be found, and it is important to avoid stereotyping institutional care as being inevitably unsatisfactory. Moreover, although many children in institutions can be seen as both vulnerable and powerless, some display a remarkable degree of resilience. It has been reassuring to find some institutions in which young people themselves have found ways of shaping and improving their environment, providing some compensation for an otherwise depriving and emotionally sterile existence.

In examining the alternatives to institutional care, *Roofs and Roots* will present the reader with something of a paradox. On the one hand, there is a general dearth of imaginative programmes designed either to prevent the need for children to leave their families, or to provide substitute family care for children for whom separation is unavoidable. On the other hand, where attempts are made to promote new approaches, there are often grounds for optimism, both in the capacity of programmes to meet the needs of children and in their potential for cost-effectiveness in comparison with the high costs involved in residential care.

In many developing countries, large sections of the population are experiencing progressive impoverishment, while at the same time structural adjustment programmes severely limit expenditure on social services. Given that family poverty is a highly significant factor in the large majority of admissions into institutional care, it seems likely that the next decade will see ever-increasing numbers of children being referred for care away from their families.

With the rapid increase in HIV and AIDS infection in some parts of the developing world, it is anticipated that the numbers of orphans having no member of the extended family able to provide care will increase rapidly. The HIV/AIDS pandemic adds urgency to the need to develop and promote community-based approaches to the care of orphaned children, to develop substitute family care for children who cannot be cared for within their own families and communities, and to find ways of developing child-centred but affordable approaches to residential care.

Background to the study

This book has its origins in concerns expressed by Save the Children that standards of care for separated children in many of the countries in which it works frequently fall far short of those required by the UN Convention on the Rights of the Child, 1989. Many of SCF's programmes have developed around a concern for children in institutions, and have resulted in projects ranging from improving the quality of life for institutionalised children to promoting preventive approaches; from developing fostering and adoption to programmes of family tracing and reunification. However, many of these programmes operated in isolation from each other, and found themselves either making the same mistakes, or the same discoveries, in the absence of a systematic means of exchanging knowledge. Many also found themselves struggling to adapt theoretical concepts, good practice and research knowledge to cultural, economic and social situations far removed from the Western countries from which they were, in the main, derived.

Save the Children therefore decided to commission a global research programme to examine a broad range of issues concerning separated children. The principal aim of the research was to learn from the organisation's own experience and that of its project partners across the globe, and to find ways of analysing, systematising and disseminating that experience. Although the main emphasis was on the developing countries of Africa, Asia, Latin America and the Caribbean, an attempt was also made to draw on relatively recent experience in Eastern and Central Europe, where – though the cultural, political and economic contexts were very different – many of the issues facing separated children were found to be remarkably similar.

The impetus behind this book, then, was a real desire by SCF to learn from its experience, to examine that experience in the spirit of honest self-criticism, and to make these lessons available to a wider readership. Some of the most useful lessons have been derived from less successful programmes, especially where those involved have been able to look critically and self-critically at their work.

Field visits were made to almost twenty countries, and material was gathered from a number of others. A comprehensive literature review was undertaken, and observation visits were made to numerous institutions and to programmes offering preventive approaches or various forms of substitute family care. Semi-structured interviews and focus group discussions were carried out with children, parents, residential staff and personnel within governments and non-governmental organisations (NGOs). Fourteen case studies were commissioned, each of which examined more systematically a particular approach. These case studies were usually written by people working in the country concerned and, where possible, by researchers rooted in the local culture. They are being published separately (the full list appears at the end of the book), but are referred to extensively in the text. Some of the case material is presented anonymously in order to preserve confidentiality.

The book does not attempt to provide off-the-shelf answers or universally applicable solutions to the problems posed by children separated from their families. Rather it seeks to share experiences and to analyse issues in the hope that the lessons so derived can be used in other contexts. But generalisations across cultures present many difficulties, and any conclusions found in this book will need to be adapted to fit the unique circumstances of other cultural, social, political and economic situations.

Roofs and Roots is designed so that it need not be read sequentially. Each of the three parts is designed to be self-standing, and can therefore be read independently of the others. However, since one of the main messages of the book is that the full range of approaches to care should be explored by agencies active in this field, a complete reading is recommended.

Save the Children is a children's rights organisation. Throughout the book, reference is made to the United Nations Convention on the Rights of the Child. Adopted by the UN General Assembly in 1989, the Convention has now been ratified by 167 countries (as of December 1994), and provides a set of internationally agreed principles, many of which are highly relevant to the themes explored in this book. However, the gulf between rhetoric and the reality is frequently found to be very wide, and it is hoped that SCF's research will provide some useful ideas which will enable countries to bring their policies and legislation more into line with the principles of the Convention.

Roofs and Roots is intended for an informed, but not necessarily specialised, readership which includes planners and practitioners in many parts of the world. It seeks to find reference points not only in the experience of work in the developing world, but also in the practice and research experience of the West. At times it draws parallels between social history in the UK and the experience of developing countries. The book attempts to convey concepts in straightforward language which is free of jargon in the hope that it will be read by people for whom English is not the mother tongue.

Scope of the book

Residential care ostensibly caters for a wide range of different categories of children and problems, and includes the following:

- homes for orphaned, abandoned, rejected or destitute children;
- homes, schools and hospital units for children with various forms of disability;
- correctional and training establishments for young offenders;
- children in adult penal establishments;
- residential homes for mothers and babies.

This list is by no means exhaustive. In addition, there are different types of residential homes and hostels provided to facilitate children's access to education, and various forms of hospitals and clinics designed to meet the health and nutrition needs of children. This category would also include some nutrition and therapeutic feeding centres.

An important issue, considered in more detail in Chapter 1, is that, in practice, many residential institutions admit children whose situation falls outside the stated referral criteria – for example, orphanages admit children who are not orphans; juvenile training centres admit children who have not been convicted of an offence, and hospitals find themselves caring for healthy but abandoned children.

The principal focus of this book is on those categories of children whose parents are unable or unwilling to care for them – orphaned, abandoned, rejected and destitute children, and those who have become inadvertently separated through such circumstances as armed conflict or natural disaster. This book does not explore in any detail the situation of disabled children or young offenders. These are both specialised areas which fall outside the scope of the research.

Terminology and definitions

The term 'institution' tends to have a negative connotation in Western societies, often conjuring up images of large mental hospitals, Dickensian orphanages, or other 'warehouse' models of care. The terms 'residential care' and 'residential home' are now generally preferred as describing, in more neutral language, the phenomenon of group-care. Outside Western countries, however, the term 'institution' is used more widely, though not necessarily with the negative connotations implied elsewhere. Terms such as 'residential care' are generally unfamiliar, and possibly appear somewhat specious. In general, the more neutral term 'residential care' is preferred in this book, though this and 'institutional care' are used interchangeably.

It is not easy to define the phenomenon of residential care precisely. However, the following working definition was adopted for the research:

> a group living arrangement for children in which care is provided by remunerated adults who would not be regarded as traditional carers within the wider society.

Various terms are used in the literature to describe the different groups of children who need, or who are placed in, either residential care or other forms of substitute care, including 'parentless', 'homeless' and 'deprived'. The generic term preferred here is 'separated children', which indicates the fact of separation without necessarily implying anything about the causes or consequences of that separation.

Different terms are used to describe the various countries included in

SCF's research. 'Developing countries', 'the Third World' and 'countries of the South' are used interchangeably, though none of them is very satisfactory. It is hoped that this book will also be relevant to readers concerned with child welfare issues in the countries of Eastern and Central Europe.

Wherever possible, gender-biased language has been avoided. However, rather than constantly repeating expressions such as he/she and his/hers, the masculine or feminine pronoun is used interchangeably to refer to children of either gender, unless the context specifically indicates reference to boys or girls.

Part I

Institutional care

In all actions concerning children, whether undertaken by public or private welfare institutions, courts of law, administrative authorities or legislative bodies, the best interests of the child shall be a primary consideration.[1]

Introduction to Part I

Few countries in the developing world have a long history of institutional care for children: the concept of the institution was commonly introduced by missionaries or by government departments which modelled themselves on their counterparts in the colonial power, often emulating the pattern of residential care which was widespread in Western Europe in the earlier decades of the twentieth century. Despite the strong traditional patterns of extended family obligations towards parentless children which exist in virtually all non-Western societies, large-scale institutional care has continued to be the norm for organisations providing care facilities in most parts of the developing world, with programmes of substitute family care often remaining at a relatively embryonic stage of development. Although it is extremely difficult to estimate the numbers of children in institutional care, a report from Defence for Children International (DCI) suggests a worldwide and conservative figure of 6–8 million.[2] Although some Western countries, notably the USA, have large numbers of young people in penal institutions, it is likely that the majority of institutionalised children are found in the countries of the South.

In Western societies there has been a significant shift away from residential forms of care, so that in the UK, for example, it is rare for institutions to be seen as a permanent form of care for children: instead they are used in a limited way to prepare young people for fostering, to facilitate family rehabilitation, or to offer treatment in respect of abusive experiences or behavioural disorders.

The move away from residential forms of care has, to a large degree, been prompted by a growing awareness of the potentially damaging effect on children of some of the characteristic features of institutions, especially on young children. It has also been motivated by financial considerations and, arguably, has led to an excessive reliance on fostering, despite depressing

11

evidence about the outcome. The effects of institutional care on children's development are discussed in detail in Chapter 1, which argues that, while sweeping condemnations of the concept of residential care are unjustified, there are certain features of institutions which do have a negative impact on child development. However, it is not clear how far our knowledge of the effects of separation and of institutional care can be applied to non-Western cultures in which, for example, shared parenting is the norm. Chapter 1 reviews the available evidence on this issue, and draws some tentative conclusions.

SCF's research of institutions in the developing world raises many profound concerns, ranging from institutional abuse to the inappropriate and unnecessary separation of children from their families; from gross and life-threatening physical neglect to a sometimes total disregard of children's emotional needs. On the other hand, some institutions which (using the yardstick of Western research findings) appear grossly unsatisfactory, in reality seem to have unexpectedly satisfactory outcomes (especially when they build on local cultural norms and practices). Chapter 5 argues that the influence of the peer-group may be of particular importance in meeting the emotional needs of children. It is also important to look beneath the surface of institutions in the developing world, and to discover hidden strengths and resources which may not feature significantly in Western societies.

It is also important to avoid assumptions about the appropriateness of Western approaches to substitute family care: some of the alternatives to residential care in Western societies have been promoted despite growing evidence of their high costs and unsatisfactory outcomes. The high failure rate – sometimes approaching 50 per cent – of foster care is an obvious example.

Part I of this book aims to provide an overview of the most important issues involved in the field of residential care, focusing both on the *concept* of residential care and the appropriateness of this form of care to the needs and resources of developing countries, and on the *practice* of residential care, including assessment and planning; contact with families; the meeting of children's need for affection, closeness and security; preparation for leaving care, and institutional abuse.

Chapter 1 provides a foundation for subsequent chapters by taking a critical look at the concepts of attachment and separation. Chapter 2 examines the concept of residential care, taking a historical look at the development of residential care in the developing world, and the relevance of institutional forms of care to developing countries. Chapter 3 considers the question: 'For whom do institutions for children exist?' It examines the different categories of children who are placed in residential care, asks why these groups are admitted, and who benefits from their admission. Chapter 4 identifies and discusses two crucial issues which emerge from the preceding analysis: gatekeeping (the process of assessment, planning and admission of children to care) and contact between children in care and their families. Chapter 5 brings together the available knowledge about the effects of residential care, drawing on the theoretical framework provided in Chapter 1, a wide range of observations made during the research undertaken for this study, and the case studies which were commissioned. Chapter 6 attempts to distil the ingredients of residential care which is 'good-enough' (to borrow from Winnicott's phrase, 'good-enough parenting'),[3] and considers the circumstances under which residential care is considered the most appropriate option for separated children.

Chapter 7 examines the process of introducing changes to the practice of institutional care, leading logically into Part II and Part III of the book, which consider preventive strategies, and non-institutional alternatives for separated children.

1 Attachment and separation: Child development in a cross-cultural context

This chapter reviews the evidence concerning attachment, separation and institutionalisation, and explores the relevance of this evidence in the context of different cultural environments. Much of the now extensive knowledge in this area has been derived from research in Western societies. This means that children have been studied primarily in the context of upbringing within a nuclear family: the children studied will have experienced child-rearing practices which will not necessarily be characteristic of other cultures, especially those in which 'parenting' by more than one caretaker is the norm. The extent to which our knowledge of the child's separation from her parent-figures, the effects of privation and the likely implications of an institutional upbringing are transferable to different cultural environments are important questions to which we have only partial answers.

Beginning this book with an examination of the literature on attachment and separation might seem to invite a charge of Eurocentricism. However, the reality is that little research has yet been undertaken to test the utility of attachment theory in non-Western cultures. Moreover, given that institutions were, in the main, introduced into the developing world by Europeans, it seems appropriate to begin with an examination of research derived from the West, while at the same time considering the extent to which it can usefully be applied to cultures in which multiple caretaking is the norm.

Background: A framework for understanding child development

Ever since the publication of John Bowlby's highly influential monograph, *Maternal Care and Mental Health*,[4] there has been a great deal of interest in the phenomena of attachment and separation, though little research has been undertaken on a cross-cultural basis. What follows is a distillation of some of the main themes from the research into attachment and separation, and then an examination of their applicability to child care in a cross-cultural context.

Michael Rutter's definitive book on this subject offers a broad review of the literature.[5] This chapter relies heavily on Rutter's work, and also draws on Erik Erikson's framework for understanding the complex process of child development.[6] The term 'maternal deprivation', used by early writers such as Bowlby, now seems inappropriate in the light of more recent research. This book is not just concerned with mothers, but with a wider range of adults (and sometimes older siblings) who offer nurturing to children; not just with deprivation (the loss of something), but also with privation (the lack of something). Therefore the term 'parent-figures' is used to describe the people who provide children with 'parenting' – the range of tasks which need to be performed to enable children to grow and develop normally.

The newborn infant is totally dependent upon her parent-figure(s) not only for physical survival, but also for the social and emotional growth which are essential for human development. It is now generally accepted that Bowlby's initial emphasis on the need for infants to have a close and intimate relationship with their mothers was too narrow, and that other people can provide appropriate 'mothering'. What does this mean?

Erikson suggests that the main task during the period of early infancy, the first of his 'Eight Ages of Man', is the establishment of 'a sense of basic trust',[7] and this is achieved as a result of close, loving, warm interaction between the infant and a committed, concerned adult-figure who is usually, but not necessarily, the child's mother. While Bowlby has continued to assert that the child has a propensity to attach herself to a single parent-figure, there is good reason to believe that more than one person can fulfil the child's needs for attachment, and that, in many societies, the parenting of young children is shared among a number of people other than the mother. McGurk et al. comment that:

> the diversity of child care and child rearing arrangements that can be observed cross culturally is extensive. They include: exclusive mother care; shared care between mother and other adults, both female and male, kin and non-kin; shared care between mother and other children, male and female, usually siblings but not exclusively so. Shared care is by far the majority experience, more nearly universal than exclusive mother care. Moreover, under shared care arrangements, the mother is by no means the majority partner, even during infancy.[8]

Attachment has been described as a dialogue between child and parent-figure – the infant signals her need for food, warmth and comfort, and the parent-figure responds accordingly. The infant soon learns that certain signals will elicit predictable responses – not only does crying tend to bring relief from physical discomfort, but smiling leads to affectionate responses, and the intimate interaction of smiles, cuddles and babbling becomes self-rewarding to both parent-figure and infant. By the age of about 4–6 months, the infant has learned to recognise one individual from another, and attachment becomes specific to her parent-figure(s). Approaches from strangers may create fear, and increasingly the infant may find it difficult to tolerate separation from her trusted and familiar caregiver(s). Here, however, cross-cultural variations are to be expected; for example, the repeated experiences of separation which would normally be involved in shared parenting arrangements may possibly serve to diminish the child's reactions of fear and anxiety.

Salter Ainsworth et al. have demonstrated the importance of secure attachment in providing a base from which the young child has the security and confidence to explore her world, and suggest that it is sensitive responsiveness on the part of mothers which is the principal factor in facilitating the development of an attachment relationship.[9] An essential component of parenting during early infancy is stimulation – the range of parenting activities which expose the child to sensory experiences which are essential to her development – sounds (talking, singing, music), sights (colour, movement, shapes), smells and tastes, and, of course, touch, whether through the functional activities of changing and cleansing, the affectionate responses of cuddles and caresses, or the movements of the person to whose back the child is strapped in many cultures.

A young child who has experienced a sense of being loved and valued, and who has felt a sense of predictability that her basic needs will be adequately met by her parent-figures, is likely to emerge into 'toddlerhood' with Erikson's 'basic sense of trust', which will give her a sense of well-being, hope and security. The capacity to endure separation from her parent-figure will be damaged unless the child has had the stability of one or more caregivers during these early months.

From the ages of approximately 1½–5 years, the child experiences rapid physical growth and mental development. Erikson describes this period as one in which the growing child develops a sense of autonomy and self-control without which she is likely to experience feelings of shame and doubt. This necessarily requires the child to internalise the norms and restraints of her parent-figures: the emotional ties she experienced with them during infancy enable her to identify with them and accept their prohibitions and restrictions without feeling a loss of love.

At this point, cultural differences in the socialisation process are very obvious. LeVine has made the interesting observation that, in societies in which there is a scarcity of subsistence resources, socialisation of young children is likely to emphasise compliance in the undertaking of roles and tasks which assist the family in its economic and subsistence responsibilities.[10] It is only in relatively prosperous cultures, where child participation in economic activity is unnecessary, that more independent and self-assertive behaviour can be permitted.

Erikson's 'Third Age of Man', which emphasises 'initiative', is probably more reflective of Western socialisation practices than cultures in which children are active participants in the family economy. His next stage, however, in which the child's sense of 'industry' can be enhanced, or 'inferiority' and low self-esteem reinforced, would seem to typify middle-childhood in any cultural environment. During this period (later middle-childhood and pre-adolescence), children invest a great deal of their energy in mastering new skills – the household or economic skills determined by culture and gender, or the educational and leisure skills which are more characteristic of industrialised societies.

In most Western countries, adolescence has become a prolonged period lasting from the beginning of sexual maturity through to economic independence which, for young people going through higher education, may not be until their early twenties. In other societies, where education may be unlikely to continue into the teenage years and full economic productivity is expected at an early age, marriage may come much earlier, and socialisation into adult roles (such as agricultural and pastoral work and domestic duties) may begin at an early age. On the other hand, marriage will not necessarily confer full adult status.

During adolescence, peer-group relationships begin to assume enormous importance in Western cultures, not least because peers reflect back to the individual an image of her emerging adult identity, and because of the great need for a sense of 'belonging' outside the immediate family. Nevertheless, in almost all societies, the growing adolescent continues to need the kind of secure personal base which an attachment-figure will generally provide – whether the young Western student who continues to be dependent upon his parents for material and moral support into his twenties, or the teenage Indian girl whose parents will choose her husband as well as determine her occupational role, and will continue to play an influential role in the upbringing of her children. There are significant differences between cultures in the extent to which adolescents are allowed or encouraged to loosen the shackles of childhood conformity and develop individuality in tastes, mores, occupational roles, choice of partner, and so on.

Erikson describes the adolescent period as that in which the young person's adult identity begins to emerge – a 'moratorium, a psychosocial stage between childhood and adulthood, and between the morality learned by the child, and the ethics to be developed by the adult'.[11] The danger in this, the 'Fifth Age of Man', is that of 'role confusion': a failure to bring together and integrate the multitude of childhood experiences into a mature adult identity.

Separation

What effects does separation of the child from his parent-figure(s) have? Clearly, separation at different ages and stages will have different meanings and implications for the child, and the experience of separation will vary from one culture to another: for example, children brought up in a situation of multiple caretaking, in which separations are very much a part of everyday life, are likely to experience separation quite differently from the child who has had an exclusive relationship with a single adult, in most cases the mother.

It should also be borne in mind that separation does not occur in isolation from other events. A child who is orphaned in war, for example, will have to cope not just with permanent separation from her parents, but also with grief and the violent circumstances in which the parents were killed. In contrast, abandoned children will have to live not only without parents, but also in the knowledge of being unwanted and rejected. They may therefore invent explanations of the circumstances of their abandonment, such as their own worthlessness. Moreover, such children will find it difficult to grieve for parents they have lost, but whose whereabouts may continue to be unknown. A third example is the child whose parents have placed her in an institution in the belief that this will afford her a 'better life' than they could offer. The effects of separation may be quite different in all three examples. Individual differences of temperament, and previous experiences of separation, will also create differences in the individual child's reaction to separation from familiar parent-figures.

In considering children's reactions to separation, the loss of, or the continuing lack of, mothering (or parenting) is of prime significance. In reviewing the research evidence, Rutter suggests that there are several essential components of mothering.[12]

First, the relationship between the child and the caregiver needs to be 'loving'. This is obviously difficult to define, but the relationship needs to be characterised by warmth, acceptance and closeness.

Second, while the emphasis placed by Bowlby on the central importance of the child's own biological mother is now very much in doubt, bond-formation relies on the same person having contact with the child over a prolonged period of time. The intensity of the interaction is also important, since more transient parent-figures are unlikely to be able to 'read' the individual child's signals and adapt their parenting behaviour accordingly – they will lack the parental sensitivity which Ainsworth regards as so important.[13] It has become increasingly clear that attachments can be made not only to mothers, but to fathers, siblings, grandparents and others who will not necessarily be the principal providers of physical care. In some cultures, the most significant attachment-figures may not be parents.

Third, there needs to be continuity, though this is not to imply that transient separations are necessarily harmful to the child's development. While it is clear that institutional care for infants rarely offers the level of continuity required for healthy development, 'shared parenting' (for example, between a mother, a grandmother and an older sister) does not necessarily lead to abnormal development.

Fourth, mothering requires stimulation of the infant for the normal development of language and intelligence, but this again can be provided by a variety of people other than biological parents.

The age of the child is a critical variable in any assessment of the likely effects of separation. It is self-evident that an infant of 9 months will react quite differently from a 9-year-old or a 15-year-old to a similar event of separation from the family. It is generally agreed that, for infants under the age of about 4–6 months, separation is not normally associated with distress, provided the child's needs for food, warmth, comfort and stimulation are met. The reason appears to be that, up to this age, the infant has not yet learned to recognise her individual carer, and is therefore not yet attached to an individual, but is still highly dependent on the parent-figure(s).

It is generally acknowledged that the greatest distress is caused by the separation of children aged from about 4–6 months to 2 years, to whom most existing research applies. It is during this period that the infant's attachment-figure(s) provide the 'secure base' from which she can explore her environment and relate to other people. In reviewing the evidence on the effects of maternal deprivation, Rutter makes a useful distinction between short-term effects (those which are observable immediately the separation occurs and during the following few months) and long-term effects (which may be seen after a period of months or years following either a brief or more prolonged period of separation).

The short-term effects of separation

Two principal types of response to separation have been observed: (1) an observable response of distress immediately after separation, and (2) developmental retardation, which, in young children and in certain types of environment, follows quite quickly after the separation and may have longer-term implications.

Some of the most influential work in the area of 'distress' has been undertaken by the Robertsons, whose films, *Young Children in Brief Separation*, played an important part in influencing policy and practice in hospital visiting and in residential nurseries in the UK.[14] From various studies emerged the typical picture of the young child's reaction to admission to the impersonal environment of hospital or residential nursery: first, an immediate reaction of acute distress and tearfulness (the phase of 'protest'), followed by an increasing sense of apathy and misery (the 'despair' phase), and finally a period in which the child appears resigned to her situation and loses interest in parents (the phase of 'detachment').[15]

It is difficult to assess the extent to which these reactions are culture-specific. It does appear that the children filmed by the Robertsons were living in a relatively isolated situation within a nuclear family, and consequently separation may have been experienced as a more traumatic event than would be the case where children have a wider circle of relationships. Weisner and Gallimore suggest that:

> Polymatric families utilising child caretakers should have infants with lessened attachment to a single primary caretaker and lessened separation-anxiety reactions when separated from the mother.[16]

However, there is little empirical evidence to confirm this.

Developmental retardation can also follow separation: the most frequently observed areas of retardation are in respect of language and social responsiveness and motor development, which have been observed in children as young as 2 months, but more global developmental retardation has also been observed.

From the considerable amount of research evidence available, Rutter has distilled the following main points regarding the short-term effects of separation:

1   Developmental retardation is not caused by separation as such, but by the lack of stimulation characteristic of many of the children's institutions observed by researchers. The lack of opportunities for secure attachment with parent-figures in many institutions also reduces the child's capacity for exploratory behaviour (which may be perceived positively by institutional staff as 'compliant' and 'undemanding' behaviour), which will also result in developmental delay. This is 'privation' rather than 'deprivation', and, while the environment of so many institutions for young children causes developmental retardation, this is not an inevitable consequence of institutionalisation.

2   In contrast, the 'distress' so commonly observed in young children separated from their carers is a reaction not to privation, but to deprivation. Bowlby interprets this as a kind of grief reaction – what is significant is the loss of the *person* rather than the loss of the *care* which he or she has provided.

3   Distress is also related to the strangeness of the environment in which

children are placed, though there is some evidence that the distressing nature of strange environments is partly mitigated by the presence of familiar people and (possibly) objects: for example, children separated from their parent-figure(s) but with siblings (even though the latter may not play any nurturing role) seem to be less distressed by the experience. Similarly, if the child is placed in an environment in which there are other familiar people (for example, if she has already visited the environment or has met people who will care for her) the level of distress may be reduced.

4   Substitute care which facilitates continuing personal interaction between the child and a parent-figure may also serve to minimise the distress reaction.

5   Distress reactions are the likely result of separation from any person to whom the child has become attached, not just from the child's own mother. Although research is lacking in this area, it is reasonable to assume that a child who is attached to several people (for example, mother, grandmother and older sister, who all play a significant part in her care and nurturing) will suffer distress when she is separated from them collectively, but that this distress will be mitigated by the presence of any one of these people.

6   While most of the relevant research has been undertaken in respect of children experiencing very brief periods of separation, there is reason to believe that the longer the period of separation, the greater the distress, though the Robertsons' study of children in hospital suggests that the 'detachment' phase is one in which the child's great distress can be misinterpreted as acceptance (see below for possible long-term effects of premature and chronic 'detachment').

Individual variations will obviously be found in response to separation: little is known about the effects of temperament on a child's reaction to separation, but some children will clearly be more resilient than others. Moreover, as already indicated, previous experiences of separation may serve to mitigate – or, conversely, exaggerate – the worst effects of separation. The individual circumstances of separation – its causes and consequences – are also likely to be highly significant.

The long-term effects of separation: Evidence from the Western research literature

Concern about the possible long-term consequences of what Bowlby termed 'maternal deprivation' go back to his earliest writings on the subject: for example, he noticed an association between delinquency and the phenomenon of the 'affectionless psychopath' with early or multiple experiences of separation and institutional care.[17] Language retardation and learning difficulties, physical growth retardation, and depression in later life have all been cited as potential consequences of maternal deprivation.

There appear to be a number of important variables in assessing the long-term effects of separation. First, the age of the child at separation is especially important, and, though empirical evidence is not entirely unequivocal, it does seem that the period from about 4 or 6 months to 2 or 3 years is particularly important for the formation of bonds and the development of attachment behaviour. Given that physical growth and maturation are extremely rapid during this period, it is likely that the effects of privation at this time may be the most marked. Language development in older children may be a significant factor in enabling the child to understand the nature of separation and the reasons for it, and this may serve to reduce the stressfulness of the experience.

Second, the duration of separation is important. The evidence suggests that very brief periods of separation, even in this 'critical period', are unlikely to have serious long-term consequences, though there is some evidence that separation in this early period for a month or more does carry a slightly increased risk of subsequent psychological disturbance, notably of an antisocial type.[18] Most studies into the effects of institutions on children indicate that the longer the stay in the institution, the greater the likelihood of emotional or behavioural disturbance and cognitive impairment.

Third, the environment into which the separated child is placed is of great importance. Some characteristics mitigate the potentially damaging effects of separation (many of which are significantly lacking in the institutions visited in the course of SCF's research). The availability of stable adults to whom the child can become attached is of utmost importance. One of the most damaging aspects of institutional care is the rotation of nurses, none of whom has sufficient time or opportunity to provide the kind of individualised and personal care and continuity which is necessary for bond-formation. Similarly, children may also be 'cycled through the system' by having to move from a 'babies' ward to a 'toddler group', and so on through the institution, and possibly on to another institution at a prescribed age. Continuity of staff is also important in enabling children to develop their capacity to maintain affectionate and intimate relationships: the high turnover of staff in some institutions is potentially damaging, especially to children in the pre-school years. In addition, a stimulating environment is a necessary precondition for normal intellectual and language development. In part, of course, this reflects the amount of individual care provided by staff within the institution, and, while stimulus deprivation may be a feature of many institutions, neither the fact of separation nor the fact of living in an institution automatically lead to impaired cognitive growth. *What matters is the quality of experience.*

The combined effects of good sensory stimulation (especially language) coupled with a high quality of personal interaction with caring, warm adults offering a good degree of continuity are likely to enable most children to survive a separation with minimum psychological damage. The most likely cause of severe and lasting emotional impairment, including the 'affectionless psychopathy' phenomenon described by Bowlby, is not so much the disruption of bonds with a parent-figure, as the failure – especially during the sensitive period between 4–6 months and 2–3 years – to establish an attachment to a parent-figure. Although the evidence suggests that the effects of such privation are reversible, it is also clear that permanent damage may be done if emotional privation persists into the third year of life.

There is some evidence that the disruption of bonds with parent-figures can lead to a higher incidence of depression in adulthood. Interestingly, it seems that parental loss during adolescence is more likely to have this particular long-term consequence than loss in early childhood. Erikson's child development framework (summarised earlier) may provide a possible explanation, for it is in the crucial period of identity-formation that parental models may be particularly important. Therefore the loss of a parent-figure – perhaps especially that of the same gender as the child – may be particularly critical at this stage.

Although Bowlby's work focused mainly on the effects of separation of young children from their families, he also asserted that:

> a well-based self-reliance ... is usually the product of slow and unchecked growth from infancy into maturity during which, through interaction with trustworthy and encouraging others, a person learns how to combine trust in others with trust in himself.[19]

It is no wonder that so many children who have been brought up in an institutional environment which has not provided the security of trusted and accessible adults often experience enormous difficulty in adapting to life outside the institution and in becoming independent adults. Moreover, the lack of experience of attachment to trusted adult-figures may be a significant factor in subsequent difficulties in forming mature, intimate relationships.

The early writings of Bowlby and others were highly influential in changing policy and practice in respect of institutional child care during the 1940s and 1950s in the West. The discontinuity of relationships for very young children cared for by a roster of nurses, the lack of individual attention and stimulation, and the harsh and regimented regimes of institutions which were typical in the early part of the twentieth century in the UK are now things of the past. Policy and practice on hospital visiting have also been changed to minimise the short-term distress felt by hospitalised children.

Before examining the features of institutions in the developing world, it is important to consider whether these research findings can be transferred to other cultural environments.

Separation, deprivation, privation and institutionalisation in a cross-cultural context

Psychologists and anthropologists have paid scant attention to this area of child development. The little research which does exist is sketchy and piecemeal, but some significant writings on the subject do offer important evidence. Werner concludes that attachment is a universal human phenomenon, and that, for most infants, attachment by 7 months is essential. Moreover, 'given normal development and an average endowment, there should be relatively little cross-cultural variation in these behaviours.'[20]

Outside Western societies, parenting is commonly shared amongst a wider group of people than the nuclear family: grandparents, other adult kinsfolk, older siblings, and sometimes unrelated adults or children may play central roles in the rearing of young children. It is attachment that is important, not attachment to any particular individual.

In one pattern of child-rearing described by Sarah and Robert LeVine, attachment to the mother is a short-lived phenomenon in Gusii society; breast feeding may continue into the second year, but the period of maternal indulgence is very short. After about 3 months there is little eye contact between mother and baby, and almost none by 7 months. Mothers tend to ignore their infants' attempts to engage them in reciprocal play, their role being confined to physical nurturing and pacification. Three reasons for this pattern of maternal behaviour are identified: (1) mothers have many other demands on their time; (2) playful behaviour is not seen as an appropriate part of the maternal role; (3) as mothers had not experienced playfulness with their own mothers, it would have been seen as inappropriate to engage in an activity such as play or conversation which is not directed towards a specific utilitarian goal. However, this is balanced by the role of grandmothers and older siblings, who readily engage in playful and soothing behaviour with infants, who learn in the process to direct their social behaviours away from their mothers. The LeVines conclude that, in Gusii society, there is little evidence of resistance from infants to separation from their mothers, or of behaviour disorders among children.[21]

The majority of writings on cross-cultural child development do not consider issues of separation, but an interesting study by Rohner attempts to assess the effects on children's emerging personalities of parental acceptance and rejection. He reviewed a large number of ethnographic sources, and compared the findings with evidence from research studies in Western societies. Rohner concludes as follows:

> all humans have a profound, but generalized, need for positive response from the people who are important to us. This need for positive response is rooted in man's psychosocial and morphological evolution, and when we are denied love, esteem, and other forms of positive response, pernicious things happen to us ... parental rejection in children leads to hostility, aggression, passive aggression, or problems with the management of hostility and aggression; dependency; probably emotional unresponsiveness and negative self-evaluation ... and, probably, emotional instability as well as a negative world view.[22]

It needs to be emphasised, however, that Rohner's study does not concern children who have been separated from their parents or brought up by alternative carers; it focuses on different child-rearing approaches and the extent to which children are afforded warmth and acceptance by their caretakers. In other words, children in cultures where the level of warmth and acceptance is low, experience a style of parenting which is 'normal' for their culture, whereas children being cared for by substitute parents may be experiencing a style of care which is quite abnormal. The value of Rohner's study is that it confirms that lack of acceptance, love, warmth and affection leads to certain predictable consequences for the personality of the developing child, regardless of cultural background.

Conclusions

The phenomenon of attachment, and the consequences of separation, often seem to have broad cross-cultural applicability, especially for young children. However, in many non-Western societies, grandparents and older siblings play significant roles in the growing child's socialisation from the age of weaning, so that the child experiences multiple attachment-relationships. Separation therefore has to be seen in the light of multiple parenting, and not in the context of Bowlby's emphasis (in his earlier writings) on the importance of the child's biological mother. The nature of the environment into which the separated child is placed is also critical. The consequences of lack of stimulation for children's language and motor development are clearly seen in institutions in a wide range of different cultural environments, though the long-term consequences of separation and institutionalisation are more difficult to observe, and empirical evidence is extremely scarce.

Chapter 5 will return to the theme of attachment and separation, and examine more closely the effects of some of the characteristic features of institutional care which have been observed in the developing world. The intervening chapters will examine the phenomenon of institutional care, firstly by posing the question of why institutions have been introduced into the developing world, and then by discussing their appropriateness and relevance to the needs and circumstances of their country contexts.

2 Why institutions?

One of the themes which runs throughout this book is the distinction between the *concept* and *practice* of residential care. Chapter 1 argued that institutions are not intrinsically damaging to children, but the evidence suggests that certain features of institutional care are likely to have a detrimental effect on children's development. This chapter focuses on the *concept* of residential care. Why have residential institutions been introduced into developing countries, and are they appropriate?

Why have residential institutions been introduced into developing countries?

This is a complex question; residential institutions have proliferated in some countries, yet in others, with similar characteristics, they are virtually unknown. The following factors seem to be significant.

Missionary activity

In many countries of the South, institutions were introduced by missionaries, fulfilling a variety of purposes, including education and care for children who had been orphaned or abandoned. It is worth noting that, in Europe, the Christian Church has played an important role in providing care for abandoned, orphaned or destitute children since the time of Constantine.[23] During the colonial period, religious orders brought with them not just a concern for the deprived and a commitment to the provision of health and education, but possibly also an institutional frame of reference stemming from their own experience of residential living.

Colonial legal and welfare structures

Colonial powers often bequeathed both a legal framework and a pattern of social service delivery derived from their own domestic situation.[24] In a number of African countries, for example, the current legal framework is substantially derived from UK laws governing the care and protection of children derived from the 1930s and 1940s, which reflected the 'rescuing' and 'training' emphases which were current at the time. Moreover, the limited services made available by the colonial powers reflected the particular concerns of the European expatriates during the colonial period – the protection of property and the control of 'deviant' behaviour such as delinquency, vagrancy and prostitution. These services, which were mainly remedial by nature, included approved schools and other forms of residential care.

In the post-colonial period, some governments have perpetuated this framework without re-evaluating its appropriateness. This has often resulted in a continued emphasis on the individual focus of social welfare departments (rather than the adoption of a wider community-development philosophy), and a continuing preoccupation with institutional forms of care. Although many countries have made legal provision for services such as adoption and fostering, they were often designed around the needs of the expatriate population, and have rarely been extended to meet the needs of the indigenous population. A case study, *The Role of Substitute Families in Mozambique*, illustrates this.[25]

Government policies

In countries such as Uganda and Mozambique, governments have made clear policy statements which have served to limit the development of institutions. Elsewhere, there has been no restriction on the activities of individuals and organisations which have wanted to promote institutional care.

In some countries, it is clear that institutional forms of care have evolved in part as a response to the State's perceived need to exercise control over groups who are perceived as posing a threat to social order (and especially to the security of the wealthy). Brazil offers an extreme example of a country in which government institutions for young people were developed in circumstances reflecting the harsh and authoritarian regime prior to the restoration of democracy.

The federal-level department, the National Federation for the Welfare of Children (FUNABEM), established large, closed institutions primarily for the education and training of young offenders, but they came to be used for a range of other purposes: street children were rounded up by the police and incarcerated there, along with orphaned, abandoned and destitute children. Most were detained without the possibility of redress through the courts, but only a small minority were offenders. Significantly, a large majority were black. The institutions offered extremely harsh, regimented and militaristic regimes, in which violence and abuse of children's rights were common.[26] These infamous institutions became something of a symbol of a repressive and authoritarian regime; when the regime collapsed, there was a strong tide of opinion in favour of non-institutional approaches to care.

Institutions as a response to growing urban social problems

Urbanisation is a significant factor in the development of institutions. The abandonment of young children, which is a comparatively rare phenomenon in rural areas, is more common in cities. Poverty, unemployment and poor housing add to the stresses on families, and may increase the demand for alternative care provision.

It is in urban areas that a clear trend towards the nuclear family may be found, lacking the support from the extended family and community which is more likely to exist in rural areas. Young people may also be perceived as a particular threat in cities: the high incidence of street children, for example, in some cities is seen as justification for developing institutional responses where street children are perceived as a threat to the order of society.

Institutions as a response to war and natural disasters

Residential care may proliferate as a response to overwhelming problems, such as a high incidence of separated children as a result of civil war. For example, in South Vietnam in the early 1970s, an estimated 19,000 orphans were being accommodated in institutions.[27] Significantly, these institutions tended to admit not just children who had been orphaned as a result of war, but those who had become separated from their families for other reasons, not least the widespread poverty which was a significant indirect effect of the conflict.

Indigenous institutional frames of reference

In some societies, indigenous organisations either provide institutional care for children, or offer a model which has influenced the development of residential institutions. In Thailand, for example, Buddhism has been a significant factor both in the provision of residential care by Buddhist organisations, and also by virtue of the traditional role played by Buddhist temples in providing education, including that provided to 'temple boys' on a residential basis.[28]

Institutions and donor-appeal

A final and potent factor in the development and maintenance of institutions for children is the high level of 'donor-appeal' they seem to elicit. There seem to be various issues at work here, but most significant is the fact that institutions offer a highly visible and tangible product of giving, which seems to appeal to both individual and organisational donors. Residential institutions can be seen, visited and touched, providing a concrete outcome of giving, whose occupants can be easily persuaded into offering token gestures of gratitude. A gratifying sense of satisfaction can be experienced by donors. By way of contrast, fostering, adoption and preventive programmes are less tangible and less visible, more difficult to understand, and hence have less appeal to donors.

Questioning the concept of the institution in the developing world

Is there really a need for large-scale substitute care, and, if so, are residential institutions the most appropriate means of providing it? The second of these questions is considered in Part II; this section examines the relevance of institutional care to the problems and needs of developing countries.

While the need for substitute care is well-established in most Western societies, developing countries differ in the following respects:

● Responsibility for the care of children is not seen as the prerogative of the child's parents. Throughout Sub-Saharan Africa, for example, children are seen as the responsibility of the wider clanship group. In parts of Mozambique, 'a woman's family receives money or goods on marriage creating a social contract with economic implications. The man's family not only has a perceived right to the children of the union; it is also their obligation to care for them.'[29] Another illustration comes from a study of orphans towards the end of the Vietnam War.[30] In examining the situation of orphans living with their extended families, researchers concluded that 'the family bonds in these cases were surprisingly strong and stable. This accounted for the fact that, though most of these families lived in poverty, their children seemed to feel very safe psychologically.' Moreover, support and material assistance were readily obtained from neighbours, the village being conceived as 'a big family'.

● In many societies (as the Vietnamese study referred to above demonstrates), a sense of community obligation as well as family responsibility exists. Where such supportive extended family and community structures exist, one may question whether any form of substitute care is necessary. However, in some urban situations, such extended-family obligations are being eroded, and an unwanted child can be abandoned anonymously with great ease, thereby excluding the extended family from a potential caring role. Moreover, in many urban settings, abandoned children are more likely to survive, and the nature of communities is such that community networks are less likely to be effective in providing care for parentless children.

● Institutions may override existing obligations towards the child, and may detach him from the support systems which are likely to exist within the extended family and community. The consequences of this phenomenon in countries lacking adequate State social welfare provision can be extremely serious as the child grows into adulthood. An additional problem for children from rural communities is that, given that institutions are usually located in towns and cities, there is often a tendency for institutionalised children to feel increasingly alienated from the communities into which they were born. This is graphically illustrated in a study of children's institutions in Lesotho,[31] and is discussed further in Chapter 4.

● It is rare to find a pattern of care provision in developing countries which supports the *discriminating* use of residential care within a range of resources (which might, for example, include fostering, adoption and various means of supporting the child within the extended family). Institutional care becomes a 'blunt instrument', which does not enable individually identified needs to be met with sensitivity. In part this reflects deficiencies in assessment and planning, and the absence of alternative means of supporting vulnerable children and families are issues which are explored later in this book. The point to be stressed here is that institutions have been imported into situations in which there are insufficient resources to ensure that the concept can be translated into practical ways to meet the needs and rights of children.

● Residential care is based, for many children, on a purely material concept of the 'best interests' of the child. As a means of facilitating the physical survival of children, institutionalisation has some validity in extreme circumstances (though this research suggests that physical survival is certainly not assured in some institutions). But institutional care often denies other basic rights,[32] such as protection and care, the principle of the child's 'best interests', the right to live with parents unless this is deemed incompatible with the child's wishes, the right of freedom of expression, and the right to protection from abuse.

The point which is emphasised throughout this book is that many (though by no means all) institutions promoted in the developing world are responding, not so much to legitimate *needs*, as to *demands* that they themselves have created. In so doing, they separate children from the family and community networks which form the principal means of support throughout life, with extremely serious consequences for the individual. In urban environments, however, where extended family and community systems are weaker, institutional care may be a less negative alternative, especially for genuinely orphaned or abandoned children, or for those who need to be removed from abusive or neglectful households, if options such as adoption or fostering do not exist. These issues are explored in depth in Chapter 3.

Even where more enlightened practices in institutional care have been promoted, the *concept* of institutional care is rarely challenged with sufficient rigour. For example, Espert's study of institutions in Latin America for UNICEF offers a useful framework for considering the process of change in institutions without once questioning the *concept* of institutional care and its relevance and appropriateness to the needs of children themselves.[33] The assumption is that residential care is required, and will be able to meet children's needs if standards of practice can be improved.

A similar example comes from a comprehensive study of children's homes in Sri Lanka undertaken by Redd Barna, the Department of Probation and Child Care Services and a local research team.[34] The study provides a detailed and insightful analysis of a large number of children's homes and produces some excellent recommendations in respect of children's psychological needs. However, the almost exclusive focus is on *practice* issues: there is no questioning of the need for institutional care in the Sri Lankan context, despite the fact that analysis of reasons for admission shows that only 10 per cent of children were full orphans, and that more than a third had both parents living. The need for a thorough assessment of the circumstances of each child who is referred to institutions and for an active searching for alternative forms of care were self-evident from the findings of the study, but are absent from the conclusions. These two examples are typical of the literature on institutional care.

The concept of institutional care must be questioned whenever such care is promoted in situations where families and communities, even under stress, have the capacity for providing care for homeless children. Many children admitted into institutional care could be adequately cared for within their own families or communities, but, once established, institutions tend to exert a 'pull effect', drawing in children whose need for substitute care is questionable. A key issue linking the concept and practice of institutional care is the process of assessment and planning for children separated from their families, which is essential if residential care is to be offered only to those who *need* to be away from their families, who cannot be placed within their own communities, and for whom other alternatives (such as substitute family care) are unavailable. These and other practice issues dominate the rest of this book.

3 Institutionalised children: Who are they?

One of the recurring themes in SCF's research is that institutions frequently draw in children who do not need to be there. Moreover, the developing world abounds with examples of child care institutions where the stated purpose of the establishment conflicts with the reality of its admissions practice. This chapter examines the three principal categories of residential institution – generic children's homes, homes or schools for disabled children, and establishments for young offenders – and considers in each case the extent to which the stated purposes of admission coincide with what happens in reality.

Residential institutions for orphaned, destitute and abandoned children

The great majority of residential child care institutions in the developing world come under broad headings such as 'orphanage' or 'children's home'. The aims of such institutions are frequently expressed (if at all) in vague terms, for example: 'to provide care for children unable to live with their family', or 'to care for orphaned, abandoned and destitute children'. Ostensibly, most such 'multi-purpose' residential homes see it as their task to provide for children who are orphaned, abandoned, unaccompanied or destitute, although admissions criteria are rarely defined clearly, and, as this chapter shows, the reality is often that children outside these categories are admitted anyway. First, however, some brief comments are necessary on the terms used to describe children admitted to this category of institutions.

Orphaned children

The term 'orphan' is used in a variety of different ways, and has different connotations according to cultural context. Sometimes the term is used to describe a child who has lost one parent, while in others it is reserved for a child who has lost both. The loss of either parent is frequently cited as a reason for admission to residential care: the loss of a father may create economic difficulties which may lead the mother to place the child in residential care, while the loss of the mother may create a situation where a father can neither provide care himself (in many societies it is unusual for fathers to take on an active caring role) nor find a culturally appropriate alternative caregiver. In Vietnamese society, for example, the idea of 'a rooster caring for its chicks' is unthinkable: a local proverb states:

> Lose the father, still something to eat; lose the mother, nowhere to sleep.[35]

Remarriage of a widowed parent often creates family tensions, with variations on the theme of 'the wicked step-parent' appearing in folklore in cultures right across the world. Again Vietnam offers an interesting illustration of the deeply ingrained negative images of step-parents. All terms for 'step-mother' carry negative connotations; one is translated literally as 'mother bitter and cruel'.

Throughout Sub-Saharan Africa, children are regarded as belonging to the clan and lineage, and, traditionally, orphaned children would be absorbed, as a matter of course, within those networks. Writing of Kenya, Colton states:

> before the arrival of the Europeans ... if a child lost a parent or parents he was automatically taken in by the most immediate relatives since in most tribal customs children were regarded as a responsibility of the clan as a whole. The changing lifestyle engendered by contact with Western civilization resulted in the advent of the homeless child. [36]

To some extent the exercise of traditional obligations toward children has been eroded by the combined effects of urbanisation and poverty, though this has sometimes been overstated. However, once 'orphanages' are established, they may serve to relieve members of the child's extended family of their sense of obligation, providing an 'instant solution' in situations in which other and more appropriate family-based care might be available.

Abandoned children

The term 'abandonment' is also used in different ways, and sometimes carries an inappropriately perjorative connotation.[37] It is often used to describe situations in which a child, usually a baby, is abandoned by a parent or caregiver, usually in some public place, with the obvious intention of creating a permanent separation. But 'abandonment' is also used in situations in which a parent places a child in a residential institution without the intention of relinquishing the child permanently. However, short-term intentions can easily become long-term realities, and, with the tendency for parental contact to diminish, such children can become, in effect, abandoned. In an article based on experience in Brazil, Rizzini demonstrates that poverty is a major factor in the placement of children by parents in institutions, and shows how this often becomes, over the longer term, a form of abandonment.[38] The issue of parental links for children in institutions is considered in Chapter 4.

Unaccompanied children

This is usually used as a generic term for children separated from their parents, usually in situations of war or natural disaster. Children so described will include those who have become separated accidentally from their families (for example, in the process of flight), as well as orphaned and abandoned children, young people who have been abducted or conscripted into armies, and those who have chosen to leave their families.

Destitute children

This is also a term which covers a wide range of family circumstances. It is used to describe families living in poverty, to varying degrees, but may also be used, as an admission criterion, to cover situations such as a single mother who needs to work but has no access to appropriate non-residential child care facilities.

Are children who fall into the categories described above appropriate to be admitted into residential care? An orphaned child having no one within the wider family able to provide care; the abandoned child of unknown family origins; the unaccompanied child in a refugee camp, or the child whose parents are literally destitute – all these might be seen to be in need of care which an institution can offer. However, SCF's research has uncovered a great many examples of residential institutions which, in the absence of clearly articulated admission criteria, have admitted children from a very wide range of social circumstances. Even allowing for a broad interpretation of terms such as 'orphan' and 'destitute', many residential institutions in almost all of the countries included in this study admit children who fall outside their admission criteria. The underlying reason for admission is poverty, coupled with the perceived advantages of institutional care (shelter, food and access to education), rather than lack of alternatives.

For example, in her study of children's institutions in Lesotho, Simms reveals a picture of widespread admission into institutional care for children who could readily be cared for in the community (Box 3.1).[39]

Box 3.1   Admission to residential homes in Lesotho

The study revealed that large numbers of children are institutionalised because consideration was not given to placement of children within the extended family. Two main reasons lay behind admissions. First, widespread poverty: case studies undertaken as part of the research indicated that 78 per cent of the children studied had been admitted because of poverty. Second, free and privileged education made children's homes attractive to parents, who expected the children to return home for holidays.

However, Simms found that, once admitted, children tended to be permanently institutionalised; she cites one home where children were retained despite requests from both child and family to return home, even though the home had no legal powers to do so.

In a study of a large institution for supposedly unaccompanied Ethiopian refugee children in Mogadishu, the capital city of Somalia, it was found that the large majority of children admitted were not unaccompanied at all (Box 3.2).[40]

Box 3.2   An institution in Somalia

Admission was sought by parents partly because their children were assured of shelter, a good diet and access to a quality of education unavailable in refugee camps. An additional motivation was to establish their child in the city, with all the opportunities it presented, to act as an 'anchor' to enable the whole family to settle there as a means of escape from an uncertain future in remote refugee camps.

What was particularly interesting in this institution was that the family circumstances of many of the children were unknown to the institution's staff, with many parents and children giving false information, and a great deal of contact with families occurring covertly. Both children and their parents were afraid that children would be sent home if their true circumstances were known.

The changing philosophy of residential care is graphically illustrated in a fascinating history of residential care provided by the Guild of Service (Central) in Madras, South India.[41] As a result of a growing awareness of the disadvantages of institutional forms of care, a decision was made to explore the possibility of children returning to the care of their families from a home providing care for 'orphaned and destitute boys'. No less than two-thirds of the children were returned to their families, who were offered a programme of material and social support. Once again, it was clear that children had been separated from their families and admitted to care primarily because of poverty.

In her study of seven children's institutions run by the National Foundation for the Welfare of Children in Rio de Janeiro (Brazil), Altoé noted that, although these institutions ostensibly catered for deprived and abandoned children, less than 10 per cent were orphans, and the majority had both parents living. Moreover, she concluded that these institutions (each caring, on average, for more than 300 children) exhibited some of the worst characteristics of institutional care.[42]

In another study from Brazil of an institution run by a Catholic foundation, Rizzini demonstrated that children were admitted primarily because their (single) mothers needed to work, usually in domestic service.[43] But the mothers were placed in a curious 'double-bind': on the one hand, they were pushed into 'becoming better parents' and absorbing 'Christian values'; on the other hand, they were denied opportunities to exercise parental responsibility for their children, and excluded from participating in their lives. Rizzini's conclusion was that such institutions 'serve as agents to perpetuate and promote the abandonment of children'.[44]

These examples are typical of virtually all the countries studied in SCF's research. The underlying factor is the role of poverty, combined with the availability of residential care as an apparently attractive 'instant solution' to the problems facing hard-pressed families striving to meet the needs of their children. The case studies and literature review suggest the following conclusions:

● Only a small minority of children living in children's homes are there because they have been permanently abandoned by their immediate family, or are fully orphaned.

● Even in cultures where there are strong traditions of care within the extended family for parentless children, the majority of children in many institutions *do* have parents or other members of the extended family who could potentially provide care for the child.

● One of the principal reasons for this situation is that the staff of the institution, or social workers within their parent agency, fail to undertake an assessment of the situation and needs of children who are referred for care. Gatekeeping policies and practices are *essential* if institutional care is to be used as an appropriate means of caring for separated children; these are explored in more detail in Chapter 4.

• Placing a child in residential care is often a survival strategy used by parents as an immediate response to the desperation caused by poverty, without thinking through the long-term consequences. However, given the propensity of institutions to 'take over' the child, parental contact tends to diminish over time, and what was seen as a short-term solution becomes a long-term arrangement. Parents rarely perceive the disadvantages of residential care.

• The availability of free education is a major factor in prompting parents to place children in residential care as a means of seeking an escape from poverty. Children's homes (or orphanages), however, are quite different from boarding schools, in that they tend to *replace* parental roles. Boarding schools seek to *supplement* parental roles and responsibilities: parental responsibility remains intact, and children normally return home for holidays.

• It is self-evident that residential care is a wholly inappropriate response to poverty. It fails to address the root causes, is a relatively expensive way of responding to a minute proportion of children and families living in poverty, and is likely to create long-term problems for the child who spends an extended period in residential care.

• Residential institutions exert a 'pull effect' because of the immediate advantages they offer of shelter, food and education. It has frequently been observed that the characteristics of many of the children admitted are not significantly different from those of other children living with their families in impoverished circumstances in the community. It is the *availability* of residential care rather than an objectively determined need that lies behind many, and probably most, admissions to children's homes.

Institutions providing education, social and medical care for children with disabilities

Although the principal focus of this study is not on children with disabilities, some broad observations regarding the situation of disabled children in institutions can be made.

It is common to find a high percentage of children in residential care who have a disability: this reflects not just the significant numbers of institutions specifically for children with disabilities, but also the fact that disabled children, in many cultures, may be significantly more likely to be abandoned or rejected than their able-bodied peers, and, once in residential care, are less likely to be placed for adoption or fostering (assuming such placements are available at all).

The enhanced susceptibility of children with disabilities to abandonment and rejection reflects a number of factors, including the stigma attached to having a disabled child in some cultures; the sense of social isolation that parents may experience as a result; the lack of support services, both for disabled children and for their parents, and, in particular, the difficulties of gaining access to educational opportunities. Children with disabilities are also likely to make additional demands on their mothers, for whom time may be a scarce commodity. Underlying all these factors are individual and social attitudes which view people with disabilities as 'different', unable to contribute to their own family and community, and requiring special, segregated care.

In many countries, the mere fact of having a disability is still considered to be an appropriate reason for a child to be admitted into residential care. Although the trend in many Western countries is towards the integration of disabled children into their communities and into local and mainstream educational provision wherever possible, this is by no means a universal phenomenon. It is common in the developing world to find organisations still committed to the philosophy that residential facilities are the most appropriate means of meeting the needs of children with disabilities.

There appear to be many reasons for this pervasive attitude. First, a belief that disabled children are 'too difficult' to be managed at home. Second, lack of resources to enable the child to be integrated into local education and other facilities. Third, social attitudes which limit the acceptability of disabled children in their own communities. In situations where there is a highly-developed institutional sector for children with disabilities, there is a danger that a vicious circle will develop: the more that children with disabilities are perceived as requiring a specialised and institutional response, the less incentive there is to promote community-based provision and to foster attitudes which will help disabled people to be more fully accepted by and integrated within their own communities.

There is, however, growing acceptance of community-based rehabilitation as the most appropriate and cost-effective means of meeting the needs of the majority of children with disabilities, so that residential care should be seen as an inappropriate and expensive means of meeting the needs of a tiny minority of disabled children.[45] Furthermore, residential care has frequently been shown to be ineffective in enabling disabled children to become independent. This is not to deny that certain types of disability may require more intensive and specialised care, treatment and education – for example, some children with multiple disabilities and those with profound sensory impairment.

In her study of residential institutions for children in Lesotho, Simms examined two homes for physically disabled children, one for boys and the other for girls.[46] She found that children with moderate degrees of physical disability (the most severely disabled children were not considered for admission!) were admitted for a range of reasons, which included poverty, distance from educational and medical facilities, and, in some cases, the mere fact of disability. However, research showed that the majority of children admitted had previously lived in areas with relatively easy access to both medical and educational facilities, and that, in the great majority of cases, children were admitted solely because of poverty. Paradoxically, the great majority of disabled children who were living in locations where access to medical and educational facilities was difficult were not offered any kind of assistance.

The experience of residential care in this case not only failed to prepare children for adult life, but also served to alienate them from their extended families, and hence to deny them the vital support they needed after discharge:

> Once admitted, children invariably were permanently institutionalized, whether there was still a good reason for this or not ... Reared in conditions inadequate to provide for their psychological development and alienated from skills and philosophies normally acquired from extended family members, the prospects of these youngsters coping in the future are bleak, despite their privileged education. They are therefore particularly in need of the social security and support, normally provided by the extended family, from which they have, in many cases, been alienated.

Some institutions, far from providing a regime which helps children to overcome their disabilities, actually serve to exaggerate them. Writing about institutions in St Petersburg, Dammann notes:

> if a child cannot say 10 words in Russian at a year old, he will be classified as mentally handicapped. The doctors often classified children this way because caring for the mentally handicapped means a 40 per cent pay increase for the staff.[47]

In Romania, children with learning difficulties were sent to homes for 'irrecuperables'. Once so labelled, it would be surprising *not* to find care practices which served to reinforce the child's perceived disability.[48] These issues are treated in more depth in Chapter 5, but the following preliminary conclusions emerge:

● In many cultures, there will be an over-representation of children with disabilities in residential care, reflecting both their greater vulnerability to abandonment and rejection, and perceptions that disabled children need specialised residential help.

● Residential care is an extremely expensive way of meeting the needs of, at best, a tiny proportion of the total population of children with disabilities.

● The promotion of residential forms of care for disabled children may serve to detract from the need to develop community-based rehabilitation, to encourage educational integration and to promote acceptance and integration of people with disabilities.

● Residential care tends to have a negative impact on the identity and self-worth of children with disabilities: rather than helping children to see themselves as full and participating members of their own communities, institutional care tends to encourage children to identify primarily with other disabled children in a sheltered situation, and to discourage them from seeing themselves as able to interact, on an equal basis, with others.

● Once labelled as 'disabled' (or worse still, as 'handicapped' or 'irrecuperable'), there is a tendency, in some institutions, to treat children as such and to fail to help them to achieve their potential. Institutions may further *disable* children if their focus is on disability rather than ability.

● Unfortunately, homes and schools for children with disabilities tend to have a particularly high 'donor-appeal', presenting a picture of 'something being done' for disabled children, and creating a visible and apparently appealing outcome of giving for individuals and agencies.

Residential institutions for young offenders

Although a discussion of the particular problems and issues involved in the field of juvenile justice is also beyond the scope of this book, it is important to note that significant numbers of institutions for children have as their ostensible purpose the punishment, treatment, care, education or training of young people who have, or who are alleged to have, committed offences. Recurring themes in residential institutions for children throughout the world – such as a lack of clearly stated objectives, unclear admission criteria and a disjunction between what children actually experience while in care and the reasons why they have been placed there – are particularly evident in residential institutions set up to respond to the problems and needs of young people who have committed offences.

Countries vary widely in the range of responses to the problems of young offenders. As indicated in Chapter 2, one of the factors behind the initial development of institutional forms of care was a concern, particularly during colonial rule, for the protection of property and for the control of behaviour which was regarded as deviant. Many former colonies in the developing world have modelled their systems for the control of delinquency on those of the colonial power, often remaining largely untouched for the past half-century or more. These systems centred on the removal of young offenders from their family and community surroundings, and the provision of a range of institutional facilities which emphasised discipline and, in theory if not in practice, training. These include approved schools, remand homes and other forms of custodial institution.

What is lacking in most of the countries covered by this book is the infrastructure required to ensure that a discriminating use is made of residential facilities, and the resources required to provide the courts with a range of possible sentences according to the nature and gravity of the offence and the child's individual needs and circumstances. The result is an excessive use of custodial sentencing for children, and, worse still, the detention of children in institutions without due legal process. Many children in institutions have been committed because of alleged 'status offences', or behaviour which, in adults, would not be seen as warranting incarceration (for example, uncontrollable behaviour, promiscuity and running away from home). Not infrequently, children are found in adult prisons;[49] they are sentenced to long periods in custody for minor offences and on first conviction, and detained in institutions for young offenders even though there has been no conviction for any offence. Moreover, children who have not been convicted – or even accused – of any offence may be compulsorily detained in institutions for young offenders. For example, children found to be living and working on the street may be rounded up by the police and detained in institutions on the assumption that, if they are street children, they must be young offenders or drug addicts.

In Brazil, for example, government institutions which existed ostensibly for young offenders actually admitted children from a wide range of circumstances, including street children rounded up by the police, along with supposedly orphaned or destitute children. All were exposed to a harsh and rigid militaristic regime. Information from former residents now working for CEAP (the Centre for the Mobilisation of Marginalised Populations) suggests that only 8 per cent of children admitted were actually convicted of offences.[50] The institutions had become a dumping-ground for society's unwanted and rejected children, who were then exposed to an inhumane regime which was designed around the perceived needs of young offenders.

In summary, the following points are particularly significant:

● Many institutions which were set up to provide care, treatment, custody or training for young offenders actually admit young people from a wide variety of backgrounds – for example, orphaned and abandoned children – who are then treated as though they had been convicted of serious offences.

● The objectives of institutions for young offenders are rarely defined clearly and precisely: it is even more difficult to find examples of institutions which work *purposefully* towards those objectives.

● It is not unusual to find young people admitted to a custodial institution without being convicted by a court of law. An even more frequent occurrence is the committal of young people to custodial institutions for trivial or first offences.

● Children's behaviour which does not contravene the law may still be equated with delinquency. Children who have been deemed to be beyond parental control, or who are alleged to be promiscuous, for example, may be treated as though they were offenders, and placed in an institution.

● It is rare to find that any purposeful follow-up work is undertaken with young offenders after their release: little is therefore known about the pattern of offending after release.

Who benefits from institutional care?

Having reviewed the main categories of children found in institutions in the developing world, this chapter concludes by considering the question, 'Who benefits from institutional care?'

The primary beneficiaries of institutional care are frequently *not* children. It is often the needs of their parents or other caregivers which dictate the seeking of admission: poverty is the most pervasive influence, compounded by others, such as poor housing and lack of day care facilities for young children. The parents of children with a disability may seek admission because of a sense of shame, social isolation, or lack of support services. In some cases, society can be seen as the primary beneficiary: in the case of children incarcerated because of their offending behaviour, the system is motivated by the perceived needs of society, not those of the individual child.

It is difficult to avoid the conclusion that many institutions exist primarily to meet the needs of the individuals or agencies responsible for providing them. Institutions are sometimes motivated by factors which range from straightforward financial gain through to evangelism, sometimes by extreme religious sects.[51]

To what extent, therefore, do residential institutions exist to meet the needs of children? The evidence gathered by SCF's research suggests that only rarely are children admitted to residential care as a result of a carefully considered judgement that this course of action is most likely to satisfy the needs and views of the child. As a report from Defence for Children International suggests, 'placement in an institution solves the problem of the placers, and not those of the placed'.[52]

4 Critical practice issues: Gatekeeping and family contact

This chapter concentrates on two related issues of central significance. First, the process of assessment and planning for children, including the important issue of admissions policies and practices in institutions, referred to here as 'gatekeeping'. Second, contact between children in residential care and their families, which is of great significance not only in facilitating the growing child's sense of self-esteem and personal identity, but also in making it possible for children to return to a more normal life within the family.

By way of introduction, it is worth noting once again the tendency for institutions to admit children whose circumstances and needs fall outside their formal (or assumed) admission criteria. Organisations are social systems which seek the attainment of a particular type of goal,[53] and residential institutions for children can be seen as one form of organisation.[54] One of the features of institutions is their tendency to depart from their stated goals. As Etzioni states:

> once formed, organisations acquire their own needs, these sometimes becoming the masters of the organisation ... In such instances, organisations reduce the service to their initial goals in order to satisfy their acquired needs, rather than adjust the service of their acquired needs to that of their goals. *Sometimes organisations go as far as to abandon their initial goals and pursue new ones more suited to the organisation's needs.* [emphasis added][55]

It would be difficult to find a clearer demonstration of this process than residential institutions for children in the developing world: indeed, SCF's research suggests that the needs of children have become a secondary consideration in many of the institutions visited.

Some examples of this phenomenon have already been provided. The home for unaccompanied Ethiopian refugee children in Mogadishu (Box 3.2) illustrates how a large institution, ostensibly set up to cater for

49

unaccompanied refugee children, provided care for a completely different clientele. Similarly, in Brazil institutions ostensibly for young offenders provided for a wide range of other children, including orphaned and abandoned children and young people rounded up off the streets (see Chapter 3). A third example comes from Uganda (Box 4.1).

Box 4.1   Institutional care in Uganda[56]

The civil war in Uganda during the 1980s created large numbers of children separated from their families – some had been genuinely orphaned, others had become separated in the chaos caused by the conflict. In response to this situation, a large number of NGOs and individuals set up children's homes to provide care for this growing number of separated children. However, in the post-war period, significant numbers of these children were able to return to the care of their families, but many of the children's homes then admitted other categories of children, many of whom had family members who were willing and able to care for them.

The combination of material provision (food, clothes and shelter) combined with the availability of free and good-quality education made residential care an apparently attractive option for families struggling to rebuild their lives after the war. The government Programme of Family Tracing successfully reunited many of these children with their families, and the introduction of new rules governing the conduct of residential homes restricted the inappropriate admission of children, and led to the closure of many institutions.

The admission into institutions of children who fall outside the stated admission criteria is not, of course, confined to the developing world. Writing of institutions in the USA, Wooden concludes that:

> far too often we find a mixed bag of children within institutions designed to help in areas other than where help is needed. I have seen hundreds of retarded children in jails and many normal children in mental hospitals or mental retardation facilities because the states either don't screen them properly or lack the resources to fulfil a child's needs.[57]

Gatekeeping

'Gatekeeping' is the term used here to describe the process of assessment and planning of children's needs and circumstances which should precede admission into residential care, and contribute to their onward progression – back to their families, into a form of substitute family care, or, in the case of older youngsters, moving on to some form of independent living.

SCF's research shows that gatekeeping is a particularly crucial aspect of institutional care, and that gatekeeping policies and practices are significantly deficient, or wholly absent, in the great majority of residential institutions visited in connection with this study.

Careful and detailed assessment and planning has, for many years, been seen in Western societies as crucial for the long-term well-being of children in care. Since the publication of Rowe and Lambert's highly influential study into the problems of children requiring long-term substitute family placement in the UK,[58] growing emphasis has been placed on the importance of assessment and planning to prevent the damage which is done to children when they spend indeterminate periods of time in institutional or other forms of non-permanent care. In the developing world, it is rare to find any systematic attempt to assess the needs of children referred for care, to consider the various alternatives which might be available, or to make careful plans for the child's future, both within and beyond the residential home.

Assessment and planning needs to be considered at three critical stages:

- prior to the child's admission;
- following admission;
- prior to leaving residential care.

Pre-admission assessment and planning

Assessment and planning before placement is of the utmost importance in determining the future course of events for the child. All too often, residential care is seen as 'the solution', without an exploration of 'the problem', and children are admitted on an indeterminate basis with no consideration of future alternative forms of care. However, in the rare examples where gatekeeping policies have been put into practice, it has proved possible for significant numbers of children to be diverted from residential care, and for children who have been admitted to return to their families. Two examples will serve to illustrate this process (Boxes 4.2 and 4.3).

Box 4.2   The Seva Samajam Boys' Home[59]

This residential home in Madras admitted older boys, many of them having been transferred from an institution for younger children run by the same organisation.

A number of events led to a major revision in the philosophy and policy of the boys' home, including a growing awareness both of children's needs for a level of emotional support and affection which an institution cannot offer, and of the difficulties being experienced by boys in the institution during adolescence, and

continued

Box 4.2 continued

especially on leaving the home.

As the result of a major review of the home, a new philosophy was adopted, which emphasised children's need for their families, and the need for residential care to be offered only when other forms of family support have proved to be inappropriate or unsuccessful.

It was found possible for about half of the residents to be returned to their families, with various forms of support. By offering a range of supportive interventions to families in the community, the flood of requests for admission was drastically reduced.

Box 4.3   Inhambane Children's Home

Despite the very large numbers of orphaned and unaccompanied children in Mozambique, stemming from the combination of a long civil war and drought, the government of Mozambique have pursued a systematic policy of promoting non-institutional care for separated children.

In the Province of Inhambane, for example, government staff undertake a full social history in respect of all separated or abandoned children. Before consideration of admission to the Provincial residential home, other options are considered, including tracing the family (where the child has become separated as a result of civil conflict), and, where circumstances require it, various means are found to support the family, especially during critical periods. Where circumstances do not permit the child to remain with her family, consideration is given to substitute family care, though this is not a well-developed programme.

Children are only admitted to residential care if strict criteria are met, and, when a family does seek admission for a child, a contract is always made with the Department of Social Action. Adhering to these procedures means that admissions are kept to a minimum, and periods in residential care now tend to be short.

Underlying both these examples are a number of crucial features:

- an open and honest acknowledgement of the disadvantages of institutional care for children;
- a systematic approach to the assessment of children's needs and family circumstances;
- a willingness to explore other options, whether some form of family tracing and reunification, support to the family, or substitute family care;
- a recognition of the importance of the family and the need to maintain family ties while the child is in care.

It is noteworthy that, in the case of Mozambique, this approach was sustained despite the large numbers of unaccompanied children and the very limited resources available. *Good gatekeeping is more a matter of attitude and philosophy than the availability of resources.* Indeed, good gatekeeping practices enable institutions to make optimal use of their resources.

Planning for children already in residential care

Once admitted into residential care, the tendency is for the child's stay to become indeterminate unless there is active planning for him to return to his family, or to be placed in substitute family care. Even when children are admitted because of a family crisis requiring care on a short-term basis, it is all too easy for the placement to drift into long-term care: links between the child and his family tend to drift unless they are perceived by the staff of the institution as important, and are therefore encouraged and nurtured. Even when children are admitted into institutions because of a need for permanent care, inactivity on the part of staff often leads to a situation in which children languish for long periods in institutional care: with the passage of time, it becomes less and less likely that the child could be considered for adoption.

This is graphically illustrated by Rizzini's work in Brazil.[60] She found that many children who are potentially available for adoption are never actually placed in families because the inactivity of the State institutions involved leads to delays of months or years before the child can be considered for adoption:

> When this occurs it is already too late. Older children have greater adaptation difficulties and the period they spend in care hinders their development in every sense, turning them into 'problem' children with far fewer chances of being adopted.

Effective planning for children in care requires multi-sectoral co-operation, and, where this is weak, the planning of permanent placements can be impeded. In India, for example, the process by which abandoned children can be declared to be available for adoption is complex, and relies heavily on the active involvement of the police, who do not necessarily regard this work as a high priority; long delays may therefore ensue.

In Mozambique, planning procedures have been established to ensure that children do not drift into indeterminate care (see Box 4.3). Although both adoption and fostering rely on interested families approaching the Department of Social Action (resources not permitting a more pro-active programme of substitute family care), Mozambique has succeeded in limiting the admission of children to institutions and shortening the length of time spent in residential care.

Article 25 of the UN Convention on the Rights of the Child requires agencies providing care to review periodically the treatment provided to the child. In the UK, regular reviews have long been recognised as an important means of avoiding 'drift' in placements.

Planning for leaving care

A third area in which planning is deficient is the discharge of older youngsters from residential care. In almost all the countries covered by SCF's research, problems experienced by young people in moving out into independent life in the community are widely acknowledged, but it is rare to find any purposeful work being undertaken to address these issues.

The problem is not difficult to explain: when children spend substantial amounts of their childhood in large, impersonal institutions, cut off from their families and from the wider community, it is not surprising that many will face the future with great anxiety. They may feel ill-equipped to cope with the demands of marriage, family life, work and personal survival in a world from which they may have been insulated for many years.

The problems and issues surrounding children leaving care are addressed in more detail in Chapter 5. At this point, what needs to be emphasised is that leaving care is a major transition, requiring careful planning and preparation. Where is the child going to live? Does he have the social and life skills required for independent living? Has the young person had appropriate opportunities for vocational training and work experience? Has he had sufficient experience of different roles to be able to take on culturally appropriate roles and tasks?

All too often, these problems are not addressed until children are about to leave care and are forced to face the daunting task of living in a society from which they have been isolated for many years. Institutional care, by its very nature, should have as its ultimate aim the preparation of young people for adult life: planning for the future should not, therefore, be approached as a simple and practical task to be undertaken as the child approaches adulthood, but as an intrinsic feature of the whole experience of residential living, with planning beginning several years before the child leaves, in order to ensure that she has been given a whole range of experiences to enable her to cope adequately in the adult world. This process requires an honest acknowledgement of the disadvantages of institutional living, and the will to provide for the child a range of experiences appropriate to her assessed needs.

Contact between children in residential care and their families

When institutional goals begin to dominate admission, parents and other 'outside figures' come to be seen not as partners to be engaged in the process of caring, but as a hindrance to the smooth operation of the establishment. It is much easier for an institution to replace parents than it is to work in co-operation with them. However, the UN Convention on the Rights of the Child specifies the right for children to maintain 'personal relations and direct contact with both parents on a regular basis, except if it is contrary to the child's best interests'.[61]

Research in Western societies has emphasised the importance of parental contact for children in care. One of the most influential of the studies was undertaken by the Dartington Social Research Unit in the UK.[62] The researchers followed up a large group of children who had been admitted to care for a wide range of reasons. They found that, at the outset of the care episode, three-quarters of the children experienced great difficulty in maintaining contact with parents. After two years away from home, four-fifths experienced 'severe barriers' to maintaining contact with their families, even though in two-thirds of these cases there were no professional reasons for excluding the natural family from the child's life. The researchers described this phenomenon as one of 'withering links'. Contact with family members tends to be eroded over time, and a good pattern of family contact has to be actively supported and nurtured by social workers and the child's carers if this is to be avoided. These findings emerged from a study of a relatively well-resourced pattern of local authority child care provision in which each child had an assigned social worker to deal with issues such as family contact.

Although it is dangerous to make assumptions about the relevance of this research to the very different context of the developing world, the research evidence that does exist tends to echo the findings. Furthermore, in cultural contexts in which family bonds are extremely strong, regular family contact assumes a central importance in the growing child's sense of identity. In this context it is particularly disturbing to find situations in which contact between children in institutions and their families has been lost. In Simms's study in Lesotho, the following picture emerges:

> In the homes for 'normal' children, the amount of contact between children and their families is particularly inadequate. Case studies were completed on a random sample of nine children. Of these, six do not go home in the holidays and in only two cases was there any reason for this ... Seven children were not visited by their families either. A total of six children have no contact with their family whatsoever.

In another home:

> no child was allowed to visit its family in the holidays despite many having been admitted only for reasons of poverty and despite the majority of children and families wanting the child to return home permanently. In nearly all cases, it was estimated that there was no good reason this could not occur.

The situation for children in homes for disabled children was even more serious. Children were admitted primarily because of poverty, and:

> once admitted, children invariably were permanently institutionalised, whether there was still a good reason for this or not.[63]

It is clear from this study that the main hindrance to family contact is not an unwillingness on the part of the family to maintain links, but the institution itself. A young disabled adult who had spent much of his childhood in a government boarding school for physically disabled children told SCF's researchers that:

> My parents used to totally forget about me because I became the property of the government – I no longer belonged to my parents.[64]

The residential institution for unaccompanied Ethiopian refugee children in Mogadishu (see Box 3.2) offers an interesting illustration of the maintenance of contact by families in a covert way: children were literally climbing over the perimeter wall in order to visit their families. Fortunately, this was not impeded by the director of the institution. However, because of the inadequate admissions procedure and the lack of satisfactory documentation, contact between children and their families was left very much to chance, and the link with some families became broken permanently.

The problems of family contact emerged as a significant issue in Wijetunge's research into children in institutions in Sri Lanka:

> For many children, entry into an institution amounts to a permanent breakage of family ties. This may cause severe psychological suffering in adolescence and adult life, as the young person perceives him/her self without roots in a family culture.[65]

The effects of isolation from family are considered in more detail in Chapter 5, but it is worth noting that most of the children in the institutions studied in Sri Lanka had at least one parent living. However, in the case of children whose mothers were known to be living, only 56.9 per cent of mothers visited their children.

A study of institutions in Latin America and the Caribbean by UNICEF identifies geographical distance, poverty, and institutional attitudes as being significant in the lack of contact between children and their families.[66] Reference is made to the practice of '"deportation" – the placement of children in institutions far from their homes, which emphasises [the child's] convict condition by estranging him from his family and social environment ... This impeded or completely broke the ties between the child, his family, and his community of origin.'

Other evidence comes from Brazil, where, in her study of three institutions in Rio de Janeiro, Rizzini notes that, although 80 per cent of the children had parents, 58 per cent had only sporadic links, or no links at all, with their families.[67] In most cases, children were placed in institutions because of poverty, but, in effect, this became a form of abandonment, with obvious consequences for the child's sense of identity and future security.

The emotional implications of this form of abandonment are graphically illustrated by a Brazilian girl who was living on the streets after a long period in institutional care:

> You think I am an orphan because I am in [an institution]. It is for poor children. At one time my parents visited me but then they stopped coming. Today I wander the streets. I see a face in the crowd and wonder if it is my father ... I see another face and I wonder if it is my mother.[68]

Lack of planned and nurtured contact between children in residential care and their families was found to be an almost universal phenomenon in the countries covered by SCF's research. It is extremely rare to find any institution which positively values family contact. A notable exception, however, is the Seva Samajam Boys' Home in Madras, whose philosophy includes the following statement:

> Services of the institution shall not be only child-centred but family-oriented. Efforts to strengthen the family to make the environment conducive to the child to be brought up in will be the focus. Institutional care shall not be a permanent arrangement and will not encourage dependency.[69]

The implications of 'withering links' with parents are profound. They include:

- the child's sense of rejection or abandonment;
- the loss of opportunities of close and intimate interaction with loved family members;
- the lack of a sense of personal, family and clanship identity.

All are highly significant during childhood, and have long-term implications for children's adjustment to the adult world after leaving the institution.

Chapter 5 explores this crucial issue in more depth.

Conclusions

This chapter has highlighted several key issues which are conspicuous by their absence in most of the countries studied in connection with SCF's research programme:

● Careful and thorough assessment of the child and his family and community context are essential if inappropriate admission into institutional care is to be avoided and alternatives explored.

● Regular reassessment and planning are necessary in order to avoid exposing children to the uncertainty and insecurity which stem from indeterminate placements in residential care. Both transfer to substitute family care (where this is available) and discharge from care on the part of young people about to enter the world of independence will be facilitated by the careful and continuous assessment and planning of the youngster's needs, problems and resources.

● Empirical evidence has shown time and time again that family contact among children in residential care tends to wither away unless it is consciously nurtured by staff, and seen as important not just for the child's security in the future, but also for his developing sense of self-esteem and personal identity.

5 The impact of institutional care on children

The discussion of separation in Chapter 1 concluded that it is common for children (especially young children) to experience distress on separation from parent-figures, and – in the case of longer-term separation – for a period of despair and, ultimately, a reaction of detachment to set in. Developmental retardation experienced by separated children should be regarded not so much as a reaction to separation, as a response to living in an unstimulating environment; particularly significant is the absence of opportunities in many residential institutions for affectionate and spontaneous interaction with adults who take a personal interest in the child.

The long-term effect of separation on mental health is not just a reaction to the loss of parents or parent-figures; it also reflects the general lack of opportunities in residential institutions for children to experience warm, close and reasonably continuous relationships with trusted adults, or, in some situations, with peers. However, there is some evidence that this 'detachment' phase can become a chronic and defensive reaction to separation, and may lead to long-term depression and an impaired capacity to make intimate relationships. Although existing research has focused on very young children, it is clear that older children also need opportunities to develop close and intimate relationships. It must be re-stated, however, that research undertaken in Western societies cannot be applied wholesale to cultural environments in which multiple parenting is the norm, and that a key determinant of the impact of institutions is *the quality of the caring environment* into which the child is placed (rather than institutionalisation *per se*).

There have been few attempts to adapt Western models of residential care to different cultural contexts. This is clearly essential, although there are *some* parallels between the current experience of developing countries and past experience in the West.

In both contexts, many institutions are large, overcrowded, poorly resourced, understaffed, neglectful and, in some cases, overtly abusive. Pinchbeck and Hewitt's assertion[70] that as many as 80 per cent of children aged under 3 years admitted to some British workhouses during the eighteenth century had died within twelve months finds echoes in countries such as South Vietnam during the 1970s, where a mortality rate of over 90 per cent was reported in some institutions supposedly 'caring' for children.[71]

Much of the Western literature on residential and other forms of care for separated children paints a very negative picture of residential care – for example, Bowlby's work on residential nurseries; very high reconviction rates from custodial institutions; the significant number of recent inquiries into allegations of ill-treatment in various forms of residential care in the UK, and the frequency with which neglectful or abusing parents are found to have had an institutional upbringing themselves.

Similarly with adults, Goffman's influential writing in *Asylums*,[72] the 'warehouse' image of many residential homes for disabled adults,[73] the drive to close down Victorian mental hospitals in recent years, and the picture of institutional life portrayed so graphically in films such as *One Flew over the Cuckoo's Nest* all tend to reinforce the idea that residential care is something to be avoided at all costs. It is, however, something of a paradox that so many UK parents from the middle and upper classes still see institutional care and education as providing the most effective pathway to a successful and influential adult life. When residential forms of care are criticised, reference is more likely to be made to approved schools and mental hospitals than to Eton, or to Kings College Cambridge!

In their writings, Jack and Barbara Tizard have argued that blanket condemnation of all forms of residential care does not square with the evidence.[74] They point out that many of the classic studies of institutional care for children have been carried out in institutions which are obviously unsatisfactory (overcrowded, understaffed, and under-resourced) and have therefore conveyed an unbalanced view of residential care. The Tizards compare the functioning of different types of institutions caring for children which share similar characteristics, and, from this comparative analysis, identify the characteristics of institutional regimes which contribute to satisfactory and unsatisfactory outcomes for children. In respect of certain outcome measures, such as language development, they found that not all children were adversely affected by their residential experience: 'In the best residential nurseries the children we studied were not only healthy but intellectually normal, linguistically advanced, and exposed to a near-normal range of general experiences'.[75]

However, there is little research in developing countries which examines the complex interactions which affect the personality development of children brought up in different types of residential environment, and there are enormous methodological difficulties in the kind of longitudinal research which would be needed in order to isolate specific variables in the complex experience of children in institutional care.

The view taken in this book is that institutions are not intrinsically damaging to children, but that certain characteristic features of institutions are likely to have predictably negative effects on children's development. Furthermore, the developing world abounds with unsatisfactory models of residential care, so that the negative characteristics are more common. Before exploring these characteristics in detail, three points need to be emphasised:

● Appearances can be deceptive. SCF's research has demonstrated how some institutions, despite obvious and visible limitations, provide an unexpectedly good quality of care: an example is the Families for Children Institution in Mogadishu, in which the informal culture of the young residents in many ways provided for the nurturing needs of children, despite the limitations imposed by staffing levels and quality of care.[76] Conversely, other models of care may provide impressively good physical surroundings and a high quality of personal care, but create both a dependency on the institution and difficulties in readjusting to life in the world outside.

● It is important to view residential institutions in their local context, and to avoid imposing Western assumptions and expectations. It is entirely inappropriate, for example, to judge the material condition of residential homes by standards other than those which prevail in the surrounding society.

● It is important to underline the point that empirical evidence of the outcomes of residential care placements in the developing world is almost entirely lacking. A close examination of residential homes can reveal both strengths and weaknesses, and sensitive discussions with children, parents and staff can yield valuable insights into perceptions of residential living. However, the outcome of residential care can only really be evaluated by reference to the subsequent adjustment of the young person to adult life – and perhaps, in particular, to parenthood. Empirical evidence on these long-term effects of residential care in non-Western societies is almost entirely unavailable.

In the meantime one can only rely on the best available information. The rest of this chapter draws evidence from relatively superficial visits to a large number of institutions within the countries covered by SCF's research, a more detailed study using participant observation in a small number of residential homes, and a review of the available literature.

Physical care

Chapter 4 emphasised that many children are admitted to residential care primarily because of poverty: large numbers of parents in almost all the countries studied sought admission of their children to residential care because of their perception that their children's physical survival would, at least, be assured.

The level of physical care in the majority of institutions visited during the research was at least of a minimally acceptable standard. In some instances, the quality of physical care was excellent, but this cannot be taken for granted. In her study of children's institutions in Maharashtra (India), Naidu found that the proportion of malnourished children actually rose after admission.[77] For example, using height-for-age criteria for assessing severe malnutrition, the proportion of severely malnourished children in the institutions in her sample rose from 80.9 per cent on admission to 86.1 per cent at the time of the study.

Other examples of unsatisfactory physical care came from SCF's own research. The first is an extract from a government researcher's report in Africa:

> This home accommodates 57 children. [It] faces serious problems because of an apparent lack of funding ... Children go without food and other basic necessities. Also children are not encouraged to go for holidays despite the fact that they have got their parents and/or relatives ... The optimum number of children that can be looked after is 25.[78]

The second example comes from Latin America:

> In at least 60% of the institutions the on-duty staff ate different food at separate tables, using dishes, while the children ate on trays, in silence, and under strict and severe supervision. Thus on top of the poor quality and frequently scarce meals, social and educational functions were totally absent ... Dormitories with rickety beds ... toilet doors off their hinges or broken or eliminated so there was no privacy when defecating ... classrooms in name only ... Recreation areas either non-existent or underutilised, neglected in the same manner as the rest of the institution.[79]

The third example comes from Asia:

> The babies' section of this large government institutional complex gave me great cause for concern. The place was spotlessly clean and tidy, but children were left in their cots for most of the day ... the older ones were sitting on the floor in groups of three or four being fed by a nurse using the same spoon. Some disabled children were being hurriedly fed individually, but many were obviously 'slow feeders' and were clearly not getting enough food: the matron referred to 'severe staff shortages', yet other staff were standing around doing nothing.[80]

A fourth example of inadequate physical care is explored in more detail in *A Babies' Home in Africa: A Case Study* conducted as part of SCF's research.[81] Reputed to be one of the better babies' homes in this country, closer investigation revealed that a staggering 46 per cent of children had died in the institution during a seventeen-year period: deficient nutrition and inadequate care seemed to be responsible.

The psychological effects of such poor physical standards of care on individual children are more difficult to predict, but it seems likely that poor care and nutrition will also have a serious impact on children's overall sense of well-being and self-esteem.

Care for the 'whole child'

A great deal of residential practice observed during SCF's research suggested a lack of knowledge of child development and children's psychological needs. In many instances, this lack of knowledge was extreme, evidenced by the existence of models of care in which the meeting of physical needs (not always satisfactorily) and the maintenance of order were the primary or sole objectives being pursued. 'Custodial' or 'warehousing' models of care in the developing world are distressingly common.

What are the characteristics of institutional care which contribute to this unsatisfactory state of affairs? This section considers five:

- residential philosophy (the stated or implicit beliefs and assumptions which underpin the practice of the residential home);
- the quality of child–adult interaction, a vitally important area which is linked to the management and leadership of the institution;
- the level of stimulation which is offered to children;
- the pattern of organisation, methods of discipline and daily routines (sometimes referred to as the 'regime');
- the significant role of the peer-group in providing for some of the non-material needs of children.

Residential philosophy

One of the clearest observations to emerge from visits to residential institutions during this study is that the most satisfactory models of care are usually found in institutions where there is a clearly-articulated, though not always written, statement of philosophy. The significance of a clearly-stated philosophy is that it requires the institution to articulate the characteristics of the children for whom it is intended. As Chapter 4 made clear, a common feature of institutions is the mismatch between the stated (or at least assumed) purpose and 'target group' of the institution, and the characteristics of the children who are actually admitted. The home for supposedly unaccompanied Ethiopian refugee children described in Box 3.2 is an example. The formulation of a philosophy requires that such inconsistencies be confronted.

A stated philosophy is also important because it requires some statement of objectives. These may, of course, be expressed in such generalities that little is actually conveyed (for example, 'to provide care for ...'), but may, in some cases, indicate the desired outcome of residential care – for example, 'to enable children to return to their families', or 'to equip children to become useful adult members of their community'.

A statement of philosophy will usually say something about the means by which the objectives are being pursued, as in the following case:

> A child deprived of a normal family needs love and care, in conditions as closely approximating a home as possible ... Services of the institution shall not be only child-centred but family-oriented. Efforts to strengthen the family ... will be the focus.[82]

Finally, a stated philosophy is important in that the *process* of its formulation requires staff and managers to enter into a debate about what they are trying to achieve and how they are attempting to achieve it. This seems to help in achieving a sense of purpose, almost regardless of the actual content of the statement which emerges.

Child–adult relationships

This is clearly a crucial aspect of residential institutions, though not one which is easy to analyse. What is depressingly widespread in the developing world is a model of institutional care which responds only to children's physical needs (and not always effectively and appropriately). Care staff are frequently employed as little more than domestic servants, accorded a very low status and pay, and, not surprisingly, perceive their role only in terms of children's need for cleanliness, food, clothing, sleep, and so on.

One of the recurring themes in SCF's research is the link between the organisational structure of the institution and the quality of care provided. Particularly important are the role of the person in charge (referred to here as the 'unit manager'), the pattern of delegation, and the way in which the tasks of care staff are defined – themes which are echoed in some of the Western research literature too.

It is now more than twenty years since King, Raynes and Tizard published their famous comparative study of institutions for children with learning disabilities.[83] The authors had noted huge differences in the ways in which children's lives were organised in different types of institutions, and that certain types of organisation seemed to facilitate the development of children's abilities (such as speech and life skills) more than others. Very broadly, they were able to categorise residential units as either 'child-oriented' or 'institution-oriented': the differences could not be explained solely by reference to unit size, to staff–child ratios or the degree of disability among the children. The more child-centred units had more flexible systems of staff deployment which afforded greater continuity of relationships for the children: the assignment of tasks to staff was less rigid. The unit managers spent more time with children, and interaction between care staff and children was both greater and warmer.

Tizard et al. summarised the findings thus:

> the more that unit heads were involved in the everyday care and supervision of the children, and the more they talked to them, the more likely were junior staff to behave warmly towards their charges, and the more child oriented were the patterns of care in the unit.[84]

In trying to explain these findings, the authors concluded that, in child-centred units, unit managers enjoyed a good deal more autonomy and had more responsibility delegated to them; they were also more likely to have received child care training, rather than nurse training, which tended to be associated with a 'hospital' model of staff deployment.

Barbara Tizard and her colleagues also found that the structure of the institution had an important effect on staff and child behaviour (measured by reference to language development).[85] The residential nurseries selected for the study were all run by voluntary agencies and offered high standards of physical care and concern for the psychological well-being of children. However, one group of nurseries was characterised by a lack of delegation by the matron, even though the institution was divided into small 'family groups'. The daily routine was carefully timetabled, children were kept together as a group throughout the day, the matron supervised each unit closely, and delegated little or no responsibility to the staff in each group. This structure had profound implications for the role of care staff: their function was effectively reduced to 'minding' the children and keeping order. Their responses to the children were superficial, with commands and 'supervisory' comments being observed – usually involving short sentences and restricted and repetitive vocabulary. The staff often appeared bored, with little investment in their work. Closeness between staff and children was discouraged by the matron, and staff tended not to relax their disciplinary grip in order to engage children in play.

In contrast, a second group of nurseries delegated responsibilities to staff in each family group, housed in a self-contained flat or cottage. Staff had autonomy to plan the day's activities, and there was a more flexible response to children by staff, whose role was closer to a foster mother. Consequently, the quality of verbal interchange between staff and children was wider, and children's levels of language development were higher. There was more closeness between staff and children, and greater continuity in relationships.

The Tizards' research is relevant to institutions in the developing world. One of the recurring features of the institutions is the way in which staff roles are defined by the limited range of tasks given to them, usually in the context of a hierarchical organisation in which little or no responsibility is delegated. As Barbara Tizard says: 'if given a limited role to perform [staff] will behave in a limited way'.[86] A typical example is given in Box 5.1.

Box 5.1   A babies' home in Africa[87]

In this babies' home, staff had a very limited 'supervisory' role. This was an institution in which the unit manager engendered a powerful and negative ethos through a combination of non-delegation of responsibility, a harsh and critical management style, and a lack of demonstrable interest in child care. Staff worked on a task-centred basis, with no sense of responsibility for the 'whole child': close relationships were discouraged, children were moved around the institution as they grew older, and were exposed to a large number of staff working on a rota basis. The babies spent long periods lying passively in their cots. Although some play materials were provided and staff were observed in play sessions with children, there was little evidence of spontaneous interaction between staff and children: staff again seemed to occupy 'supervisory' roles, with little sense of engagement with the children.

In this cultural context, mothers would not normally spend a great deal of time playing with their children: however, older siblings, grandparents and other adults would do so. In the artificial environment of an institution, children would have to rely on staff to undertake a range of 'parenting tasks' which traditionally would be shared amongst a number of people in the child's family and community. However, in this institution, there was no encouragement for older children to take responsibility for the care of younger ones.

These features are typical of institutions observed in SCF's research:

- low adult–child staffing ratios, coupled with a high turnover of staff;
- the deployment of staff who do not see it as part of their role to offer affection and close personal care to children, and may be actively discouraged from doing so;
- the rotation of children through the system;
- the deployment of staff on a shift basis, which offers no continuity of care.

These factors are often compounded when children have to progress from one institution to another (for example, from a babies' home to a children's home, and possibly a third institution at the age of puberty). What are the consequences of these characteristics for children's development?

First, children (especially young children) require close and affectionate relationships with parents or other caretakers in order to engender a sense of trust and to develop the capacity for making and sustaining relationships (see Chapter 1).

Second, it is through close and intimate relationships that children feel wanted and valued, and hence come to develop a sense of self-worth and to avoid the danger of what Erikson referred to as a 'sense of inferiority'.[88] It is, however, significant that, in some institutions in the developing world, the peer-group seems able to meet some of these needs in young people, a conclusion which is discussed below.

Third, children require the security and comfort of close relationships in order to overcome the sense of loss which stems from their separation from their own families. John and Elizabeth Newson use the term 'memory bank' to describe one of the functions of parents in helping children to recall and understand the past in order to integrate past events with present experiences.[89] Although the Newsons describe this as a parenting role, it is equally important (and perhaps more so) for children who have experienced disruption and separation in their lives. Recalling earlier experiences and fitting the past into the present is an essential process which helps the child to become a fully integrated person.

Most research into the effects of these characteristic features of institutional care has focused on very young children, and it seems clear that the greatest and most enduring damage to children will occur when children aged from about 6 months to 2 or 3 years are deprived of close and personal care. Consequently, it is in respect of residential nurseries and children's homes providing care for the very young that the greatest concern is to be expressed. But older children also need affection, personal care, a sense of being important to someone else, and the availability of a trusted person with whom to share their concerns and inner feelings.

Stimulation of children

The earlier discussion of attachment and separation (see Chapter 1) highlighted the importance of stimulation to child development (cognitive abilities, motor skills, social relationships and language). For young children, the quality of the surrounding environment is extremely important in determining the range of opportunities available for exploratory play and interaction with adults and other children. Sensory stimulation is especially important – touch, verbal interaction, access to play materials of different shapes, colours and textures, and so on. The least satisfactory institutions are deeply depriving in this respect: young children left alone in their cots for much of the day; limited verbal interaction; a depressing and drab physical environment; few play materials (which need not be expensive toys), and lack of opportunities for physical activity.

The babies' home described in Box 5.1 offers a typical example: an unstimulating physical environment, infrequent use of outdoor play space, the complete absence of visits to the nearby park and the fact that the home's playroom has been out of use for many years all illustrate a lack of understanding of the crucial importance of stimulation for the healthy development of young children. The inevitable developmental delays, especially in language, were clearly observable.

Some of the most dramatic effects of unstimulating environments have been seen in institutions in Romania and other Eastern European countries. The homes for 'irrecuperables' in Romania, for example, contained children who gave the appearance of being mentally retarded, but whose condition probably reflected the grossly depriving environment to which they had been consigned.[90] Once labelled 'irrecuperable', they were denied the stimulating environment which might have helped them to develop their potential, thereby creating a self-fulfilling prophecy.

Another illustration comes from Latvia (Box 5.2):[91]

Box 5.2   An institution for disabled children in Latvia

In the rooms for babies, the children spent long periods of the daytime lying passively but awake in their cots. The staff in these rooms – described as 'nurses' – saw their task as the physical care of children, and made few attempts to offer any kind of stimulation.

It appeared that children were suffering delay in the development of motor skills and language as a result of these depriving early experiences. Indeed, it seems likely that many of the children who were labelled 'mentally handicapped' were simply severely developmentally delayed as a result of their institutional experience.

Older children also need stimulation for healthy development. Kenneth Wooden, writing of institutions in the USA, suggests that 'boredom, although not overtly violent, is just as cruel as the beatings and verbal abuse.'[92] Inactivity and boredom are frequently-observed phenomena in institutional facilities in the developing world, especially those set up for young offenders. The UN Convention on the Rights of the Child includes 'the right of the child to rest and leisure, to engage in play and recreational activities appropriate to the age of the child'.[93] Observations during SCF's research confirmed that boredom tends to lead not to aggression and deviant behaviour (as in the West), but to passivity bordering on depression, as evidenced by the following report by an SCF researcher:

> In the Remand Home there was virtually no purposeful activity. I went into the older boys' dormitory – forty or more boys in a room designed for less than half that number. They were locked in, with no staff and no educational or leisure materials of any kind. They appeared apathetic and depressed. The six staff spend the vast majority of their time escorting children to and from court: they do some counselling work, but this leaves one member of staff on duty at a time – hence a custodian role. There were supposedly three teachers, but none in evidence, the schoolroom used for storage.[94]

This passivity among young people may be convenient for staff as a means of social control, but extremely damaging to children. Children may be denied opportunities to learn the traditional roles and tasks defined by their culture, provided with limited opportunities for study and constructive activity, and compelled to spend long hours in inactivity. As a result, they will almost inevitably find themselves ill-prepared educationally, socially and psychologically to take their place in the adult world after leaving care. This issue is discussed in more detail in Chapter 11.

Residential regimes

One of the results of poor gatekeeping (see Chapter 4) is that it is rare to find institutions which make any real attempt to provide an individualised programme for children in their care. Individual needs are subjugated to the needs of the institution for routine, order and uniformity. An extreme example is given in Box 5.3, but other less dramatic examples of regimented care can be found throughout the developing world. 'Block' treatment is a very common phenomenon, including rigid routines and fixed times for going to bed and waking up, centralised catering with meals taken in large groups, regimented activities, and an absence of opportunities for individual

---

Box 5.3   Large government institutions in Brazil[96]

A former resident from Rio de Janiero described how children were addressed by number rather than name, and were given uniform clothing and identical haircuts. Methods of discipline emphasised militaristic training – for example, children were required to stand to attention at the blowing of a whistle.

The resulting loss of a sense of personal identity is not surprising, though this former resident described how the children themselves struggled to uphold each other's sense of identity by using nicknames, and maintaining a sense of solidarity within the peer-group.

play or leisure pursuits. These features of residential care help to develop an environment in which children can lose their sense of personal identity and individuality, denying them the opportunity to develop skills, interests and personal characteristics. The worst examples of regimented institutional care have many of the hallmarks of the 'total institution' described by Goffman.[95]

A significant, but tentative, conclusion from SCF's research is that the peer-group may play a particularly important part in mitigating some of the worst effects of institutional care in the developing world.

The role of the peer-group in institutional care

The contrasting socialisation practices which characterise different cultures were considered in Chapter 1. Western patterns of family upbringing tend to emphasise individuality, self-assertion and competition, while, in the developing world, children tend to be encouraged to be compliant and obedient, with an emphasis on co-operation and the prioritisation of wider family and collective needs over those of individuals. Such patterns of behaviour are well suited to social situations in which children contribute to the family economy from an early age, and in which children receive a great deal of care, nurturing and supervision from older siblings.[97]

In this context, it is not surprising to find a relative absence of the sibling rivalry which characterises many Western families. Equally, the lack of rivalry and aggression observed among children in institutions studied by SCF is predictable, and stands in sharp contrast to the typical dynamics of residential homes in Western societies. Neither is it surprising that depression appears to be a more common reaction to institutional experiences than physical aggression and other forms of self-assertive and rivalrous behaviour (especially among adolescents).[98]

It is difficult to find empirical evidence of the possible beneficial effects of peer relationships in residential care, though one study does provide a picture which confirms some of the observations made during SCF's research. In his study of two contrasting models of group-care (both of which offered 'family-orientated' care) Wolins found no evidence of deficiencies in the children's intelligence, personality and value development, even for children who had been subjected to early and prolonged deprivation.[99] In one of these models (the 'Kinderdorf') there were strong and affectionate ties with a housemother; in the other, the 'Djete Dom' in the former Yugoslavia, there was more reliance on other, and usually older, children for their affective ties. These 'brothers and sisters' played highly significant roles in a range of tasks which included nurturing, washing, feeding and helping with homework.

In another study, Uri Bronfenbrenner showed how cultural variables affected the extent to which peer-group influences uphold or undermine adult influences in day and boarding schools.[100] He concluded that peer-group influences are likely to mirror adult norms in societies which value conformity and the acceptance of adult authority. Peer-group influences are likely to be more in the direction of adult-approved norms than in societies which value individuality, assertiveness and autonomy.

These findings are echoed in some of the institutions observed in SCF's research. The institution for unaccompanied refugee children in Somalia showed a very high level of nurturing and care exercised by the older children, in the absence of a pattern and level of staffing which might otherwise have provided for these needs.[101] However, it is important to recognise that many of these children were also maintaining active contact with their families, who also played an important part in the children's psychological development.

What have rarely been observed in SCF's research have been the powerful but potentially destructive peer-group influences which are well documented in Western research into residential institutions. For example, Polsky observed the sub-culture in a small residential unit for 'unmanageable' delinquent boys in the USA.[102] He found that the power of the peer-group was so strong that adults, far from counter-balancing, actually became co-opted into this delinquent sub-culture, not only colluding with undesirable behaviour, but actually participating in it.

In another study which attempted to understand the influence of the peer-group on boys in residential care (approved schools), it was found that the informal social system of the residents in some institutions exerted a powerful influence on the boys in reinforcing delinquent behaviour and attitudes and undermining the authority and influence of the staff.[103] However, where the school was structured to prevent informal social systems exerting such an influence (for example, through the introduction of small-group living arrangements, the development of small activity groups, and the use of elaborate systems of rewards and punishments), the boys were more likely to identify with the formal norms and goals of the school, and the pastoral systems of the school became more accessible to them.

These findings are particularly interesting when compared to the observed influence of the peer-group in the institution for unaccompanied refugee children in Somalia. In the study of approved schools cited above, the influence of the peer-group reinforced delinquent attitudes and behaviour when structures allowed this. In the Somalian institution, the same lack of structures seemed to release positive peer-group influences, encouraging older children to meet many of the nurturing needs of younger peers.

In Nepal, a meeting between SCF researchers and a group of former residents of a large residential institution for boys revealed an illuminating picture of the value they placed on their residential experience, despite the harsh and uncaring attitudes of staff:

> Sometimes we feel so sad at not having a mother and father to love us and do other things for us, but in our group we don't feel so bad.

> We were close as brothers.

In both cases (Somalia and Nepal) the structure of the institutions allowed a degree of free interaction within the peer-group which made it possible for older youngsters to offer nurturing and emotional support to younger children. Moreover, the way the peer-group operated seemed to complement and support the work of the staff. In the Nepalese example, this was despite the contempt with which the former residents viewed many of the staff.

However, free interaction between older and younger children is not a common feature in institutions. In another institution in Nepal, for example, teenage girls, when talking with SCF researchers, were highly critical of the fact that they were allowed to play no part in the care of younger children, thereby denying both them and the younger children the experience of traditional roles and relationships. In societies in which older siblings (rather than parents) play with young children, it is particularly important for older children in institutions to be allowed to fulfil this role.

The following tentative conclusions emerge from the research:

● In societies in which socialisation practices emphasise co-operation and conformity, and in which the peer-group is seen to offer support rather than rivalry to children, peer support and nurturing in institutions may compensate in part for inadequate parenting by staff, provided the structure of the institution allows for this. This may help to explain why some young people in a few institutions studied by SCF seemed to survive what appears to be a deeply depriving institutional upbringing without the level of psychological damage that might be expected.

● On the other hand, it needs to be emphasised that the potential for peer-group rivalry, competition and exploitation also exists within institutions, particularly in highly structured and harsh institutional environments. This is discussed below under 'The Institutional Abuse of Children'.

Lack of preparation of children for leaving institutional care

The problems associated with young people leaving care and adjusting to adult life in the community are well documented in the social work literature of the West. Unfortunately, there are very few systematic follow-up studies in the developing world.

One exception is a recent study undertaken in Thailand, which attempts to compare the life-adjustment skills of young people who had experienced at least eight years of institutional care with those of a matched sample of young adults who had not been separated from their families.[104] A complex set of indicators was used which attempted to measure adjustment in the areas of family life, careers, peer relationships, in relation to the community, and in relation to themselves (self-understanding), each broken down into a number of sub-categories. The study concluded that, in virtually all areas, young people who had been in institutional care had adjusted less well than the control group: however, the differences were, in the main, small.

Methodological difficulties limit the usefulness of these findings: in particular, the sample of institutionalised young people was almost certainly biased in the direction of the more settled and successful. But it seems likely that, had the researchers gained access to a more representative sample, the differences from the control group would have been even more marked.

Aside from this study, the evidence relies mainly on observations and interviews with children. Although this evidence does not give a very precise view of the problems associated with leaving care, a number of important themes are clear.

I have no idea what it's like to live in a family.[105]

This simple quotation from a teenage girl who had spent most of her childhood in a large institution in Nepal illustrates graphically what is possibly the fundamental problem with most models of institutional care: they fail to equip young people with the knowledge, skills, experiences and emotional reserves which are necessary for them to cope with normal life in the community. The major features of institutional living which contribute to this problem are as follows:

● Institutions rarely provide children with appropriate role models. The Nepali girl quoted above had no clear memories of family life, and now lived in a predominantly female environment, in which there was no attempt to recreate the kind of roles and relationships which would be present in a typical family. She feared for the future, having no perception of the role she was expected to play as an adult woman, and no picture of what she should expect of adult men. In a society in which most marriages are arranged, she had no family behind her to help her to plan and manage her future life: in such societies, girls are particularly vulnerable. Even the simple practical roles and tasks which are traditionally assigned to women were unfamiliar to her; her institutional experience was characterised by centralised purchasing and catering, so even buying food in the market and cooking were unfamiliar. Although there were younger children in the institution, she bitterly resented the fact that she was not allowed a role in helping to care for them, as she would do in a family.

● Institutional care detaches children from their families, even when the reasons for admission concern poverty rather than family breakdown, orphanhood or abandonment. This has extremely serious implications in societies in which the extended family, and possibly community systems, provide the principal sources of support throughout adult life. This was highlighted in Simms's study in Lesotho, referred to in previous chapters:

> some [children] lost contact with their families who are so essential to them. Reared in conditions inadequate to provide for their psychological development, and alienated from skills and philosophies normally acquired from extended family members, the prospect of these youngsters coping in the future are bleak, despite their privileged education.[106]

A graphic illustration of this pattern comes from interviews conducted by SCF in a home which had formerly cared for boys with a physical disability, also in Lesotho:

> A partially sighted boy had returned home on leaving the institution, but he felt alienated from his family and community and sought re-admission to the boys' home. This was refused, but, on the basis that 'this is my home', he made a makeshift tent immediately outside the gates of the institution, and this he regards as his permanent home. During the day, he earns money as a beggar: he displays some of the symptoms of psychotic illness.[107]

● Institutional living tends to breed a sense of dependence and a marked lack of self-motivation. As the Guild of Service in Madras found when it reviewed its experience:

> Generations of inmates in the homes were found to be without motivation or a clear sense of identity, without loyalty to the concept of belonging to a large family and yet quite pathetically dependent upon the support of the structure. It seemed that they were living rather like automatons dictated more by the need to remain supported than to draw sustenance and then launch out on their own as secure citizens.[108]

In a context in which everything is provided, where life is lived in accordance with rules and routines, and where even mildly deviant behaviour is punished, it is not surprising to discover, across the globe, that young people experience huge difficulties in adjusting to life outside the institution when this requires independent and self-directing behaviour. Neither is it surprising to find at least anecdotal evidence that a disproportionate percentage of the inmates of prisons and mental hospitals had been in institutional care as children.

● A common characteristic of residential institutions is that they tend to be isolated from the community in which they are located. In this regard, children in large institutions are particularly disadvantaged, especially when the institution has its own facilities such as pre-school, school and sports facilities which may mean that residents rarely have the opportunity to step outside the gates. Large institutions are also likely to have centralised catering and bulk purchasing, so that involving children in shopping in local markets is perceived as being inappropriate or unnecessary.

Well-resourced institutions may actually face particular difficulties in integrating with the local community. A large Children's Village currently under construction in Lesotho has the appearance of a homely fortress, surrounded by a high barbed-wire fence. This institution is being constructed despite the clear government perception that it is an unnecessary resource, and it would appear that the need to protect the institution's material wealth has become more important than the need to integrate children into the local community.

Particular problems are created when the institution is located far from the child's home community, or in a different type of environment. For example, institutions in urban environments may result in children from rural areas feeling alienated from their community: institutions in rural areas may pose similar problems for children from an urban background. This sense of alienation is particularly significant in the context of the need for institutions to prepare youngsters for life in the wider community.

● Many institutions fail to enable their residents to learn appropriate social and life skills. A young man who spent a considerable part of his childhood in one of the infamous government institutions in Brazil told SCF's researchers:

they don't give proper tools to survive in society.[109]

Although many institutions do place emphasis on vocational training, it is rare to find institutions that provide young people with opportunities to learn the basic skills of living in the community – finding accommodation, using the telephone, communicating with members of the opposite gender, applying for a job, cultivating the garden, and the thousand-and-one other skills which most children acquire through the experience of living in a family in the community.

● Although there are some notable exceptions, most institutions seem to place little emphasis on supporting young people after they have left care. As the young Brazilian quoted above said:

> they throw you out into society with no kind of structure to survive.

The development of follow-up programmes was a particular recommendation of the Thailand study referred to above.[110]

To summarise: most institutions across the globe fail to prepare young people for independent life in the wider community. What is needed is a greater emphasis on both children's emotional and educational needs. Children need both the quality of personal care in order for them to feel a sense of self-worth and self-confidence, and opportunities and experiences which enable them to acquire a wide range of social, life and vocational skills to enable them to survive in the world of work and independent living. These themes are examined in more detail in Part II of this book, which looks at supporting young people after leaving institutional care.

The institutional abuse of children

The UN Convention on the Rights of the Child states that:

> States Parties shall take all appropriate ... measures to protect the child from all forms of physical or mental violence, injury or abuse, neglect or negligent treatment, maltreatment or exploitation including sexual abuse, while in the care of parent(s), legal guardian(s) or *any other person who has the care of the child*. [emphasis added][111]

It is extremely difficult to gain an accurate picture of the susceptibility of children in institutions to abuse in the developing world. In their report *Children in Institutions*, Defence for Children International go so far as to assert that 'the use of institutional placements is in itself a form of violence on the child', and that 'avoidable physical and psychological violence – both legitimate and clandestine – takes place within all types of institutions'.[112] These conclusions are not, however, supported by evidence, and the implication that the *concept* of the institution necessarily involves abuse or violence to the child does not seem justified.

Recent years have seen significant numbers of allegations of physical, emotional and sexual abuse of children in residential care in the UK, and it may well be that these are only the 'tip of the iceberg'. Children in institutions are, almost by definition, in a singularly powerless situation, and the potential for abuse by staff, and sometimes by older children, is an ever-present reality. It is also well known that closed and punitive institutional regimes tend to have a brutalising effect on staff as well as children.

Young people with a learning disability may be particularly vulnerable to abuse in institutions. Reviewing the evidence in this respect (primarily from North America), the Roeher Institute concludes:

> it must be estimated that between 39 and 68 percent of girls with development disabilities and between 16 and 30 percent of boys with developmental disabilities will be subjected to sexual abuse before they reach 18 years of age.[113]

Whilst it is extremely difficult to estimate the relevance of these findings outside the context in which the research was undertaken, it seems reasonable to assume that the situation in the developing world will be no better. Indeed, the relative isolation of many institutions, coupled with the widespread lack of accountability and inspection of residential homes, suggests that the situation could be very much worse than Western research suggests.

The following issues have emerged from SCF's study in relation to institutional abuse:

● Anecdotal evidence about the physical, emotional and sexual abuse of children in institutions abounds, and it is not surprising that firm evidence about its incidence is extremely difficult to find. However, a sufficient number of allegations were encountered to suggest that abuses are far from being isolated occurrences.

● In the developing world it is rare to find any internal or external mechanisms for facilitating and investigating allegations of child abuse or other violations of children's rights. The potential for abuse in institutions is rarely acknowledged.

● As already noted in Chapter 4, there is a tendency for institutions to emphasise *organisational* goals at the expense of their stated *child-centred* goals. Maintaining a sense of order, and 'not rocking the boat', ensuring job security for staff and protecting the good name of the institution are accorded higher priority than the safeguarding of children's rights. All of these factors militate against treating allegations seriously and ensuring that they are properly and objectively investigated.

● The lack of *advocates* for individual children makes it more possible for abuses to go undetected or unchallenged. Where there is active parental involvement in the life of the child in residential care, or where children have access to a confidant, it is more likely that abuses will be reported, and this is likely to act as a deterrent. The reality for the majority of institutions visited in SCF's research is that parental contact is usually weak (see Chapter 4), and becomes weaker the longer the child is in care.

Abuse in institutions can be interpreted as an act of commission by members of staff, but it can also be argued that passive forms of abuse are widespread – for example, depriving children of affection, comfort, or purposeful activity. Another type of passive abuse observed in the research is the failure on the part of staff to protect children from abuses by other children. The following observation illustrates this:

> Older boys could bully the young boys and sexually harass the girls. The elder boys cooked and served the food, but the young boys and girls would sometimes go without food.[114]

The abuse of children's labour also appears to be relatively common. For example, children may be required to undertake unpaid work in the gardens of staff, as in this Ugandan child's testimony:

> there was a lot of digging in the gardens of the institution and those of the staff.[115]

On the other hand, institutions which deny older youngsters the opportunity to work and derive benefit for themselves or their families from work, may be depriving them of something which is valued not just because of the material rewards of work, but because work may enhance their sense of self-worth.

Conclusion

Although this chapter has focused primarily on the most negative aspects of residential care, these are not inevitable characteristics of institutions. Institutions are not, *by nature*, damaging to children. Nevertheless, SCF's research does show that the vast majority of residential institutions in the developing world offer an unacceptably poor quality of care, and thus violate children's rights for protection, survival and development.

6 'Good-enough' practice in residential care

Chapter 5 emphasised the negative characteristics of institutional care in the developing world and their likely impact on the development of children. In this chapter, the emphasis is on identifying those features of residential care practice which contribute to a satisfactory quality of care for children. In borrowing Winnicott's phrase 'good-enough parenting',[116] the intention is not to paint an ideal picture of residential care, but to determine the principal characteristics of residential care which help to create an environment which is 'good enough' in meeting the needs of children. The definition of 'good enough' needs to be considered in the context of the reality of developing countries, where high staff–child ratios, a high level of staff training, and good material provision are going to be difficult, if not impossible, to achieve. The emphasis, therefore, is on identifying steps which can be taken without incurring unrealistic costs.

The ideas presented in this chapter are not based on empirical evidence linking residential processes with outcomes: such research is lacking, and in any case is intrinsically difficult to conduct. Instead, the conclusions are based on direct observation of many residential institutions, discussions with children and staff, and the available literature. Consequently, the conclusions must be regarded as tentative.

The components of 'good-enough' residential care

Philosophy, objectives and gatekeeping

Residential care should be based on a clear but simple philosophy which is understood and subscribed to by staff and (where possible) by the families of referred children. The philosophy should clearly indicate the characteristics of the children for whom the institution exists, and admissions policies and practices should reflect the need to avoid unnecessary or inappropriate admissions. The assessment of potential admissions should reflect a pro-active search for non-institutional options, and, once children are admitted, the organisation providing care should constantly review the child's progress and explore more appropriate, non-institutional placements. There should be an honest acknowledgement of the disadvantages of residential living for children.

All residential institutions should work in a purposeful way with young people, aiming always to equip them with the knowledge, values and skills necessary to function adequately and independently in the wider community. This means meeting their physical, emotional, social, educational, cultural and spiritual needs.

The physical environment

The physical environment of a residential institution for children should reflect the material conditions within the wider culture. Excessively spartan conditions, or excessively generous material conditions, can be equally unhelpful to children in equipping them for life in the outside world. Where possible, buildings should be in keeping with those in the surrounding area and not stand out as 'different'.

Physical care should reflect prevailing family norms as far as possible, provided that these include an understanding of children's age-related nutrition and health needs. Care needs to be taken to avoid the spread of parasites and infectious diseases, especially when large numbers of children are living in close proximity.

Bearing in mind that many children in residential care will have experienced poverty and various forms of family disruption, an adequate diet and individual health monitoring and medical treatment are vital ingredients of effective care.

The pattern of daily living

Children's experience of care should reflect the full range of children's needs, and not just the institution's need for order, control and routine. Central to the pattern of daily living is the child's need to establish and maintain close and trusting relationships with caring and committed people who see it as part of their task to offer nurturing, affection, guidance and discipline appropriate to both age and culture. Although in most instances these needs will be met by residential staff, in some situations it may be appropriate to develop models of care in which some are met by older youngsters.

Consistency and continuity of relationships are important, and, wherever possible, children's experience should be structured in such a way that they can invest in relationships with a relatively small number of adults and other children. Where it is culturally appropriate, children should both receive and offer nurturing and care to other children. Both of these needs are more readily provided if children live in relatively small groups of mixed ages and, where culturally appropriate, genders. In some cultural contexts, it may be appropriate for older children to exercise responsibility for younger children, to the benefit of both. In turn, this may make it possible for an institution to function on lower staffing levels. Although the aim is not necessarily to recreate a family atmosphere, what is desirable is that children experience similar opportunities to those which others experience within their own families – a range of relationships characterised by a sense of belonging, and in which children feel secure and valued.

The experience of daily living should provide children with opportunities for play, stimulation, recreation and leisure, appropriate to their age. These should include opportunities for children to be alone, and for them to play freely and spontaneously. Daily living experiences should equip children with the skills required within their culture to play the different roles required of adult life. Many of these skills and roles require the modelling of appropriate behaviour and attitudes by male and female adults (and possibly older children) who are trusted and respected. Children should be given opportunities to practise their religion.

Methods of control and discipline should reflect cultural norms. Rules should be rational and intelligible to the children, and controls should be experienced as firm but benign, and aim at fostering a sense of self-discipline. Punishments should reflect cultural norms, but also be consistent with children's rights to protection from abuse and maltreatment. The experience of daily living should encourage a sense of independence and self-reliance appropriate to the age and circumstances of the individual child. 'Institutional dependence' should be consciously avoided at every opportunity.

Educational opportunities

Children who have experienced family breakdown, community disruption or separation may already be educationally disadvantaged. Moreover, children who are unlikely to be able to return to their families may have to survive as adults, with little or no family support. Good educational opportunities, including vocational training and work experience, are therefore of the utmost importance. Where possible, these opportunities should be gained outside the institution, enabling young people to interact with others who have not had an institutional upbringing.

However, an excessively educational orientation should be avoided. A schoolroom ethos should not permeate the children's whole experience of daily living and deny them opportunities for a warmer and more intimate atmosphere.

Contact with families

The UN Convention on the Rights of the Child asserts the child's right to maintain contact with both parents, unless this is contrary to her best interests.[117] Residential institutions must acknowledge and respect children's need for contact with their own families, even if circumstances dictate that this contact must be limited. Residential staff need to be non-possessive of children, seeing themselves as supplementing rather than replacing children's own families, and constantly and actively working to help children to foster family contact despite the difficulties this sometimes creates for residential staff. Siblings should be kept together whenever possible and consistent with their needs and wishes.

Community integration

Central to the task of every residential institution is the need to enable young people to become integrated adult members of their community and culture. It is unlikely that this will be achieved unless children have adequate opportunities to mix with other children (for example, through pre-schools and schools, temples, churches or mosques, as well as through informal opportunities to interact with children living outside the institutional context). The acquisition of daily living skills requires children's participation in such activities as shopping in the local market, using public transport, taking part in festivals and other community events, and so on.

Staff should strive to develop a positive image of the institution in the local community, and to avoid practices which may stigmatise children – for example, uniforms and regimented rules.

Management and leadership in the institution

There are clear links between the quality of care provided to children, the quality of management and leadership, and the organisational structure of the institution (see Chapter 5). There needs to be managerial commitment to meeting children's needs as the highest priority for the institution. Managers who emphasise institutional needs above those of children place their young residents at serious risk of deprivation.

Residential managers (both the unit manager and agency management structures such as boards of governors) need to openly acknowledge the risk of abuse within the institution, both from staff and from older youngsters, and take steps to monitor the behaviour of staff, to make known how allegations will be responded to, and to provide communication channels for children with trusted adults outside the institution.

Children are influenced by the way staff relate to each other: with this in mind, staff management practices should model behaviour which will positively enhance the experience of the children. Residential staff who are valued by their managers are more likely to help children to feel valued themselves.

The expressed views of the children

In many cultures it is not considered appropriate to involve children in discussions and decisions about their future. However, the UN Convention on the Rights of the Child specifically identifies the child's right to express an opinion where he is capable of forming a view.[118] Children in institutions are often in a particularly powerless and vulnerable situation, and it is therefore of the utmost importance that staff take steps to enable children to understand their situation and to articulate their views about their future.

In summary, the residential environment should be one in which the needs of the whole child are acknowledged and responded to appropriately: it should facilitate the development of a positive sense of self-esteem, and should equip the growing child with a range of experiences which are designed to facilitate her entry into the world of work and relationships, and enable the young adult to play a positive role in society.

> In all actions concerning children ... the best interests of the child shall be a primary consideration.[119]

The cost of 'good-enough' residential care

Residential care is an expensive form of care, bearing in mind the required capital investment as well as recurring costs.[120] As a response to family poverty, residential care is not only inappropriate, but considerably more expensive than the likely costs of helping to support the child within her own family. If residential care is expensive, then it seems reasonable to assume that the costs of 'good-enough' residential care will be even higher. If residential care is improved even to a minimally acceptable level, the costs may be prohibitive.

It is certainly true that some of the worst models of residential care are seriously under-resourced: low staffing levels, a complete lack of training, low levels of pay, poor buildings and a general lack of material resources may all be significant. But SCF's research shows that 'good-enough' residential care need not be prohibitively expensive. The required improvements to institutions often depend not on greatly improved resource levels, but on significant changes in values and approaches. The process of change may require significant resources, including training (see Chapter 7), but many of the characteristics of 'good-enough' care are not expensive to implement.

For example, the steps required to meet children's needs for nurturing, affection, stimulation and continuity consist not so much in high staff–child ratios, as in the role-definition of staff and the pattern of organisation of the institution, and a good understanding of children's needs.

Training may, of course, be an appropriate means of improving staff knowledge and skills, and staffing levels must be high enough to allow time for tasks beyond those of basic physical caring. But the kind of changes required to create small-group living units, to ensure greater continuity of staff, and to give staff more responsibility for care of 'the whole child' require attitudinal changes rather than resources. Indeed, the kind of small, mixed-age units which are probably the best way of meeting children's needs might require a *lower* staffing level, in view of the potential of involving older youngsters to a greater degree in the care of younger children, where this is culturally appropriate.

One of the most significant features of 'good-enough' residential care is a clear admissions policy, coupled with gatekeeping practices which ensure that children's needs are carefully considered prior to admission, that alternative options are considered, and that residential care is a planned and purposeful experience for each child. This, of itself, is costly, in terms of deploying skilled staff to undertake a demanding range of tasks: but this is an *essential* feature of 'good-enough' care. On the other hand, when children are admitted into residential care on a more considered and discriminating basis, the costs of inappropriate admissions can be avoided, and residential resources can then be directed at those children most in need. This avoids wastage of resources, as well as the social and psychological damage caused by inappropriate admissions.

Residential care: First choice or last resort?

Part III of this book examines various forms of substitute family care. The general conclusion of SCF's research is that agencies committed to the care of children who are unable to live with their own families should always take steps to promote family alternatives – in a substitute family within the child's existing community, or in various forms of adoption or fostering. Where such family-based care arrangements are available, they are to be preferred to institutional care in most cases.

However, promoting adoption and fostering is, in many cultural environments, both difficult and costly, and requires a long-term commitment of resources, perseverance and tenacity on the part of the agency, and a supportive framework of legislation and social policy. Experience suggests that the search for substitute family forms of care can, in the long term, prove to be rewarding. In the meantime, however, residential care for some children may be the only realistic form of care if options within the child's family and community networks have been exhausted. The challenge then is to ensure that residential care is 'good enough', that children's rights are respected and upheld, and that more appropriate alternatives for individual children are constantly reviewed.

In the field of juvenile justice, residential forms of care and treatment or training should rarely, if ever, be advocated, except possibly in the case of persistent, serious offenders for whom other approaches have been tried and have failed. Although this area of practice is seriously under-researched in the developing world, virtually all the evidence from research in Western societies suggests that, far from altering offending behaviour, residential care or custody tends to immerse young people in a criminal sub-culture, to reinforce their delinquent tendencies, and to serve to further alienate them from the norms of their wider society.[121]

Disabled children should, wherever possible, be helped to remain within their own families and communities: community-based rehabilitation, and the promotion of integrated education, are more appropriate and cost-effective options than institutions. There is a stronger case for providing residential education for children with certain types of disability, such as severe sensory impairment and multiple handicap. However, even in these cases, the high cost of 'good-enough' residential care, medical treatment and education, coupled with the likelihood of meeting the needs of only a tiny proportion of children who are disabled, may mean that such facilities should not be given a higher priority than the development of community-based approaches.

There are, however, some situations in which residential care can appropriately be considered the placement of choice, even if family- and community-based options are also available. This is true, for example, of children who have been so damaged by abusive experiences within their family that a period of emotional recovery in the more neutral environment of a supportive residential home may be more appropriate than immediate substitute family placement. Similarly, children who experience a breakdown in substitute family care may benefit from a period of stability in residential care. In the UK, research has demonstrated the important role of residential care in complementing fostering programmes, especially in the context of high rates of fostering failure.[122]

Some older youngsters who have become separated from their families may prefer to remain together in some form of group-care. In refugee camps, for example, groups of adolescents who have shared a common experience of fleeing from conflict may prefer some form of group living, possibly on a self-help basis, to dispersal among unrelated families. Similarly, some groups of young people who have lived together on the streets and who have clearly expressed a desire to return to a more regular living situation but are unable to return to their families may also find that some form of group-care is preferable to substitute family care.

In these situations, it is particularly important that the young people are given an opportunity to express their own views and to be accorded an appropriate degree of self-determination.

In practice, residential care in the developing world is almost always a full-time and long-term placement for children, but this is not necessarily the case. One of the case studies in SCF's research describes a facility for street children provided by an NGO in Nepal which includes both a minimal 'shelter' facility and a 'transit home', which is a short-term residential facility designed to help young people, if they so choose, to move away from life on the streets.[123] The home provides a time-limited residential facility, with clear objectives and purposeful work undertaken to support them.

Although the main aim of this book is to promote non-institutional approaches to child care, the reality is that institutional care has become the mainstream form of substitute care provided by State agencies and NGOs in many developing countries, and that the development of substitute family care may prove to be both complex and expensive. In addition, some categories of children can benefit from residential care as the placement of choice, and it is important that their needs are not overlooked. Raising the standards of care in residential institutions should be seen as a high priority on the part of agencies concerned with children in difficult circumstances.

7 Achieving change within residential institutions

In previous chapters it was suggested that concerns about institutional care cluster around three sets of issues: (1) questions about the appropriateness of the *concept* of the institution, which include, for example, whether institutions are needed and whether children who are admitted could be cared for more appropriately within their own families, or in substitute families; (2) questions about the *practice* of institutional care, ranging from unsatisfactory physical care to lack of awareness of children's psychological needs, and from gross environmental deprivation to institutional abuse and violations of children's rights; (3) the process of *gatekeeping*, which links these two issues together.

This chapter provides a practical model to assist in the process of planning interventions in residential care, or in the wider systems within which it is located. Four examples of attempts to achieve change in residential institutions are presented and discussed, using a theoretical framework provided by research on innovations.

Innovations

The literature on innovations is extremely diverse, but particular reference is made in this chapter to the work of Everett Rogers, who reviewed a large amount of material on innovations and distilled out a number of useful generalisations.[124] The focus of this chapter is on change and innovation within residential institutions. Although, as has been made clear, an acceptable level of physical care for children in institutions in the developing world cannot be taken for granted, the primary concern about the quality of care in institutions focuses on the capacity of the institution to meet the child's psychological needs. Particular concern is felt over practices such as:

- the lack of opportunities for children to form attachments to adults;
- the lack of personal, individualised care and emotional support;
- discontinuities of staff created by shift systems, children being rotated through the institution, and so on;
- harsh and inappropriate methods of discipline;
- rigid, routinised care;
- the tendency to see children as detached from their families and communities.

This chapter looks at attempts to change the overall provision of unsatisfactory care, rather than the specific practices which improve the quality of life for children in institutions. 'Innovation', in this context, means an attempt to introduce what can described in shorthand as *child-centred*, as opposed to *institution-centred*, practices.

The literature on innovation uses the term 'change-agent' to describe the role of the person involved in introducing the innovation, and this term is used throughout this chapter. However, in Third World institutions, the impetus for change often comes from outside both the institution and the social systems in which it is located: the starting point for change will frequently reflect the advocacy role of organisations like Save the Children rather than a perceived need for change on the part of the organisation providing residential care. The principal agenda on the part of the organisation which agrees to external intervention may not be an agreed need for innovation, but the material resources which may be offered, or the kudos of an association with an overseas agency.

This is particularly significant in understanding some of the difficulties in achieving change in institutions in developing countries. Moreover, the cultural gap between the institution's staff and external change-agents can create additional difficulties, as the case examples show. As Smale comments: 'communication across ethnic, racial, class, professional or other cultural boundaries needs particular care if preconceived assumptions and prejudices are not going to lead to misunderstanding or worse'.[125]

A framework for planning interventions in residential care systems

Most attempts to improve the quality of life for children in institutions in developing countries have focused on residential care *practice*, without questioning the *concept* of institutional care, and without attempting to influence the other factors which impinge on practice issues. Attempts to influence *gatekeeping* polices and practices have rarely been made, though one notable exception will be examined below.

The framework which is elaborated in this chapter has six key elements:

1 *Concept*: Is residential care consistent with the cultural, social, political and economic circumstances of the country concerned? As indicated in Chapter 2, residential institutions for children have proliferated in many countries, despite their questionable appropriateness. Examining the appropriateness of the concept of the institution in any context prompts consideration not just of cultural norms and coping mechanisms, but of the overall framework of social policy, the availability of resources to support vulnerable families, and the legal framework surrounding family support, institutional care and substitute families.

2 *Philosophy*: It was suggested in Chapter 5 that a key determinant of the quality of care in any individual institution is the existence of a clearly-understood philosophy. A statement of philosophy provides the value base on which the institution is run. It influences the objectives of the institution, and also the means by which those objectives are met.

3 *Structure*: The term 'structure' covers the overall organisation of the institution. Chapter 5 highlighted the link between quality of care in institutions, the pattern of delegation by the unit manager, and the level of autonomy of care staff. The way in which staff roles are defined has profound implications for the quality of work undertaken with children.

4 *Resources*: While the availability of resources is only one of a number of determinants of the quality of care in residential institutions, it is self-evident that good-quality care requires a minimum level of resourcing in areas such as physical facilities and provisions, staffing levels and quality, and access to educational, vocational and recreational opportunities.

5 *Gatekeeping*: The process of assessment, planning and decision-making regarding the admission and discharge of children is a vitally important means of ensuring that residential care is used purposefully for children who need such care and can benefit from it.

6 *Practice*: This describes the wide range of tasks and roles undertaken by the staff of the institution, both directly with children and indirectly in the provision of material resources. It also covers the patterns and structures of daily living, and the rules and norms of the institution.

How are these six elements linked together?

With some notable exceptions, attempts to improve the quality of residential care reviewed in SCF's research have focused on *practice*. One worrying implication of this is that, if intervention succeeds in improving practice, the institution may become more attractive to families, and consequently an increase in inappropriate admissions may follow unless careful attention is given to ensuring that appropriate *gatekeeping* policies and practices are implemented.

Similarly, attempting to change the *practice* of the institution without questioning the *philosophy* of care being pursued may result in the appearance of change, but the continuance of inappropriate attitudes and values. For example, there is little value in teaching care staff new approaches to control and discipline in a training centre for young offenders unless this is accompanied by an examination of the attitudes and values of staff towards young people, their behaviour and their family circumstances.

The *structure* of the institution is of central importance in determining the quality of care provided, as discussed in Chapter 5. There is little point in providing staff with new skills if their role is defined in a way which provides no opportunities for exercising those skills.

Similarly, if training opens up new ways of working with children, but the level of staffing *resources*, or the availability of material resources, prevents them from being implemented, the result may be frustration and demoralisation.

Hence, intervention at the level of practice is likely to have a limited impact unless careful consideration is given to the philosophy, organisational structures and resources which inform, facilitate or constrain it. Furthermore, unless the *concept* of the institution has been carefully and critically thought out, it is questionable whether any work should be undertaken to improve the institution, and unlikely that the institution will be able to meet the needs of the children in its care.

The four case examples that follow show that, where intervention aims only at practice, significant and sustainable change is unlikely to be achieved. This is echoed in Potter's research, which found that:

> the extent to which a training course can achieve its goals of promoting changes at the workplace depends on many factors, including a large number which are outside the direct control of the trainers. However, the degree to which trainers identify and attempt to influence these factors has a great bearing on the overall outcome of the training programme.[126]

What is required is a strategic and systemic approach to the planning of intervention, with long-term as well as short-term goals, and with a focus both on the institution as a complex system, and on the organisational context of the institution as a complex series of overlapping social systems.

Case examples

1 An attempt to improve inadequate institutional care for children with profound disabilities

This residential home for children with severe learning difficulties (and some with multiple handicaps) was attached to an institution for elderly people in Asia. Concerns about the home included an appalling physical environment, widespread malnutrition among the children, extremely poor hygiene practices, the lack of any kind of purposeful activity with, or stimulation of, the children, and the absence of any kind of care planning – in short, a classic picture of the worst form of 'warehousing' of children. Staffing levels were minimal, morale was low, no staff had received any form of training, and physical and material resources were grossly inadequate. Fatalistic attitudes towards disability were very apparent among the staff. The child mortality rate was thought to be high.

A team of specialists was deployed to try to improve this situation – a social worker, speech therapist and physiotherapist (all expatriates) and two local staff. They supervised an intense period of intervention which involved major environmental improvements; reorganisation of the utilisation of the building; initiation of major changes in the routines; introduction of improved practices in areas such as health care, nutrition and hygiene; the purchase of new equipment including play materials; on-the-spot staff training, largely through the modelling of good practices, and the introduction of play and stimulation sessions. They also attempted to transfer children who had been inappropriately placed, and to influence policy on the admission of children.

During this brief period of intensive involvement, huge improvements were noted in the physical environment, the physical condition of the children, and in their overall psychological and emotional growth. After the end of the programme, follow-up by SCF showed a complete failure to achieve sustainable change. A year or so after the departure of the team, SCF researchers visited the home and found that the quality of care appeared broadly similar to that noted before the programme began. The level of care was graphically illustrated when, by chance, a profoundly disabled child was found left in an unoccupied room, lying face down in a pool of faeces and urine, covered in flies. Discussion with staff about her tended to confirm the suspicion that she had been left to die.

Why was this intervention unsuccessful? Looking back over the experience, there seem to be a number of reasons.

First, this was a classic illustration of how an overseas organisation attempted to achieve change without involving members of the institution in the process of planning. There was no assessment of the need for change, and staff in the home were seen as *objects* of change, rather than *partners* in a change-endeavour over which they apparently felt no sort of ownership. The matron of the home was clearly resistant to change from the outset, but the intervention apparently proceeded without any real attempt to see her as a vital part of the change process. In his comparative case study, Potter identified the involvement of managers in staff training as a key issue.[127]

Second, the manner in which innovation was communicated was quite unsatisfactory. Rogers places considerable emphasis on the process of communication between the 'source' of the innovation and the 'receivers': he uses the term 'homophily' to describe the extent to which individuals share similar characteristics in language, personality, cultural background, values, and level of education:

> Where source and receiver share common meanings, attitudes and beliefs, and a mutual language, communication between them is likely to be effective.

> Heterophilic interaction is likely to cause cognitive dissonance, because the receiver is exposed to messages that may be inconsistent with his existing beliefs, an uncomfortable psychological state.[128]

One of the central factors in the failure of this programme was the fact that the change-agents were mainly expatriate staff, whose knowledge of the culture and language of the country appears to have been minimal. Moreover, they had a much higher educational and social status than local staff and certainly did not share similar values and philosophy.

Third, the programme attempted to achieve change in the institution without considering the wider context. If a proper assessment had been undertaken, the following factors might have been identified as significant:

- The institution was seriously under-resourced.
- Staff were of low social status and had poor levels of education.
- They were poorly motivated and there was little incentive to change their practices. Moreover, the innovations being introduced required more effort on their part, and they were being asked to take on additional and demanding roles.
- Cultural attitudes towards disability included the sense of shame that disability conferred on parents, and a certain fatalism which served to restrict perceptions about the potential for disabled people to respond to stimulation and education.
- Care staff were given little autonomy or sense of responsibility for the children in their care.
- Children were admitted without an assessment of their needs and

whether these could be met appropriately within the institution.

In short, four elements in the planning framework outlined above were ignored: philosophy, organisational structure, resources and gatekeeping. By intervening solely within the institution, focusing almost exclusively on physical improvements and practice, and ignoring the wider context, the programme was bound to fail.

What was really required was change in the whole system of the institution and its surroundings. For example, it was assumed that the grossly negligent care practices reflected ignorance on the part of staff, rather than being an understandable survival mechanism evolved by low-status, poorly-paid staff whose commitment, motivation and morale were low. Realistically, staff were not in a position to carry out the additional tasks required without increasing the staff–child ratio. The innovations being introduced had a high cost to staff in terms of additional work, complicating their already demanding schedule. For example, offering more appropriate stimulation to children led to children making increasing demands on staff.

2   The Out of Care Programme: An attempt to influence children entering residential care

The second case example reflects an attempt to move beyond institutional change to influence the inappropriate admission of children to institutional care. In one South-East Asian country, SCF had been working for some years in State-run institutions, with a broad-based programme designed to improve the quality of care they provided. This experience suggested that the principal areas of difficulty included the large number of children being admitted, the lack of assessment and of clear admission policies, and the absence of care planning for children. The combined result of these factors was a growing population in care, serious overcrowding, the admission of children who could readily and cheaply be supported within their own families, and long periods of time spent in care with no planning for the children's future.

In response, SCF decided to initiate a programme to examine the family circumstances of children in State institutions and those referred for admission in one district. The aim was to return children to their families, divert children who were referred for residential care, and introduce a system of assessment and planning, including the planning of contact between children and their families. This programme was sanctioned by the government (the Department of Social Welfare), who indicated their support for the principles of assessment, planning, gatekeeping and prevention. The venture was seen as an important pilot project which might be replicated elsewhere.

Initially, the work achieved some success in returning children to the care of their families, supporting children within their families as an alternative to admission, and gaining the co-operation of parents in visiting their children and in planning for their future. However, the work came to a precipitate end when a new institution manager was appointed. She challenged the validity of the work being undertaken, showed no interest in the principle of avoiding unnecessary admissions, preferred to work in isolation from children's families, and made the continuance of the programme impossible. As fast as children were returned to the care of their families, others were admitted inappropriately.

The Out of Care Programme went a step further than Case Example 1 in seeing the importance of the wider social systems surrounding residential care. It managed to move beyond an attempt to change care practices, and tried to influence the wider circumstances under which children enter care. In targeting the crucial area of gatekeeping, it recognised the importance of challenging the appropriateness of residential care for some children, and at first appeared to make some progress in diverting children from care and enabling some children to return to the care of their families. In this sense, the programme attempted to achieve change in the wider social system, but what it failed to do was to locate the innovation in the context of government policies and practices. The initial success depended on the co-operation of the individual manager of the institution, and, although the programme was sanctioned by the Department of Social Welfare, its unintended consequences had not been predicted. For example, the drop in perceived status *and pay* as a result of the drop in numbers of children in residence was a powerful disincentive to co-operation for the new manager.

With the benefit of hindsight, it is clear that there was no real commitment to the programme within the Department of Social Welfare, and little sense of ownership by them. For the innovation to have worked would have required a change in the 'work culture' of the department, seeing a falling admission rate as a sign of success rather than failure, and certainly not as a reason to reduce the salary of the manager of the home. Thus, although changes were achieved in the short term, they were not sustainable, and the system as a whole remained unchanged.

3   A strategy of promoting community-based policies and practices[129]

In Uganda, SCF has had a long and close association with the Ministry of Probation and Social Welfare. The situation of children orphaned or separated from their families because of the effects of civil war prompted joint initiatives to work towards tracing families and resettling children. During and after the war, large numbers of institutions within the private and voluntary sectors sprang up, and it became clear that many of them not only admitted children who could have remained with their families, but also offered an inadequate level of care. Partly as a result of a successful programme of family tracing and resettlement, both the government and SCF began questioning the appropriateness of institutional care, and a strategy was evolved to influence the context for separated children in a variety of ways.

Child care legislation was amended in order to achieve some judicial control over the admission of children to residential care: this, coupled with the family tracing and resettlement programme, led to a dramatic drop in the numbers of children in institutions, a more discriminating use of residential care, and a growing interest among the organisations who were involved in providing care to devise ways of supporting children within the community. A registration and inspection system was set up by the ministry in order to achieve a measure of control over the activities of individuals and organisations providing residential care, and to enforce the standards set out in new Rules for Babies' Homes and Children's Homes which the government introduced.

Training facilities for residential child care staff were virtually non-existent, and the geographical spread of the homes, coupled with resource constraints, made the idea of conventional forms of training unrealistic. An Open Learning Programme was therefore designed and piloted, with a package of training material produced and tested, and the course was promoted by the ministry, with the Babies' and Children's Homes Rules used as a lever to facilitate participation.[130]

In order to promote a strategy for encouraging local communities to take responsibility for the growing problems associated with children orphaned by HIV/AIDS, a programme was developed in the district most affected by the disease to assist local communities in identifying orphaned children and finding appropriate resources within the community to respond to their needs. Essentially the programme involved deploying additional government social workers, whose role was extended to community development – sensitising community groups to the problems of unaccompanied children to promote the concept of community responsibility, to advocate for children's rights and to provide some resources to facilitate the care of children within the community.

This case example is of particular interest because it illustrates an approach which aimed at change on a broader front, within a more strategic framework. Not only did the programme recognise the need to influence the wider legislative and policy context of admissions to residential care, it also succeeded in creating a climate in support of change by intervening in a wide variety of networks and across organisational boundaries, and by introducing innovations in a way which provided a multi-pronged attack on an institutional problem of great proportions, both qualitatively and quantitatively. The net result was a review of the whole *concept* of residential care.

In Uganda, circumstances enabled SCF to become involved in the legislative and policy arenas, and, by deploying staff within government structures, a wider impact became possible. Similar opportunities may not exist in other countries where the agency's starting point may have to be intervention at the level of the institution.

The main point to emphasise here is that attempts to intervene within institutions will be constrained by factors in the wider context, and a careful assessment will be required to identify what needs to be changed if sustainable progress is to be made in improving the quality of life for children in institutions.

4   The process of change in care practices in a children's home

The final case example is drawn from the experience of Rädda Barnen (SCF Sweden).[131] The aim of this programme was to improve child care practice in a State-run children's home in the Middle East, which was in many ways typical of large institutions: staff–child ratios were low; staff were poorly paid, of low status and poorly motivated; children's physical care was poor, and mortality rates were high, despite good nutrition levels. There was a serious lack of stimulation for children, and a number of children were emotionally disturbed or had learning difficulties. Little individual care was offered, and the lack of opportunities for attachment to adult-figures was identified as a major concern. Children were rotated through age-banded groups, and were exposed to a wide range of different staff during the course of each day.

A team of Swedish specialists based in a local Child Health and Development Institute were engaged in a programme of change and development which aimed at improving child care practices within the home, but with a stated long-term aim of achieving organisational change. The programme established a number of guidelines at the outset, including the assumption that it is the *system* that is wrong, rather than the *staff*; that support for change would be needed at all levels, and that change requires both time and support for the staff. The programme emphasised, from the beginning, the importance of working alongside staff, offering praise and encouragement, and of facilitating their identification of areas in which change was required. Particular care was taken to include the matron in the process of change, and negotiations within the relevant government ministry were seen as essential in order to legitimise any changes which occurred.

As members of staff began to identify areas in which change was required, Rädda Barnen's team offered on-the-spot training and modelling of good practice in different aspects of the life of the home, and care practices improved on a broad front. In this developing climate of change, discussion took place about the kind of organisational changes which were required if children's needs were to be met more effectively. The idea of creating 'family groups' within the home emerged from these discussions, to provide a more family-like experience, with greater opportunities for personal care by a relatively small number of staff.

This far-reaching innovation required high-level negotiation within the ministry, and great importance was attached to gaining a mandate from the minister himself to go ahead with the scheme as a pilot which might be replicated elsewhere. The staff for this project were self-selected, and were centrally involved in planning the innovation, in determining staffing structures, selecting children, and so on. The difficult position of the matron in implementing the programme was acknowledged, and particular support was offered to her, while continuing efforts were made to make her and senior staff within the ministry feel a sense of 'ownership' over the programme.

The 'family group' concept helped to highlight the importance of families in general, and from this stemmed an increasing awareness of the need to avoid unnecessary separations of children from their families. The innovation eventually led to a decision by the ministry to extend the family group idea.

This case example illustrates a vitally important theme identified in Chapter 5 – the link between the structure of the institution and the quality of care provided within it: good-quality, child-centred care was found to be associated with a structure in which staff were delegated responsibility for the care of children and were given opportunities to work in an autonomous way. This structure enabled staff to interact with children in ways which emphasised closeness, engagement and continuity, a better quality of verbal exchange, and a more flexible and relaxed atmosphere. For significant progress to be made, change must go beyond the level of staff knowledge and skills: what is required if significant change is to be achieved and sustained is *an alteration to the organisational structure of the institution*, and not simply changes in the way staff behave.

In the Rädda Barnen case example, what started out as an attempt to introduce changes in residential care practice ended up achieving significant change in the whole concept of the institution, involving all six elements in the framework outlined at the beginning of this chapter. In the process of change, there was a radical review of the home's philosophy, which prompted, and was prompted by, a new look at gatekeeping policies. This resulted in a drop in admissions, thereby releasing additional resources. The need for change in the structure of the home was recognised, and, in turn, this fed into the changing philosophy of the institution.

Two other factors are significant in the structural changes that were achieved: (1) the goal of organisational change was included at the planning stage; (2) this change was achieved as a result of staff themselves identifying the structure of the institution as a problem, and the planning of major structural change involved careful negotiation across organisational boundaries. In this particular case, the unit manager and the government minister were identified as key people who needed to be fully involved in the initiation of change.

Innovations in residential institutions: Some key issues

These four case examples, along with the rest of SCF's research and the findings of Rogers[132] and Smale,[133] give rise to the following conclusions concerning the successful introduction of innovations in residential institutions for children in developing countries.

● Residential institutions, which have many of the characteristics of 'traditional social systems', are less likely to adopt innovations either readily or quickly. Even modest changes in child care practices are only likely to occur if interventions are planned carefully and sensitively, and may require a considerable investment of time.

● The planning of change needs to be undertaken in a systemic and systematic manner: particular attention needs to be given not just to practices within the institution, but also to the institution's philosophy, its organisational structure, the availability of resources, its relationship with its 'parent' agency, the wider framework of residential care, alternative forms of care and the availability of resources which might help sustain children within their own families, and the wider context of social policy and legislation.

● Staff training by itself, therefore, is unlikely to be an effective means of improving poor-quality institutional care. Moreover, there are many different approaches to training, and it is particularly important to see training as a part of a wider strategy for change, and to select an appropriate approach to training. Potter's study is particularly helpful in identifying what approaches are appropriate to different situations.[134]

● Effective networking is essential for the successful introduction of innovation. It is important to identify key people who need to be involved in the programme of change. Beckhard and Pritchard make a useful distinction between the key people in the change process who 'make it happen', or who 'help it to happen, by providing resources', or who 'let it happen by not blocking the process'.[135] Effective planning requires that energy be put into social networks in order to provide a wider context that will be supportive to the innovation.

- Another vital aspect of the planning process is to identify who views the status quo as a problem requiring change. If a 'solution' is imposed without discussion of the problem(s) to which it is addressed, it is most unlikely that innovation will be successfully introduced: indeed, to some of the people involved, the innovation will be perceived as the problem. If the staff whose behaviour needs to be changed are fully involved in discussing the need for change and in planning change, they are much more likely to feel a sense of 'ownership' of change and commit themselves to it on a lasting basis.

- As well as determining what needs to *change*, it may be helpful to *identify what should stay the same*. Innovations are more likely to gain acceptance if the people involved can integrate changes with existing knowledge, values, practices and skills.

- It is important to predict the possible consequences of change, especially the unintended consequences. The loss of salary resulting from the reduction in admissions in Case Example 2 is a good illustration of what happens when consequences are not predicted. It should be remembered that change can be painful to individuals and de-stabilising to organisations: it provides losses as well as gains, threats as well as challenges and opportunities. The need to identify key people includes the identification of people who are likely to oppose change.

- Once the need for change is identified, a vital part of the process is what Rogers describes as the establishment of a change relationship. He emphasises the importance of the change-agent adopting a 'client orientation' rather than a 'change-agency orientation': an empathic understanding of the situation faced by both the unit manager and care staff is required in order to ensure that the programme of change is consistent with the needs and views of staff, as well as with the needs of children.

- The concept of homophily is particularly relevant when expatriate staff are involved in the programme of change. Barriers created by the lack of a common language (both literally and metaphorically), limited understanding of the culture and values of the staff, and disparities in social standing and educational levels, may greatly impede the communication of innovation. The change-agents must be credible in the eyes of the people with whom they work: credibility stems from perceived professional expertise as well as such personal attributes as honesty, empathy and genuineness.

● The identification of 'opinion leaders' may be important in accelerating the acceptance of innovation. In Case Example 4, key people in the institution were identified. When it came to the second phase of the programme, the decision was made to allow staff to self-select for the new 'family group' units, with the expectation that these people would influence opinion within the home.

● A participatory approach is especially important when the proposed innovation requires consensus within the institution. The contrast between Case Examples 1 and 4 graphically illustrates the need for institutional staff to feel a sense of ownership of the proposed changes, which is only likely if they feel involved in the assessment of the need for change and the planning of it. In Case Example 1, the change-agents may have been fooled by the appearance of change on the part of staff, when in reality the staff had effectively 'immunised' themselves against change.

● Linked with this is the important issue of staff morale and motivation. As well as ensuring the participation of staff in the process of planning change and in the ownership of change, it is essential that ways are found of raising morale and motivating staff to be actively involved – a point again emphasised by Potter,[136] and one seen as particularly significant in Tolfree's *A Babies' Home in Africa: A Case Study*.[137]

● An extension of the principle of participation is the question of legitimisation. Innovation needs to be sanctioned, not only by key figures who carry formal authority (the unit manager, and people in higher management within the agency, are obvious examples), but by key people who hold informal authority. Cooks, for instance, may carry considerable authority, and if an innovation involves abolition of centralised cooking in favour of care staff doing their own cooking in family group units, the legitimisation of the innovation by the cooks may be crucial if the possibility of sabotage is to be avoided. They could easily be overlooked in discussions about the innovation.

● The formulation of an action plan should reflect all the above points, taking account of the nature of the innovation required, the context of change (including the wider context of the institution) and the significant people involved. Although it is important to establish both short-term and long-term objectives, the plan must be flexible enough to respond to the situation as it evolves.

● Any attempt at introducing change should involve children themselves, especially older youngsters, whose views should be sought,[138] and whose active involvement in the process of change is likely to facilitate it rather than obstruct it.

● Evaluation is vital if the changes achieved are to be sustainable. It is not sufficient for the change-agents to evaluate the effects of an innovation positively: those involved in implementing it also have to view the changes positively if they are to be sustained.

The simplistic and patronising attempts at 'improving institutions' in Romania in recent years are well illustrated in Kelly's case study for SCF's research.[139] She illustrates the naivety, insensitivity and arrogance on the part of agencies and individuals who failed to take the trouble to understand the wider context of institutional care in Romania. They assumed that the poor conditions were simply due to staff inadequacies, and offered short periods of 'staff training' by expatriates who had no understanding of the severe constraints under which institutional staff had to work, and who failed to see the importance of understanding the staff's perceptions of their problems, needs and abilities. The result was a further demoralisation of the very staff they were attempting to help.

Such poorly-planned intervention graphically illustrates Mencken's statement that 'there is always an easy solution to every human problem – neat, easy and wrong.'[140] Many of the attempts to introduce innovations in residential institutions in the developing world have been strikingly unsuccessful: they have also been costly, not only in terms of financial investment, but also in human terms for the residential staff, who, because of poor planning, have not felt either convinced of the need for change, or positively involved in the change process. There has also been a high cost for the change-agents in terms of their frustration at what they perceived as resistance to change. But, as Smale comments, 'The question "How do we overcome resistance to change?" can be reframed as "How do we manage the process of innovation so that we provoke the minimum of resistance?"'[141]

Part II

Prevention and leaving care

The family ... should be afforded the necessary protection and assistance so that it can fully assume its responsibilities within the community.[142]

Introduction to Part II

Part II of this work addresses two related issues: preventing the need for children to enter institutional care, and preventing the long-term institutionalisation of children by facilitating their return to their families or their move into independent living.

The term 'prevention' has a reassuringly commonsense air about it – 'prevention is better than cure', as the saying goes. However, on closer examination, prevention is found to be a deceptively complex and difficult area. The term is often used without specifying what it is that is being prevented, or how preventive action is related to the problems and situations at hand. Chapter 8 therefore provides an overview of the concept of prevention, and draws some parallels between the situation in developing countries and the history of preventive approaches in the UK. A framework for analysing prevention is introduced, focusing on the changes which form the goals of prevention, and the methods used to reach them. 'Developmental' is distinguished from 'responsive' prevention: developmental prevention is concerned with promoting family and community environments in which the needs of children are most likely to be met; 'responsive prevention' describes a range of programmes which seek to respond to the specific possibility of family breakdown and the admission of children into the care system.

Chapter 9 explores the concept of developmental prevention and looks at different strategies which may influence the circumstances which may ultimately lead to family breakdown.

Responsive prevention is explored in Chapter 10, which surveys a number of approaches designed to divert young people away from the care system when problems have come to the point that referral to institutional care may already have been made.

Chapter 11 considers the issues involved in returning children to their own families or facilitating their integration into society as independent young adults.

This leads into a discussion of common themes in Chapter 12, particularly the need for an overall framework of social policy to diminish the need for institutional care and to prevent children spending long periods in institutions. As noted in the Introduction, preventing the admission of children because of disability and juvenile delinquency is not discussed in any detail.

8 Prevention: What is it and how is it achieved?

Lessons from the UK experience

The picture painted in Part I of many institutions in the developing world was similar, in many ways, to that of the UK in Victorian times: large and overcrowded institutions, rigid methods of maintaining control and discipline, a harsh physical environment and the absence of caring and affectionate responses from the staff. Further parallels are to be found in relation to prevention. What lessons can be learned from the UK experience which can assist in developing appropriate approaches to prevention in the developing world?

Forms of preventive intervention existed under the British Poor Law system as far back as the Elizabethan Relief Act of 1601.[143] In some areas, 'out-relief' was dispensed to poor families, enabling some to remain together. But after the enactment of the Poor Law Amendment Act of 1834, able-bodied people could only receive assistance on condition they entered the workhouse – the principle of 'less eligibility', which was destructive of family life by separating husbands and wives, while maintaining destitute children in the same institutions as the mentally ill, the senile, the sick and prostitutes.

The Poor Law system was based on the assumption that poverty was largely self-inflicted, blame being attached to people who needed to seek help. The emphasis in the care of destitute children lay in ensuring they were 'rescued' from their surroundings and kept apart from their families. As Barnardo himself said: 'if the children of the slums can be removed from their surroundings early enough, and can be kept sufficiently long under training, heredity counts for little, environment counts for everything.'[144] Attitudes towards parents tended to be judgemental and punitive, and the 'rescue and fresh start' approach was most dramatically illustrated by a number of UK voluntary agencies sending children abroad, a practice which continued until the 1940s. Contact between children in care and their parents was often discouraged.

In the context of such a philosophy, it is not surprising to find little or no interest in prevention. Although organisations such as the Charity Organisation Society were concerned with providing and co-ordinating charitable giving, this was rarely offered as a means of enabling parents to continue to provide care for their children: the general view was that 'out-relief' was harmful to people and should be discouraged. Preventive approaches in the Victorian era were more likely to be seen as preventing children from becoming like their destitute or feckless parents, rather than preventing separation from them.[145] Indeed, the system encouraged the break-up of families.

Such attitudes persisted into the twentieth century, and even the Children and Young Persons Act of 1933 stressed 'removal from undesirable surroundings' as a basic principle. Care and training for neglected and delinquent youngsters formed a growing part of the attitudes of the voluntary sector. The Second World War – and in particular the evacuation of children from areas threatened by bombardment – was significant in drawing the attention of the public to the conditions in which many urban children lived. Moreover, the negative effects of separating children from their families – despite the physical dangers if they remained – were increasingly realised.

The Curtis Committee, which reported in 1946 on methods of providing for separated children, provided a landmark in the development of social policy for children in difficult circumstances in the UK. Although Curtis was highly critical of the circumstances under which many children were being cared for, the committee failed to advocate policies which would enable children to remain with their families. The main thrust of the Children Act of 1948, which followed the Curtis Report, was to legislate for the processes for admission into care and methods of providing care. However, the Beveridge reforms of the late 1940s *were* based on principles which included preventing family breakdown: 'the aim ... to ensure every child against want, against going hungry, ill-clad and ill-housed ... a second principle that we should do that in such a way as to preserve parental responsibility as completely as possible'.[146]

By the mid-1950s, the Children's Departments set up by the 1948 Act were beginning to commit resources to preventing the admission of children to care, but it was not until the Children and Young Persons Act of 1963 that a duty was imposed on local authorities to provide preventive services. Over the next two-and-a-half decades, considerable emphasis was placed on prevention, though increasingly (with local authorities under severe resource constraints) the prevention of care and custody assumed greater prominence than a broader approach to prevention.

At the same time, voluntary agencies were pioneering new approaches to prevention which often emphasised neighbourhood-based approaches based on self-help, empowerment and community-development methods. Significantly, in the Children Act of 1989, the primary emphasis is on the provision of services to 'safeguard and promote the welfare of children in need',[147] although the prevention of abuse, neglect and delinquency still feature significantly.

Some parallels in the developing world

Many organisations providing institutional care in the Third World seem to adopt a 'rescue and remove' philosophy, similar to that which characterised the UK in Victorian times. They tend to show a striking disinterest in finding ways of helping the child to remain in the family, in encouraging the maintenance of children's links with their families once separation has occurred, and in facilitating the child's return to his or her family.

A second parallel is poverty, which seemed to lie behind many admissions to care in the UK up until the first quarter of the twentieth century. Chapter 3 noted that this continues to be the case throughout the developing world, and that institutional care continues to be seen as an appropriate response to destitution, notwithstanding the high cost of institutional care in relation to the cost of helping to maintain children within their own families.

Thirdly, while the immediate benefits of placing a child in an institution in the developing world may be perceived by parents, caregivers, children themselves (in some instances) and the wider public, there is little awareness of the potentially damaging long-term consequences of institutional care. It took the mass evacuation of children from cities in the UK during the Second World War to draw people's attention both to the unacceptable living conditions of many urban families, and to the damaging effects of separation, the latter being reinforced by the considerable amount of research then being undertaken into separation and institutionalisation. In the developing world, there is clearly a need for advocacy in respect of both children's needs and rights and the effects of separation and institutional care, as an essential part of any preventive strategy. This issue is discussed in more detail in Chapter 12.

A fourth parallel relates to changing ideas about methods of prevention. Recent years have seen something of a rediscovery of neighbourhood-based and community-development approaches to prevention in the UK, partly in response to the perceived stigmas attached to 'client-based' work, which is often seen as implying a judgement about parental capacities and behaviour.

As Holman emphasises, the Family Centres movement capitalised on the advantages of resources that could be made easily accessible to families, and solutions which were approachable and informal, and oriented towards the particular needs of the neighbourhood.[148] They stressed local participation and empowerment, as well as the avoidance of the stigma frequently attached to statutory services when targeted at what are perceived as 'malfunctioning' families, labelling them in a negative way. Encouraging such neighbourhood-based community-development approaches in the developing world is vital: these approaches receive particular emphasis in Chapter 9.

Definitions and stages of prevention

'Prevention' is a deceptively difficult and complex term, though it has a reassuringly commonsense feel about it: it is obvious that it would be better to prevent family breakdown than to impose on the child long-term and potentially damaging institutional care. But when the concept is examined more closely, many crucial questions are raised. What is it that is being prevented? Does prevention stop problems emerging in the first place, or is it designed to 'nip problems in the bud'? Does prevention aim to prevent children being separated from their family after a problem has reached critical proportions? Can one talk of prevention in the sense of preventing the long-term institutionalisation of children?

In medical usage, a distinction is sometimes made between 'primary prevention', which seeks to prevent even the first signs of disease from appearing (for example, by immunisation against a particular disease, or by making environmental improvements which may prevent the appearance of such diseases as tuberculosis); 'secondary prevention', which seeks to intervene at an early stage in the development of a disease (for example, screening for breast cancer before the individual first experiences any symptoms), and 'tertiary prevention', which seeks to limit the damaging effects of a disease which is already established.

Can this medical model of the stages of prevention be applied to social development? One problem in using this kind of language is the extent to which we can predict that social problems will follow a particular course or career. The idea of preventing problems emerging in the first place implies that one can predict that certain problems will become manifest in a given set of circumstances unless particular steps are taken to forestall this. Similarly, the idea of 'nipping problems in the bud' implies that early intervention in the development of a problem will prevent it becoming more serious. But, in a social context, can such predictions be made? An understanding of the typical career of a social problem cannot be equated with knowledge of the likely course of a disease such as lung cancer. On the one hand, it is clear that social circumstances do predispose families to family breakdown or the necessity of seeking admission to care. These include, for example, poverty and unemployment and the sense of despair and powerlessness which may be associated with them,[149] and a lack of pre-school facilities. On the other hand, social work experience in the UK and elsewhere suggests that a significant number of children referred for care do not have long 'problem histories' in which intervention could have been offered at a much earlier stage.

Even if such predictions could be made with reasonable accuracy, would this confirm a *causal* relationship between the situation being addressed and the intervention being offered? How can one demonstrate that it is the intervention that has led to the prevention or diminution of the problem, rather than some other factor or factors in the lives of the child/family, especially in the case of 'primary prevention'?

These difficulties should not lead us to reject the concept of prevention altogether. Very often, when a child is admitted into residential care, it is possible to make various 'if only' statements about what might have been offered to the child or family at different stages, in order to change some of the circumstances which led to placement in care. It has already been suggested that many children entering residential care in the developing world – possibly the majority – could have remained with their families if appropriate assistance had been offered at the right time. It is often possible to define quite precisely what form of intervention could have forestalled admission. On the other hand, it is more difficult to specify forms of intervention at earlier stages in the process. Nevertheless, it is reasonable to argue that the social conditions frequently associated with high levels of family stress and breakdown can be addressed very broadly by 'preventive' measures, especially if viewed from the vantage point of concerns about the institutionalisation of children.

Holman makes a useful distinction between 'promotional prevention' and 'reactive prevention'.[150] Save the Children's preferred terminology is 'developmental prevention' and 'responsive prevention'.

'Developmental prevention' describes approaches which influence the circumstances of communities, families and children to diminish the likelihood that children will need to enter institutional or other forms of substitute care. It is acknowledged that the main aim of such approaches will not usually be to prevent admissions to care, and that the cause-and-effect relationship between approach and prevention may be difficult to establish. The goal is more likely to be to provide a range of facilities or services which support families, enhance the quality of life for children, families and communities, and serve to create the social conditions in which the likelihood of family stress and breakdown is diminished. Most such interventions do not have the prevention of admission of children into institutional care as their principal aim, but they may nevertheless have a broad preventive impact.

'Responsive prevention', on the other hand, describes a more specific set of approaches which *do* aim to influence the situation of families where a tangible possibility of family breakdown already exists. This more targeted approach to prevention may be a cost-effective way of avoiding the need for care by directing resources to children and families who are specifically identified as vulnerable. It does, however, have a rather negative connotation, and may carry a danger of stigmatising people by focusing on problems rather than strengths, and therefore of creating long-term dependence.

These two contrasting approaches to prevention are not always clearly differentiated in practice, and there is frequently a great deal of overlap between them. Day care for young children, for example, may well span both types of prevention. By offering an important range of experiences for young children, and making it possible for parents to seek employment, day care may offer a significant developmental role. On the other hand, by targeting families who are identified as vulnerable, or by opening centres in particularly disadvantaged communities, day care may make a significant contribution to preventing later and more specific family breakdown. Day care may also play an important role in enabling families to resume the care of a child who has already experienced a period in substitute care.

Different strategies for prevention

In most of the countries studied in SCF's research, little emphasis is placed on the need for approaches to prevent children being admitted into institutions. Residential care is accepted as an appropriate response to a diverse range of problems and situations, including poverty and destitution, orphanhood and abandonment, disability and delinquency. But the uncritical acceptance of institutional care belies the real difficulties which children often face after long periods of care. It is significant that the implementation of preventive strategies in the West began during a period of growing realisation of the potential damage inflicted on children by long periods in institutional care.

Where the need for preventive approaches *is* recognised in the developing world, the principal methods used are individualised responses to the needs of children and families, often involving some form of material assistance. Just as the idea of institutional care was imported into many parts of the developing world in the belief that it reflected good practice in the West, many social welfare departments have modelled themselves on the practice of their counterparts in Western Europe during the middle part of the twentieth century, when individual approaches tended to hold sway. The appropriateness of such approaches to the economic and social circumstances of developing countries is highly questionable.

It was suggested in Part I that poverty is probably the underlying cause of the majority of admissions into residential care in the developing world. However, the widespread incidence of both rural and urban poverty in the Third World suggests that a reliance on individualised preventive approaches is inappropriate. Moreover, the scale of social problems in the countries of the South, coupled with the limited (and in many cases, diminishing) resource-base of many social welfare departments, makes it imperative that more cost-effective and community-based approaches are promoted in order to capitalise on existing community resources and coping strategies, promote self-help schemes, and enhance parental, family and community responsibility for the care of children.

A number of case studies were commissioned as part of SCF's research to illustrate a range of approaches to prevention. These are summarised in the form of boxes in Chapters 9 and 10. They were chosen in order to illustrate the diversity of potential approaches at different stages along the 'early–late prevention' continuum. The intention is not to illustrate 'good' or 'bad' programmes, but to suggest that there are many ways of approaching prevention, each of which should be evaluated according to its appropriateness to the particular situation at hand. Case studies are grouped under the headings of 'developmental prevention' (Chapter 9) and 'responsive prevention' (Chapter 10). As already indicated, projects cannot be neatly and precisely categorised in this way, so there is a considerable degree of overlap. Some of the case studies have aspects of both developmental and responsive prevention.

9 Developmental approaches to prevention

It is obviously preferable to address the basic social and economic circumstances of families which often lie behind admissions to institutional care, rather than rely on approaches which intervene in the lives of families when institutional care is already being considered or requested. At the most basic level, a wide range of development programmes can be seen as having an early preventive impact.

The range of programmes which contribute to the material and social well-being of families, and which may therefore serve to mitigate the danger of family breakdown or separation, is almost infinite. They include programmes which attempt to improve housing, water and sanitation facilities, or which encourage communities to seek collective action to improve their living environment; those which provide opportunities for greater economic productivity; programmes which encourage women to become literate; day care provision to enrich the lives of young children, and which also enable parents to seek employment opportunities; family planning facilities which help to avoid unwanted pregnancies; programmes which facilitate children entering, and remaining in, full-time education; vocational training, and the promotion of employment opportunities. These types of programme, and many others besides, all have a potentially positive impact on children and families, and may diminish the likelihood of family breakdown or the seeking of admission of a child into institutional care. Rarely, however, will the prevention of admission to institutional care be articulated as a specific objective of such programmes.

Similarly, in times, or areas, of extreme hardship, measures which ensure food-security, or a basic minimum level of material provision, may be highly significant in enabling families to continue to provide care for their own children, and possibly for the children of others. Chapter 3 suggested that placing a child in an institution at times of severe material privation may be an understandable survival strategy both for the individual child and for the family. In these situations, interventions which enable families to achieve at least a basic level of subsistence, coupled with other basic amenities such as shelter, safe drinking water and sanitation, may be seen as basic preventive approaches.

This chapter concentrates on a range of more specific approaches to developmental prevention, citing four contrasting examples. The first two approaches – parenting education and a day care centre – are examples of 'early' developmental prevention. Next comes the resource centre approach, which addresses a wide range of social problems in urban areas by using a combination of different methods. The fourth approach seeks to use community-development methods in preference to individualised approaches.

The parenting education approach

The first two of these case studies are based on an assessment of particular features of the society or community which were seen as significant in terms of the capacity of families to provide adequate care for their children. The first case study (Box 9.1) comes from Jamaica, where a programme of 'primary prevention' was planned in response to a specific set of circumstances seen as significant in the context of known information about the pattern of family breakdown in the country. In Jamaican society, a quarter of all children live in families headed by single women, many of whom also work outside the home. Local research revealed a growing incidence of child abuse by parents; large numbers of teenage pregnancies; a rising crime rate among young people, with particular concern about violent crime and drugs; widespread difficulties among parents in coping with adolescent behaviour, and a growing number of children living on the streets. These issues pointed towards the need for training in order to support parents to become more effective in their roles.

Box 9.1   The Parenting Education Programme in Jamaica[151]

SCF began work with street children in Jamaica in 1988, and quickly became aware that many children experienced family breakdown partly as a reflection of poor parenting skills on the part of their parents. This led to the implementation of a programme which sought to address some of the problems which seemed to lie behind many family breakdowns.

Jamaica has a long tradition of Family Life Education (FLE) which had been developed by organisations such as parent–teacher associations, Churches, youth clubs and health clinics, but the primary focus was traditionally on sex

continued

Box 9.1 continued

education and aimed mainly at women: neither parents nor men were targeted. However, the existence of a widespread network of FLE groups provided an appropriate vehicle for the introduction of parenting education.

The SCF Parenting Education Programme (PEP) adopted a multi-pronged approach to improve parenting skills in the country at large by using a number of methods, including:

- a rolling programme of training in parenting education for FLE trainers;
- strengthening institutional capacities, especially the FLE system for promoting parenting education;
- promoting national policy and programme development in the area of parenting education as a preventive measure;
- networking through Parenting Partners, a group which was established to support parents, and which developed a *Parenting Manual* to be used in school and community outreach programmes.

The PEP training courses emphasise aspects of parenting which were felt to be neglected in Jamaica, including human growth and development; the adolescent; behaviour management techniques; child abuse, and building relationships within the family.

By adopting a 'cascade' model of training FLE trainers, and by adopting a networking approach, SCF's strategy has succeeded in reaching large numbers of actual and potential parents. The impact of these activities on parenting behaviour is difficult to evaluate, and it is difficult to judge the extent to which those whose parenting skills most needed to be improved actually benefited from the courses. However – given that inadequate parenting skills were thought to cut across barriers of class, race and gender, and given that part of the approach was to use the mass media, as well as to influence educational policy – there is good reason to believe that this was an appropriate preventive strategy.

This case study is of particular interest for a number of reasons. First, it is an attempt to make an impact on large numbers of people (many of them not yet parents) by equipping them with a range of skills which are needed for effective parenting. As such, it is a good example of early prevention, though it is not possible to establish a clear cause-and-effect link between the programme and a diminution of family breakdown in Jamaica. Second, the programme evolved out of work with young people who had already experienced a breakdown in family relationships. By tracing back the history of the problems faced by children living on the streets it was possible to identify deficiencies in parenting skills as one amongst a number of significant factors. Third, although this was a developmental approach, it did lend itself to a degree of targeting towards families who were already experiencing specific difficulties in parenting. For example, probation officers used the parenting education course with parents of young people in trouble, but by using a national curriculum they were able to avoid the dangers of appearing to single out such parents for special treatment.

The day care approach

Pre-school provision is extremely important, not only in enriching the lives of young children (especially those who are seen as deprived of good stimulatory and social experiences), but also in enabling parents (especially single mothers) to engage in gainful employment without exposing their children to neglect or unsatisfactory experiences.[152] Potentially, pre-school facilities benefit children from all backgrounds, not just those who are perceived as particularly at risk of family breakdown. But careful targeting of pre-school resources can ensure not only that particularly deprived neighbourhoods are well served, but also that resources are organised in such a way that they reach those most in need in a sensitive but non-stigmatising way. Moreover, they may also be able to offer support which might seem to be outside the remit of more traditional pre-school facilities. A good example of this comes from Thailand (Box 9.2).

Box 9.2   The Nongkhaem Community Day Care Programme in Thailand

On the outskirts of Bangkok is a huge rubbish tip. A small slum community has grown up close to it, whose members gather various items of waste for recycling. Economic pressures on most families are such that adults and children alike spend long hours scavenging, and young children often have to accompany their parents in this exceptionally hazardous and unhealthy working environment.

Experience in similar communities on the part of the NGO involved, the Foundation for Slum Child Care, revealed particular concern not only about widespread family stress and marital breakdown, but also about the large numbers of children who were vulnerable to abuse, neglect or rejection by their families, or who had already experienced family breakdown and were living independently in this stressful and highly competitive sub-culture. Some of these difficulties could be traced to the early childhood years, when their mothers, who were seen themselves to have a very low sense of self-esteem, also had low expectations of their children, and hence offered a poor level of physical and emotional care and stimulation. Unsatisfactory child-minding arrangements were common.

It was therefore decided to open a day care centre adjacent to the health centre in the slum, which offered flexible hours in order to accommodate the

continued

Box 9.2 continued

needs of working parents. Significantly, the centre sought to engage parents themselves in playing an active role in the care of children within the centre, thereby learning more about good child care practice. Family outings and parents' activities were arranged, and a savings scheme was developed to enable parents to save money for their children's education – often seen by parents as a very low priority.

Outreach into the community is seen as extremely important. Most staff in the centre are recruited locally, and home visiting, health and child development education and counselling are an important part of their role. The intention is for the centre (as it develops) to become more actively involved in the local community by encouraging local leadership among women, in order to reduce their sense of isolation and powerlessness.

Like the Parenting Education Programme in Jamaica, the Nongkhaem project evolved as a result of identifying and then addressing a number of features which seemed to lie behind family breakdown. But, in addition to offering specific services to individual children and families, the programme attempted to influence the obvious isolation of families and the striking absence of a sense of community in a situation where survival and competition were more apparent than co-operation. Despite the difficulties involved, strenuous attempts were made to develop the community-development aspect of the work of the centre, and to achieve a sense of ownership of the project by the local community.

Studies of the reasons why children enter institutional care in the developing world have highlighted the particular problems associated with a combination of poverty and single-parent families. A good example comes from Brazil, where Rizzini (describing a particular institution for 120 pre-school children) emphasises that most of the children were of single mothers who, because of poverty, had sought work as domestic staff.[153] However, they were treated by the institution as 'irresponsible mothers', and were denied opportunities to maintain their parenting role with their children. Rizzini argues that, if daytime child care facilities had been available, there would have been no need for these children to be placed in institutional care.

Another approach to meeting the needs of pre-school children from particularly disadvantaged backgrounds also comes from Thailand. The booming construction industry in Bangkok has attracted large numbers of men and women from rural areas. They live on the construction site with their children, moving on to other sites in a constant search for work. The condition of their temporary housing is frequently very unsatisfactory; wages and conditions of work are usually extremely poor, and the environment is a hazardous one for children.

In response to this situation, a Thai NGO, the Foundation for Better Life of Children, initiated a programme of mobile day care centres, usually offering both a traditional day care experience for pre-school children and facilities for school-aged children who have been denied opportunities for education because of the unsettled lifestyle of their families. These facilities include non-formal education, vocational training and recreational activities. In the evenings the centre staff provide other activities for construction workers, including health care, family planning, income generation, and so on.

Broadly similar programmes are operated in India by Mobile Creches, which provides day care facilities for young children on building sites in a number of urban locations.[154]

The resource centre approach

A rather different approach, which has also specifically targeted families with young children, is the resource centre approach. Unlike the Nongkaem Community Day Care Centre in Thailand, the planning of the Hong Kong Family Resource Centre was not based specifically on the need to prevent family breakdown and the entry of children into the care system. Nevertheless, it does attempt to have an impact on families who, in a more general sense, can be identified as vulnerable.

Although Hong Kong cannot be accurately described as a developing country, it is, in many respects, not unlike the large and rapidly growing conurbations found elsewhere in the developing world. Hong Kong is one of the most densely populated cities in the world, and most public housing offers high-rise and very high-density multi-occupancy living. Many of the new towns in the colony have a poorly-developed sense of community, and this, coupled with the rapid growth of the nuclear family and a tendency by the authorities to re-house families away from their original homes, means that many families experience a profound sense of isolation. Breakdown in marital and family relationships has increased rapidly – for example, the number of divorce decrees increased from 2,060 to 5,507 between 1981 and 1989 as traditional Chinese family values have been eroded.[155]

Particular concerns are being expressed in Hong Kong about the situation of the rapidly growing numbers of single parents, and the lack of specialised services available to them, especially during the early stages of adjustment to single parenthood. An additional problem in Hong Kong was the belief that existing counselling services were not readily accessible and were seen as stigmatising their users. In response to problems such as these, a Family Resource Centre was initiated by a local NGO, the Hong Kong Family Welfare Society (Box 9.3).

Box 9.3   The Hong Kong Family Resource Centre[156]

The centre is centrally located in a large housing estate in the new town of Tuen Mun. It was originally envisaged as a twin resource, combining the functions of a drop-in centre for single-parent families and a family resource centre – though there is no strict separation of activities, which include the following:

- a play-corner, sitting area with books, magazines, newspapers and information, bulletin board and tea-making facilities, which are all available on a drop-in basis;
- a small library of books with video and audio tapes relating to child care and life skills;
- counselling services on both drop-in and appointment basis;
- various activities (for example, camps, films) and groups – therapeutic, recreational, educational and self-help – with content and format which vary according to the objectives. Some are aimed at parents, some at children (for example, social skills groups for adolescents), and others at the whole family;
- a newsletter aimed particularly at single parents;
- a respite care service which is available on an occasional basis, and a referral and counselling service for users and providers of day-minding;
- a wider advocacy service, including talks on family issues, the reception of visitors and promoting the family resource centre model.

The centre offers a relaxed and informal environment in which families can interact with each other and seek help from social workers: it is designed to be easily accessible in a non-stigmatising way.

The aim is for the centre to grow and change according to needs which are identified in the neighbourhood: the development of services in respect of day-minding is an example of a locally-identified need which the centre sought to meet. The increase in demand for counselling services in the centre has demonstrated the need for a more accessible and less stigmatising service. Sadly, as this aspect of the centre's activities has expanded, more space and resources have been committed to the centre's work, rather than encouraging further the user-led self-help approaches which would both facilitate cost-effectiveness and encourage a greater sense of this being a resource *of* the community as well as *for* it. Experience throughout Hong Kong shows that the development of self-help approaches is difficult, though there are plans by the government to facilitate such approaches throughout the Territory.

The Hong Kong Family Resource Centre does not focus its resources on families where there is a clearly identifiable danger of family breakdown.

Rather, the centre evolved out of a more general concern for families in the area. But, by offering intervention at an early stage in the development of family problems, it seems likely that the centre plays a significant 'early preventive' role.

In the context of the relatively well-resourced social service system in Hong Kong, this emphasis on professional services may be affordable. However, as Holman explains in his book about the neighbourhood-based family centres movement pioneered by voluntary organisations in the UK, one of the most valuable aspects of the family centre approach to early prevention is that:

> local resources, be they neighbours, friends or project workers, became valuable means of support to families in times of trouble, because the lack of stigma meant that parents at the end of their tether ... were prepared to seek preventative help, and because the wide-ranging activities allowed preventative work to be operational at an early stage and through very ordinary channels.[157]

In other contexts, this kind of model could be promoted with minimal professional input and a much greater reliance on user participation. Not only would this facilitate a real sense of community ownership, but it would also make such centres more affordable in situations where expensive staffing resources are not a realistic prospect.

Chapter 8 suggested that one of the factors underlying preventive approaches is an acknowledgement that children may be psychologically damaged by the experience of separation, especially if placed in a large and impersonal institution. In Hong Kong it is surprising to find a relatively unquestioning attitude towards the use of residential care, even amongst professionally qualified social workers. Although there is now a strong move away from large institutions and towards fostering and small-group homes, there is some reason to believe that many care episodes could still be averted by more targeted and purposeful preventive work with families.

The community-development approach

Uganda offers as great a contrast to the situation in Hong Kong as can be imagined. The programme considered here is set in a rural area within a country still recovering from long years of civil war, and facing huge social and economic problems, as well as the impact of the HIV/AIDS pandemic. Despite the large numbers of children who have lost their families or become separated as a result of the civil war (or perhaps because of these factors) the government of Uganda has adopted an unusually progressive policy towards the use of institutional care. There has been a recognition of the potential damage to children which can result from institutionalisation, and particular concern has been expressed regarding the practice of many institutions in admitting children who *do* have family members able and willing to care for them. One feature of the government's approach has been the initiation of gatekeeping measures in the form of legal controls over the admission of children to institutions (discussed in Chapter 4).

With the rapidly growing numbers of children orphaned by AIDS, it became apparent that conventional approaches were neither affordable nor appropriate to the situation in Uganda. Both a continued growth in residential care and an individualised, casework approach by government social work staff were clearly inadequate. A comprehensive survey of the problems associated with AIDS orphans produced some striking findings.[158] In Rakai, the district most affected by AIDS, there were estimated to be more than 25,000 orphans (defined as children who had lost one or both parents), forming almost 13 per cent of the population under the age of 18. AIDS has affected young adults particularly, giving rise to a high mortality rate among parents and economically active people. Many of the guardians of orphans were either very old or very young, but, despite the difficulties involved in families and communities coping with an increasingly difficult situation, guardians expressed a wish for assistance programmes which would enable children to remain in their homes and communities. Local administrators also expressed a wish to see self-help solutions and local initiatives in the form of income-generating activities, vocational training and employment.

Against this background, a project was developed jointly by the Ugandan Department of Probation and Social Welfare and SCF in the district of Rakai. Entitled the Child Social Care Project, the aim was to deploy Probation and Social Welfare Officers, their assistants, and ultimately Child Volunteer Advocates, in a community-development role to complement and extend the traditional role of the district staff which hitherto had emphasised individual casework in response to statutory duties.

Box 9.4   The Rakai Child Social Care Project[159]

The aim of this project was to initiate a community-development approach to problems associated with the care of orphans in the context of AIDS, poverty and resulting social pressures. Government staff were deployed throughout the district, and, in addition to the statutory duties of Probation and Social Welfare Officers, they undertook a number of new tasks, including:

- awareness-raising within communities of the needs and rights of children, by addressing meetings, liaison with local leaders and other organisations;

continued

Box 9.4 continued

- identifying problems concerning vulnerable children, providing advice and arranging assistance where necessary, and mediating in disputes over the property of widows and orphans;
- tracing the families of children who had been admitted to residential care, and facilitating their resettlement where appropriate;
- supporting and co-ordinating community initiatives and the work of NGOs and government departments concerned with children, and assisting in the training of their staff;
- recruiting, supporting and supervising the work of Child Volunteer Advocates, whose role was to work at village level to identify and advocate for vulnerable children, and offer information and advice.

By placing responsibility for the care and protection of children within the community, while at the same time offering support to local initiatives and co-ordination, the early indications are that this project has been successful in avoiding the unnecessary separation of children from their families and communities, and in promoting an awareness of their needs and rights. The deployment of volunteers has been especially important in developing an approach which is both appropriate to the local situation and cost-effective.

The Rakai Child Social Care Project is especially significant because of its attempt to break away from a welfarist approach which, in Uganda, had seen an individualised, casework response to social problems, coupled with an ever-growing expansion of residential child care facilities. The experience of this project demonstrated clearly the extraordinary capacity of local people to respond positively to the problems of vulnerable children, despite the enormous problems associated with poverty, the long-term effects of many years of civil war, and the rapidly growing social and economic effects of HIV/AIDS.

Although categorised here as a developmental approach to prevention, this project can also be seen to have some of the characteristics of a responsive approach – a focus on individual children who had already been orphaned. However, the approach clearly emphasised developmental rather than welfare objectives.

Conclusion

All the approaches considered in this chapter have aimed broadly at improving the quality of life for children and families in the community, and, although some have attempted to target particularly disadvantaged children, families or communities, the approach has remained developmental.

10 Responsive approaches to prevention

In Chapter 9, consideration was given to a range of programmes grouped under the broad heading of 'Developmental Approaches to Prevention'. It was noted that, although these programmes probably all contributed to the health and well-being of families in the community, and hence, in a general sense, helped to prevent the circumstances in which children might need to be separated from their families, the prevention of institutional care was rarely identified as a specific objective.

In this chapter a different approach to prevention is considered – the deliberate prevention of the need for children to enter the care system. This type of preventive programme directs resources towards children and their families in situations where children are already close to the threshold of care. In using the term 'responsive', the intention is to emphasise the function of these programmes in reacting to the specific circumstances in which there is a real risk of a child experiencing breakdown in his family. Clearly, however, when a child is referred for institutional care, a range of developmental resources could be considered as an alternative – for example, referring the child to a pre-school facility, involving parents in community-development activities in order to boost their income-generating potential, and so on. Indeed, an essential part of the role of responsive prevention is to provide advice, and possibly advocacy, in respect of potential resources within the community.

Chapter 2 emphasised the role and obligations of the extended family in providing care for children, and a particularly important aspect of responsive prevention is the support which may be required by members of the extended family to fulfil these obligations. The provision of material and other support to children being cared for within the extended family is not without its difficulties, but in most traditional societies the extended family is a vital resource for parentless children. This chapter begins by examining a number of approaches which provide material support to families, and follows this with a discussion of sponsorship programmes, which offer a diversity of approaches to the support of vulnerable families. Approaches which emphasise non-material assistance are also explored. Finally, the chapter discusses the situation of street children: children in institutions share many of the characteristics of children living and working on the streets of Third World countries. Furthermore, there is a two-way movement of children between life on the street and life in an institution: the final section of this chapter examines approaches to prevention which have this twin focus.

Preventive programmes which focus primarily on material assistance

In Angola, SCF's research found that one of the principal reasons for admission of children into institutions was the death of the mother, and the father's inability to afford the dried milk and other foods needed by babies. In response to this problem, the Angolan government decided to initiate a modest and carefully targeted programme designed to prevent the admission of babies where there were relatives able to provide care (Box 10.1).

Box 10.1   A programme of material assistance for orphans in Angola

In cases where female relatives, friends or neighbours are prepared to provide care for babies whose mother has died in childbirth or shortly afterwards, the Angolan government has started a scheme to provide milk and baby foods until the child is 18 months old, as a means of forestalling the child's admission to an institution. Experience has shown that children admitted to institutional care for such reasons often lose contact with their families and end up in care permanently.

Evidence of the mother's death has to be provided, and the child has to accompany the carer when milk or food is collected. The type and quantity of food provided is dependent on the child's age. The number of children receiving such help at any one time is relatively small, but the cumulative effect of the scheme is to divert away from institutional care significant numbers of children who might otherwise experience an entire childhood of institutional living.

Careful targeting and gatekeeping in this scheme ensure that it is not abused by families who are not entitled to benefit from it, and the very modest costs involved are more than justified by the avoidance of the much greater costs of maintaining children in institutions, in both material and child-development terms.

A similar but broader-based preventive programme has been initiated in the Mozambican Province of Inhambane. Here, as part of a government policy of avoiding institutional care placements wherever possible, a modest and flexible programme was devised as a means of forestalling unnecessary admissions (Box 10.2).

Box 10.2   Community-based support to prevent admissions in Mozambique[160]

This programme began in response to concerns about the long-term well-being of young children admitted into institutional care. The exact nature of the assistance offered depends on the assessed need of the individual family, but the following are typical examples:

- infant formula milk for babies whose mothers have died;
- school materials for school-aged children;
- tools for cultivation to encourage self-sufficiency among rural families.

In addition, families are assisted by Social Action (the government Department of Social Welfare) to access the modest State benefits available to some of the poorest families, or places in day care centres where necessary. Where appropriate, families are also offered counselling, and support in seeking help from relatives or other members of the community in providing care for the child.

This flexible pattern of provision has no fixed time-scale attached to assistance, and the experience of this relatively new programme is that there is no evidence of unnecessary continuance of assistance or of the creation of dependency. By intervening during 'critical periods' during a young child's life, this programme, along with rigorous gatekeeping policies in the Provincial children's home, has been demonstrably effective in preventing admissions to institutional care.

A further variant of this type of programme was initiated by SCF in Thailand in response to concerns about the escalating numbers of children being admitted to government institutions – an annual increase of about 35 per cent.[161] It was realised that the main reason for admission was not orphanhood but poverty, which motivated parents to abandon their child or place him/her in an institution. The Out of Care Programme attempted to examine the family circumstances of all children referred to the State institution in a particular district of the country, and to find ways of forestalling admission. In addition, the programme aimed to return children to the care of their families where this was possible.

The programme achieved some initial success: by using a combination of counselling, financial assistance and loans for income generation, the programme achieved some results in diverting children away from residential care, but, for reasons which were explained in Chapter 7, it failed in the longer term because of vested interests in maintaining the numbers of children in the institution.

Some programmes have directed material assistance particularly towards the support of children who have already lost their parents and who are being maintained within their extended families. An example of such a programme comes from Sri Lanka (Box 10.3).

Box 10.3   The Orphan Support Scheme in Sri Lanka

The continuing armed conflict in the north and east of the country has led to significant numbers of orphaned children being admitted into institutions, often far removed from their communities of origin. This programme sought to provide a modest level of material assistance to orphaned children who were being cared for by substitute families, as a means of relieving the financial burden of caring for an additional child, to ensure that he/she was not denied educational opportunities for financial reasons, and in order to prevent the need for institutional care.

The programme did not accept responsibility for making placement arrangements for children, but sought to support placements arranged spontaneously within the extended family and community. Although the stated objectives of the scheme included support to children via visits from project staff, this was never fully implemented, and the main focus was on material assistance, with visits designed to monitor provision rather than to offer a wider counselling service.

It is difficult to assess the impact of the scheme in preventing admissions to institutional care: although some children did come into care, clearly the programme succeeded in providing a modest cushion against some of the hardships experienced by families in caring for additional children under particularly difficult circumstances; it also enabled some children to benefit from opportunities for education and family life which otherwise would have been denied them.

Before leaving the issue of material support to the extended family, it is necessary to sound a cautionary note. Identifying individual children as the recipients of material assistance may lead to a situation in which other children in the family are seen as disadvantaged by comparison. Such targeting of assistance may have the unintended consequence of detracting from the child's integration within the family. Material assistance which is directed towards the family as a whole may be more acceptable, and, if it enables the family to achieve sustainable economic security, this will facilitate the child's long-term well-being, as well as offering the whole family enhanced future prospects.

On the other hand, income-generating programmes do not necessarily have a beneficial effect on all members of the family. Peace and Hulme conclude from their research that 'the assumption that income "trickles-down" within the household is very questionable, especially in situations where women and men have different obligations and responsibilities in provisioning the household.'[162] Moreover, they raise the possibility of income-generating programmes serving to 'increase demand for child labour (especially female children) but not provide compensations in terms of increased access to purchased items, food, education or health services'.

An additional area of difficulty, identified by Boothby,[163] may arise in communities in which significant numbers of separated children have been taken in by non-traditional carers. Financial assistance to such families may lead to a raising of expectations among other members of the community, including families who could be regarded as traditional carers. Caution needs to be exercised to ensure that such assistance does not serve to erode the traditional pattern of family and community responsibilities which exists in the local context.

Sponsorship programmes

In many parts of the Third World, sponsorship programmes have been developed by agencies as a means of assisting children within the context of their own families and communities. The term 'sponsorship' describes an approach to raising funds rather than a type of programme, though, in some countries (most notably in the Indian sub-continent), it is used more widely to describe assistance aimed at individual children or families, sometimes directed more broadly towards community-development activities. The common element in all these programmes is the link between the sponsor and the beneficiary of the programme, though, in the case of the community-development approach, this link may be somewhat notional. Child sponsorship is a controversial subject, with strong arguments being expressed both 'for' and 'against'. The focus of this chapter is *not* on these general arguments, but on how well different forms of sponsorship programme perform as responsive strategies in preventing the entry of children into institutional care.

India has a long tradition of sponsorship programmes: traditionally they have targeted 'needy' children living with their own families, and have usually involved material assistance, often in the form of school fees. This welfare model has been criticised on a number of grounds – it tends to create pockets of privilege in basically poor families and neighbourhoods; it does little to promote the economic and social development of the family and community; it tends to create dependence, and it has sometimes been argued that contact with wealthy foreign sponsors creates cultural confusion and raises unrealistic expectations for the child.[164]

In some development agencies, this approach to sponsorship gave way to a more family-orientated model during the 1970s, with less emphasis on the needs of the individual child, and a greater focus on the needs of the whole family, especially in relation to the capacity of the family to be self-sufficient economically. More recently, many organisations concerned with sponsorship have adopted a community-development orientation, with sponsorship money 'pooled' in order to direct resources towards more general activities, ranging from improvements in facilities for health and education to infrastructural development, leadership training, the development of women's and children's groups, skills training programmes and income-generating schemes. Although individual or corporate sponsors are notionally linked with an individual beneficiary, this approach has certainly evolved beyond the patronising 'gift relationship' of traditional sponsorship programmes.

Some of these programmes have found it possible both to adopt a broad community-development approach and to target the most vulnerable families within the community: while adopting a 'developmental' approach, it has also been possible to respond to the needs of individual children and families where problems may have reached the stage of there being a real risk of family breakdown. The question to be posed here is whether sponsorship programmes are effective in targeting children who are vulnerable to family breakdown, thereby providing a systematic approach to prevent admission to institutional or other forms of substitute care.

In general, SCF's research has concluded that they are not. Although sponsorship programmes in India, for example, are frequently referred to as 'non-institutional' programmes, they are seldom developed with the specific objective of preventing admission to institutions, though there are some exceptions which are discussed below. One of the surprising findings of this study is that many NGOs in India operate both institutional and sponsorship programmes for children, but that the latter are rarely used as a specific means of preventing admission to the former. The two types of programme tend to be operated in parallel, with opportunities being missed to use child sponsorship as a means of supporting children with their families where admission would otherwise be necessary. The development of the philosophy of sponsorship from an individual-welfare approach to a broader community-development approach seems to have failed to capitalise on possible opportunities for sponsorship to be used as a preventive strategy, either to forestall the need for institutional care, or to facilitate a child's return to his family. This is particularly surprising in contexts in which large numbers of children continue to be admitted into institutions largely because of poverty, and where a modest level of material support to the child's current carer would be much more cost-effective than admission to an institution, as well as more satisfactory to the child's long-term well-being.

There are, however, a few examples of the sponsorship approach being used more imaginatively to prevent the need for institutionalisation, one of which is described in Box 10.4.

Box 10.4   The Community Aid and Sponsorship Programme in India

The Community Aid and Sponsorship Programme (CASP) is a local NGO formed in 1975, now responsible for arranging more than 30,000 sponsorships. The organisation began in response to an approach by a patient suffering from Hansen's disease, who had asked the founder of CASP to take his son away in order to build a better future for him. The response was that 'the best place for a child to grow healthily is in his own family', and thus began CASP's attempts to find ways of supporting such children within their own families.

The organisation now works primarily in a community-development role, which includes supporting housing, income generation and health in urban slums and rural areas. Various more specific programmes have targeted children in particularly difficult circumstances: in addition to the children of people suffering from Hansen's disease, CASP has also focused on child labourers, the children of fathers serving sentences of life imprisonment, disabled children and children in 'utter poverty'.

Of particular interest is a programme which involved the deployment of a social worker in the local Juvenile Court. CASP found that many of the children appearing in court came from destitute, disrupted or single-parent families, and the aim of this programme was to explore the possibility of diverting young people away from institutional care. By using individual sponsorships, children were enabled either to remain with their own families, or to be placed with relatives or other substitute families. The programme was further extended into a scheme to enable children who had already been committed to institutions to return to the care of their family or relatives.

However, few other programmes have exploited the potential of sponsorships to target children who are specifically vulnerable to institutional care. In general, sponsorship programmes, where they have targeted individual children, have tended to focus on 'disadvantaged' children, broadly defined, rather than being directed towards family situations where there is an imminent danger of a child being placed in an institution.

Where poverty is widespread, developmental approaches to sponsorship whereby resources are used to promote broad community-development are to be preferred; the benefits are spread more widely, and such programmes avoid the danger of dependency and of the creation of elitism amongst severely disadvantaged communities. On the other hand, when children continue to be admitted into institutional care primarily because of poverty, there is a case for utilising individual sponsorships as a means of meeting the material needs of selected families where this would avoid the danger of long-term institutionalisation of a child.

Where assistance can be directed towards helping the family to achieve long-term economic security, rather than singling out a particular child for direct benefit, this may both avoid unhelpful dependency and ensure that the whole family reap long-term benefits from the intervention. Appropriate material assistance through sponsorship is often accompanied by counselling and advocacy: some sponsorship programmes appear to offer unsolicited counselling as part of the 'package', which may or may not be appropriate. Clearly, in some situations it will be helpful and appropriate to provide a blend of approaches which meet the particular needs of the family.

Preventive programmes which focus primarily on non-material assistance

So far this chapter has focused on material forms of intervention designed to prevent the necessity of admission into institutional care. Although poverty has been identified as a recurring reason for admission, there are other preventive programmes which have been developed to deal with non-material circumstances which are seen as relevant.

For example, within the Palestinian refugee camps in Lebanon, a particular problem emerged regarding the care of children who had either been orphaned in the conflict with Israeli forces or were living with widowed or unsupported mothers. Numerous orphanages had sprung up in the camps, offering an 'instant solution' to these problems. Although many orphaned children did have extended families in the camps, their capacity to provide adequate care was limited by a number of factors, including the general level of deprivation, the harsh and stressful environment within the camps, and the high priority given by families to supporting the political and military efforts of the Palestine Liberation Organisation. Although there was a generally-felt obligation within the extended family to provide for orphaned children, they were not necessarily accepted as members of the family, and were often treated as 'poor relations'.

Box 10.5   The Orphan Help Scheme in the Lebanon

As part of a strategy to divert children from institutional care, in 1982 SCF initiated a programme in the camps which reflected children's own articulation of their needs. Orphaned children were placed with relatives, facilitated by SCF offering a modest level of material help to the families. Children felt a strong need for social, educational, recreational and broadly nurturing opportunities to supplement the often minimal level of care provided by their relatives, so it was decided to set up a series of clubs which were available on a 'drop-in' basis to children who were attending school on one of the two shifts which the schools operated. In order to avoid the dangers of stigmatising orphans and children with single parents, the clubs were available to any children in the camps, and, as the programme evolved, they became a resource open to the whole community. Parents and carers were actively involved, and care was taken to facilitate and not undermine family responsibility for children.

The club provided various forms of support, including: supervised homework and educational help, especially for under-achievers; sports and other recreational, artistic and creative activities, and, perhaps most important of all, opportunities for interacting with caring adults who could offer informal counselling, emotional support and guidance (particularly in the context of widespread delinquency among young people in the camps), and provide good adult role models. Raising the self-esteem of children being brought up in such a stressful environment was seen as an important objective. Particular emphasis was placed on the importance of linking the work of the clubs with the families and schools in order to achieve an integrated and co-ordinated support structure for vulnerable children.

The programme outlined in Box 10.5 was planned around the identified needs of children who were regarded as particularly vulnerable to institutional care: hence it has been categorised here as a 'responsive' approach to prevention. However, it was gradually recognised that the clubs could potentially benefit any children living in the difficult conditions of the camps, and they evolved into a community-wide resource with more developmental objectives. Nevertheless, they retained a particular concern for those children who were specifically vulnerable to family breakdown.

A somewhat similar approach, but based around the needs of a very different group of children, comes from India (Box 10.6).

Box 10.6   The Ananda Mandir Club in Calcutta

The Rambangan area of Calcutta is a 'red light district', and the children of prostitutes were seen as especially vulnerable for a range of reasons: most of

continued

Box 10.6 continued

the families were fatherless, and, because of the nature of their mothers' occupation, they were left to their own devices for much of the day, especially during the evenings. A particular concern existed regarding the danger of children becoming involved in the illicit activities common in this sub-culture, including drug abuse, delinquency and prostitution, placing them at serious risk.

In response to these dangers, a group of concerned local people started a club for these children, offering a seven-day resource whose facilities included:

- nourishing meals, including breakfast and after-school snacks;
- health awareness activities;
- a variety of indoor and outdoor games, sports and recreational activities;
- a supportive environment with the availability of appropriate adult role models, counselling and group sessions;
- attempts to involve parents in the club, and in various parental education activities;
- assistance with school work.

Like the clubs in the Lebanese refugee camps, this facility sought to enrich the lives of children within their own community, but also to offer a measure of protection from the dangers associated both with their mothers' occupation and lifestyle, and with the particular sub-culture in which they were living. However, it is difficult to establish how far the programme succeeded in averting the need for institutional care. One potential disadvantage of such approaches is that they may introduce children into a welfare system which could potentially serve to channel them into institutional care. On the one hand, those involved in developing these programmes clearly saw the clubs as a community-based facility for disadvantaged children. On the other hand, they may have had the unintended tendency to heighten parental awareness of the vulnerability and disadvantage of their children, and to raise expectations that a higher level of care was needed. This tendency was clearly demonstrated in a meeting between SCF researchers and a group of children and their mothers.

A completely different approach to prevention, based on a careful review of research into the causes of child abandonment, comes from Thailand.

Rapid economic and social change in Thailand, coupled with rapid urbanisation, have led to escalating problems of child abandonment. Almost one-third of the 5,000-plus children nationwide in the care of the Department of Social Welfare had been abandoned by their parent, abandonment having become the leading reason for children entering institutional care.

A careful study of child abandonment in Thailand, conducted prior to the implementation of the Ban Sai Samphan Shelter project, revealed that the women most likely to abandon their children shared a number of distinguishing characteristics: they were usually young; educated only to primary level; had moved to the city from rural areas to seek a low-paid job; had become pregnant unintentionally; had sometimes sought, unsuccessfully, to terminate the pregnancy, and were living apart both from the father of the child and from the family of origin at the time of birth.[165] Most babies were abandoned at hospitals, and the majority were referred to institutions.

The Ban Sai Samphan Shelter for Mothers and Babies was started in response to this pattern of abandonment. It sought to identify mothers who were at high risk and provide them with a nurturing living environment in which they could establish themselves with their babies and plan for the future (Box 10.7).

Box 10.7   The Ban Sai Samphan Shelter for Single Mothers and Babies[166]

Under the management of Bangkok's Rajawithi Children's Hospital, and funded by SCF (UK), the shelter is based in a new, purpose-built building in the grounds of a Buddhist Centre at the outskirts of Bangkok. The main objective is to provide short-term support to mothers and their babies through accommodation, maintenance, counselling and training to enable mothers to avoid abandoning their child, and to plan for the future.

In addition to free accommodation and meals, mothers are provided with training in child care, nutrition, health care and family life (including family planning as well as planning for the future), and occupational training. Individual and group counselling is provided, and Buddhist meditation and chanting are regarded as an important aspect of daily life in the shelter by helping the women to achieve emotional stability. Mothers take all responsibility for domestic and child care tasks in the shelter.

Shelter staff assist in mediating with the families of the mothers and in helping to re-establish supportive contact. Counselling focuses particularly on planning for the future, and mothers are assisted in finding accommodation, employment and, where appropriate, child-minding arrangements. Follow-up visits are made to provide continuing support.

Evaluation of the shelter's work has indicated that, out of a total of 76 women who had resided at the centre, only 4 are known to have since abandoned their babies, and most of these were able to be placed for adoption. Interviews with former residents confirmed that behind this high success rate lay some important though rather intangible reasons, which included the sense of warmth and support the mothers had experienced, and a generally more positive outlook on life engendered by their time in the shelter.

One of the striking features of this programme is the fact that its costs are very modest when compared to the benefits to children, evaluated in terms of the advantages of family life rather than the high risk of abandonment and consequent experience of institutional care. Because of the care taken prior to programme design in reviewing the considerable amount of research into the phenomenon of abandonment in Thailand, it was possible to define the target group of the programme with some precision to ensure that it catered for those for whom it was planned. It is an important lesson.

Street children and preventive strategies: Some common preventive themes

The term 'street children' is used here in the narrower sense of children who are working *and living* on the streets of cities in the developing world. Although a detailed discussion of the problems and needs of street children is beyond the scope of this book,[167] it is appropriate to give some consideration to approaches which aim to prevent the inappropriate institutionalisation of children who are living on the streets.

Children come to be placed in institutions as a result of both 'push' and 'pull' factors. 'Push' factors comprise a wide range of circumstances within the child's home environment, ranging from poverty (which is usually a primary factor) to child abuse and neglect, to loss of one or both parents through death or separation. 'Pull' factors include the advantages of institutional living as perceived by the child and/or his family (the availability of adequate meals and shelter, education, and so on).

Many children who end up living on the streets have also experienced this combination of 'push' and 'pull' factors. The 'push' factors are often very similar to those of institutionalised children, with poverty as an underlying factor in many instances, and with child abuse and neglect, family conflict and rejection also as recurring themes. The 'pull' factors exerted by the street are, however, rather different: despite adult perceptions that living on city streets is fraught with risks and dangers, street life is often highly attractive to children, offering not only good opportunities for earning a living, but a level of freedom, often perceived by the child to be in striking contrast to previous experiences of restrictiveness, abuse and lack of opportunities.

Many studies also show an interesting two-way movement of children between life on the street and life in the institution. The 'solution' to the 'problem' of street children is often seen to lie in placing them in institutions. In many countries (Brazil is perhaps the clearest example), children living on the streets are perceived by the authorities as posing a threat to society. Reasons include the belief that they are involved in criminal activities (theft, drug abuse, prostitution) and the fact that they may tarnish the image of the city, with consequent impact on the tourist industry. Assumptions that street children are involved in criminal activity are often challenged by research evidence,[168] but in many countries it is still common for the police to round up street children and place them in institutions, often without any legal authority or court order. Some child welfare organisations are dedicated to 'rescuing' children from the street in the belief that institutional care offers children both protection from the dangers of street life, and better opportunities for the future. Many of these projects are providing *for* street children rather than working *with* them to help them find ways of enhancing their future prospects.

In contrast, there is a considerable amount of evidence, mainly of an anecdotal nature, though confirmed by some studies,[169] that significant numbers of children who live on the streets have *chosen* to do so in preference to their previous experience of institutional care. The decision to 'vote with their feet' often reflects children's perception of the restrictiveness, and sometimes the abuses, which they have experienced in institutions, as indicated by this 16-year-old street boy in Kathmandu:

> I was living in a large Catholic institution, but ran away after a severe beating because of an incident in which a group of us tore a curtain in one of the rooms. The other boys were not beaten … The staff were teachers, not parent-figures, and I missed the love of a father and mother.[170]

Like many other children, this teenager had found more opportunities, freedom from abuse, and supportive networks provided by other youngsters in his chosen lifestyle on the street.

Given that, in many countries, children living on the streets are vulnerable to compulsory institutionalisation, to what extent are preventive approaches different from those which have already been considered?

As far as the more developmental approaches are concerned, there is probably little difference. Clearly, programmes which attempt to alleviate poverty (both rural and urban), which attempt to support families, and which facilitate children's entry to and retention within the educational system will all help to relieve the pressures which may lead to children seeking life and work on the streets. In terms of responsive approaches designed to divert young people away from institutional care, the principal difference is that these programmes aim to influence the situation of children who are already adrift from their families.

Child Workers in Nepal (CWIN) is a local NGO which has its roots in a student-led human rights movement: it has developed an approach to working with street children summarised in Box 10.8. The programme has evolved slowly in response to street children's own articulation of their needs and the resources required to meet them.

Box 10.8   The Common Room and Transit House for Street Children in Kathmandu[171]

This twin resource illustrates an approach which aims to promote the protection, education, socialisation and empowerment of street children in a child-centred and (where possible) family-centred way. The Common Room provides a range of resources which can be freely and readily accessed by street children, including:

- a health clinic, sick room, toilets and showers, an informal library and games room, and a safe-deposit system which can be accessed by children on a 'drop-in' basis;
- an informal literacy programme, along with occasional outings, video shows and other recreational activities;
- counselling and work undertaken with children (and families where appropriate) to plan for the child's future and achieve family reunion where appropriate;
- a night shelter, comprising sleeping space in the garage of the Common Room.

The Common Room aims to provide opportunities for young people to adjust gradually to a more structured lifestyle, to consider various options for the future and, ultimately, to move away from life on the streets. The Transit House is designed to provide simple accommodation and care, on a time-limited basis, principally for the younger children who have expressed a desire either to return to their families, or to move into a longer-term residential facility.

Individual and group counselling are important components of both resources, and work is undertaken with families in order to enable children to return where this is desired and feasible. Post-reunification support – both social and material – is provided where appropriate.

An important aspect of CWIN's work is *advocacy* on behalf of street children – for example, representing their interests with the police and city authorities.

The CWIN resource is of particular interest for three main reasons. First, it has evolved directly as a result of children themselves articulating their needs and participating fully in the development of the resources provided by the organisation. Second, CWIN, while avoiding an inappropriate and patronising 'rescue' approach, have nevertheless succeeded in providing youngsters with opportunities to move away from life on the streets where this is consistent with their expressed needs and aspirations. Third, in relation to the prevention of institutional or other forms of substitute care, it illustrates the central components of an appropriate preventive strategy for street children:

- Helping to re-connect street children with their families where this is both possible and desired by the child, and to address the problems which led to the child leaving home. This is considered in more detail in Chapter 11, which looks at family reunification.

- Providing children with a range of facilities, based around the needs articulated by children themselves, and which might include resources such as health care and health education, nutrition, hygiene, non-formal education and vocational training, recreational activities, counselling, and savings schemes. Such facilities enable young people to continue in their chosen lifestyle, offer some protection from the hazards of life on the streets, and open up a range of choices for the future. Such a range of resources may be appropriately provided in a 'drop-in' centre or club, but need to be available, accessible and child-friendly if they are to meet the needs of street children.
- Advocacy, especially in respect of police and city authorities, to prevent the enforced institutionalisation of children, and abuses of their legal and civil rights. Advocacy with the general public may also be significant in changing the distorted public images of, and prejudices towards, street children, and in promoting their needs and rights.
- In some situations, it may be appropriate to provide a fourth type of resource: although the 'rescuing' of children from the streets is usually inappropriate, some children, given the choice, may prefer the opportunity of an appropriate residential home or boarding school.

11 Preventing long-term institutionalisation: Family and community integration

Chapters 9 and 10 examined two broad approaches to preventing the need for institutional or other forms of substitute care. In this chapter, attention is turned to the situation of children who are already in institutions. Do they need to remain there? Is their own family, or a member of their extended family, in a position to care for them? Is it possible that members of their family, from whom they have been separated, could be traced? And, in the case of older children, are there ways in which they can be supported to live independently in the community in the absence of available carers within the extended family?

These approaches are often described by such terms as 'family tracing and reunification', or 'rehabilitation', and they are included in this part of the book under the heading of 'Prevention' because one of their aims is to avoid the need for long-term institutional care. Appropriate intervention aims not only to avoid protracted stays in institutions for children, but also to help avert the danger (which is often associated with institutional care) of predisposing children to periods in other forms of institutions during adulthood – especially within the penal and mental health services.

Family tracing and reunification programmes often direct their attention towards children separated from their families in emergency situations. In these situations, children will not usually be living in institutions: many will be living with related or unrelated families in the community, and, in these cases, family reunification may be significant in diminishing the likelihood of children being placed in institutional care. Hence, such strategies serve an important preventive function, as well as returning the child to the love and security of her own family. Other children, however, may be in feeding centres, orphanages or other institutions, and for them family reunification serves to prevent permanent institutional care and its consequences.

Before looking in detail at family tracing and reunification, it is worth recapitulating the likely effect of institutional care on children:

- Lack of opportunities for close relationships with trusted adults may impair children's capacity to make and sustain relationships with other people.
- Lack of opportunities to learn traditional roles and skills – many young people emerge from childhood in an institution with no perception of different adult roles, and no understanding of the customs and traditions which underpin daily life.
- Institutions tend to create a deep-rooted sense of dependency, with children being denied opportunities to learn to become self-reliant and self-directing.
- Institutionalised children often lose their sense of family, clanship or tribal identity: they lack the security and strength that comes from identifying with family and ancestors. Instead, they may assume a negative identity (for example, the 'orphanage child') and face the stigma and prejudice that results.
- Where children have lost contact with their families, they will have to enter adult life without the support which the extended family and community traditionally offers in most cultures.

The situation of young people leaving institutional care in India is poignantly summarised by Chandy:

> These institutions provide training in certain low level trades and never aim very high for the children in their care. The girls are often 'suitably' married off, and these agencies are somewhat silent on the outcome of these marriages. In actual fact, these are nobody's children. Rootless, often without direction or purpose, they gravitate back towards this place which was supposedly 'home' but, as teenagers, these doors are very often closed to them permanently. They tend to take up petty jobs on the periphery of the institution and join the child labour force; eventually perhaps to duplicate their own hopelessness in their own children.[172]

This moving account of the plight of young people leaving care is a reminder that supporting young people to return to their families, or to find an appropriate independent lifestyle, may be an important measure in preventing similar problems in the next generation.

Family tracing and reunification programmes

SCF's research included a review of five family tracing and reunification programmes in Africa by Lucy Bonnerjea, whose substantial contribution to this chapter is gratefully acknowledged. This review resulted in the publication of *Family Tracing: A Good Practice Guide*, which contains a much more detailed discussion of the main issues involved in family tracing and reunification programmes.[173] A description of a family tracing programme in Mozambique can be found in *Non-Institutional Care in Inhambane Province, Mozambique: A Case Study* (see Note 160).

Family tracing programmes have most often been developed in response to the large number of children who are separated from their families in times of war or famine. Recently, however, it has been realised that the approaches and techniques involved in such emergencies can also be used to facilitate the tracing of families and the return of children where they have become separated for other reasons – for example, children who have been admitted into institutions, often inappropriately, and street children who have expressed a wish to restore their relationships with their families.

Programmes developed in emergency situations are often referred to as 'family tracing programmes', reflecting the particular issues associated with identifying and contacting the families of children who have become separated accidentally. In other situations, the main emphasis may not be on tracing (the whereabouts of the family may already be known) but on other issues, not least the reasons for the child's separation: abuse or neglect, poverty, difficult relationships with step-parents, and so on.

Sometimes children themselves take the initiative in finding their family and returning home:

> I've been living in this orphanage. I'm not related to anyone here. When they get angry, they tell me I have no origin. They say I was thrown away during the war by my mother. I would like to find my home.[174]

In other situations, the decision may be based on adult perceptions of the child's best interests, as when government policy leads to the closure of institutions and official encouragement for family-based care. In some programmes, specialist teams are set up in order to ensure the rapid development of a high-quality service: in others, the tracing and reunification work is integrated into existing networks, such as a government department of social welfare.

The five stages of a reunification programme

Reunification programmes are usually divided into five stages, though some stages will be inappropriate to some situations:

- Stage 1 is the identification of children, which involves locating separated children, not all of whom will be immediately visible.

- Stage Two is the documentation of children: this involves interviewing children (and relevant adults) about the circumstances in which they became separated, their present living situation and future aspirations.
- Stage 3 is the actual tracing, the search for family members and assessment of whether the child can appropriately be returned to their care.
- Stage 4 is the actual reintroduction of the child and placement with the family.
- Stage 5 comprises a package of support which may be required to ensure the child's future well-being, and a system for monitoring the success of reunification.

As already indicated, some of these stages will be inappropriate to some situations. For example, in some cases, the location of the family will already be known, so Stage 3 will be unnecessary.

These five stages all need careful planning: successful tracing requires an unusual blend of carefully developed procedures and systems, and sensitive, sometimes painstaking work with children and their families. A large element of lateral thinking is also required to piece together different fragments of information. It is self-evident that staff training in this range of skills is essential.

Stage 1: Identification   Separated children usually fall into two groups – those who are obviously separated and easily visible, and those who are much less visible. Children in institutions are an example of the former, young people conscripted into armies are an example of the latter. Some reunification programmes involve small numbers of visible children (for example, the residents of one particular home); others involve the initiation of a country-wide programme aimed at identifying invisible as well as visible children who are separated, which will necessitate widespread publicity and public education, as well as elaborate systems for registering, documenting and cross-checking information, and the deployment of large numbers of appropriately-trained staff.

Many large-scale reunification programmes are initiated during periods of armed conflict or refugee emergencies, when communications can be difficult, people are wary, and trust in officialdom is limited. Gaining the co-operation of people in these circumstances is no easy task, and requires a good knowledge of the local community. Systems need to be set up to register families caring for a separated child and those which have lost a child.

The need to establish family tracing and reunification programmes should be regarded as urgent. In many refugee emergencies there has been a delay of many years before even the first steps are taken to set up such programmes, with obvious difficulties when families are traced after the child has lived with another family for a period of years.[175]

Stage 2: Documentation   The key elements here are the successful eliciting of information (often of a personal and sensitive nature) from the child, and accurate recording of important data. Interviewing children is a deceptively skilled and sensitive task, often requiring a great deal of time and patience. Children may have been traumatised by their experiences which led to separation: they may have come to learn to distrust adults, and to face possible changes in the future with considerable apprehension. This is how one family tracing worker expressed the difficulties involved:

> Some children don't want to talk to you. Some have been separated so long they can't remember details. Some have had difficulties with their families and do not want to talk to you about them. Some are traumatised and do not want to remember what happened to them. Street children are also very difficult – they don't want to talk.[176]

Much has been written on the subject of communication with children, and reference should be made to these works as the subject will not be discussed in any detail here.[177] The important point to emphasise is the delicacy of the task, and the requirement that interviewing should not be simply a matter of gaining information: it should involve counselling and supporting vulnerable children.

Documentation aims to record information about the child's *past* (family members, geographical area, the circumstances of separation, and so on), the child's *present* living situation (Can the child remain while tracing takes place? Is she well supported?) and the child's ideas for the *future* (Which relatives should be traced? What are the child's views on the various options? What problems might the child face in leaving the present living arrangement?)

In planning the programme, provision needs to be made for selecting the interviewers, deciding where the interviews take place, and what training and support are required. Where children are living in institutions, there may be tensions between the staff of the institution and those doing the interviewing and tracing work. The former may be trying to keep the child settled, and perhaps to bury unhappy memories; the latter will be working to get the child moved, asking difficult questions, evoking painful memories and getting the child to face change and an uncertain future. Moreover, institutional staff may feel that their livelihood is threatened by family tracing. For these reasons, careful preparation of and liaison with institutional staff is vital.

Documentation involves meticulous recording of information which will not always be complete – especially when it has come from young children.

Carefully designed forms will help to ensure that the right questions are asked, and that information is recorded in a way which will be useful to someone else, possibly hundreds of miles away, who has never met the child, but will be able to build on the information gained (for example, finding the shopkeeper who knows the child, or finding the village without a name). Careless misspelling of names or a failure to record nicknames can lead to disastrous consequences for the child.

Documentation also involves recording information resulting from interviews with families who have lost children, and the two sets of information need to be brought together for cross-referencing. Systems for the long-term storage and retrieval of information will be required. The development of computerised programmes has enormous potential in family tracing work, but practical difficulties, especially in the difficult circumstances of conflict or ecological disaster, may prevent their potential being realised.

A large-scale programme (Operation Reunite) to reunify children separated as a result of the war in the former Yugoslavia makes use of a computerised system which reproduces both written information on separated children and parents, and digitised photographs on CD-ROMS. These are then distributed to various locations throughout the former Yugoslavia and countries of asylum. The overall programme is co-ordinated by the United Nations High Commission for Refugees, with NGOs such as SCF taking responsibility for identifying and documenting children in particular countries.

In some programmes, photographs are taken, and can be reproduced on posters with brief details of the child, to be circulated in the district of origin. In some situations, however, the practical difficulties involved in taking and processing photographs and distributing information will outweigh the obvious advantages.

Stage 3: Tracing   'Tracing' refers specifically to the search for the family of a separated child. It may involve either specialist tracers, or local staff who are given responsibility for trying to locate a child's family. Techniques include locating a broad area and then searching marketplaces or trading centres, talking to traditional leaders or shopkeepers, showing photographs, visiting schools, and so on. Often tracing requires great tenacity, extensive travel (possibly in difficult circumstances) and the willingness to face resistance from communities who are suspicious and defensive.

Taking children on such tracing trips is a controversial area of practice: it may have the advantage of using the child's memories of landmarks and people, but has the disadvantage of exposing the child to an emotionally demanding, frightening and exhausting experience – which, for some, may end in disappointment and an enhanced sense of rejection.

When travel is impossible, tracing methods can include advertising in the media, and the use of posters which are put up in clinics, markets, churches, mosques and temples, or other public places, in the hope that someone will recognise the child from the photograph or the brief information provided. A family reunification programme for street children in Nepal sometimes took advantage of certain festivals, when families tended to come together, to provide opportunities for identifying relatives who might be able to provide care for a particular child.[178]

Two things are required if the family is to be successfully traced: first, verification to ensure that the child is returned to the appropriate family; second, an assessment of the family to ensure that they are able to provide adequate care for the child. In cases where the child had previously chosen to leave the family, for example, the reasons need to be examined and reassurance sought that the same problems will not recur. An assessment of the family's material capacity to provide care is also important.

'Returning home' does not always mean going back to exactly the same family in the same place as before. Often the composition of the family will have changed through births, deaths, separations and reunions. The family may have been displaced and other significant changes may have occurred. Reunification usually involves creating a new family, not simply replacing a lost member.

Stage 4:   Reintroducing and placing the child   Tracing the family should not automatically lead to reunification. Careful assessment will help to determine the suitability of the family, but care must also be taken to ensure that the move is in the interests of the child. Particular care needs to be taken if children may be placed in a family in which they have not lived previously. Sometimes the family will refuse to have the child, or the child may refuse to move. There may be many reasons for family refusal, including economic difficulties or family conflicts. Community leaders may be helpful in resolving problems, and traditional healers may also have a role to play – for example, in carrying out purification rites if the child was believed to have been killed.

A child's reluctance to return to the family may be due to a variety of reasons. The situation of the family, a reluctance to leave the institution, anxieties about a break in schooling or the loss of valued friends may all be important. Change is almost always painful and difficult. Some programmes address these issues by making children active participants in the programme. Much can be achieved by explanation, discussion, opportunities for questions, and talking through possible anxieties. Often when children witness the positive emotions experienced by other children who return to their families, the idea of moving begins to be seen more positively. Clearly, placing a child into a potentially harmful environment, or into a situation of extreme poverty and hardship, should not be the aim of a reunification programme, and alternative arrangements will have to be considered.

When a decision is made for the children to return, making this a public event may be an important safeguard. Neighbours, community leaders, wider family members and elders can be invited to witness the return and make it a memorable event, celebrated with prayers, music or dancing (if culturally appropriate). A second safeguard is to request the family to confirm in writing that they are willing to accept the child: the less close the degree of kinship, the more important this is. The agreement may be read out in front of visitors, and the different adults may be asked to sign: the aim is to create a publicly acknowledged social, moral and economic bond.

Stage 5: Monitoring and supporting the placement   Sometimes tracing and reunification programmes see the return of the child as the end point of the programme, rather than an important new beginning which requires further support and monitoring to ensure the child's well-being. Community leaders, women's groups, elders and teachers may all have a role to play in monitoring the child's health and welfare and helping to address problems which arise. Children are likely to experience adjustment difficulties which may cause frictions in the family, and it may be that other people in the community can help those involved to understand what the problem is and respond appropriately.

Sometimes additional resources will be needed to ensure the success of the child's return. Many tracing and reunification programmes routinely offer a 'kit' of goods to assist the child and family, including, for example, a blanket, cooking utensils, agricultural tools and seeds, and water containers. Other programmes offer individual packages of material support dependent on the family's particular needs, sometimes involving sponsorship for education. Opinion among practitioners on the utility of these kits is divided. In some situations, families may simply not be in a position to feed another mouth without some extra help; on the other hand, kits may prove to be a false incentive, a harmful addition which sets up unrealistic expectations within the family and the wider community, and which has a distorting effect on the pattern of family and kinship obligations. Where kits are distributed routinely, misappropriation is common. Decisions also need to be made on whether the kit should include items just for the child, or for the whole family, and whether material help should be in the form of capital to enhance the self-sufficiency of the family (for example, a goat or cow, or a grant or loan to start a small business).

Chapter 10 included a brief discussion of material support as a preventive measure, and the issues raised there are equally relevant in the case of family reunification. Support for children may also include advocacy, and help to the family to negotiate access to other resources. A family receiving a very young child may find the availability of day care to be an invaluable support, both in facilitating the parents' continuing work, and in enriching the life of the child. Help for older children in gaining access to schools, vocational training, employment opportunities, and so on, may also be highly significant in maximising the chances of a successful re-integration into the family and community.

One final point should be made about the need for follow-up. If properly carried out, follow-up visits provide opportunities for the programme to learn about success and failure, and how procedures can be changed and improved. Visits can identify whether there has been sufficient preparation of the child, and whether sufficient emphasis has been placed on the role of community leaders; whether educational needs have been met, and whether health or nutritional problems have emerged.

One of the most important lessons to be learned from SCF's review of family tracing and reunification programmes in Africa is that such work cannot be carried out effectively without the involvement of community leaders. They open doors, link families together, facilitate access, recount history, negotiate problems and monitor children. They are an essential link in the process of transplanting children and ensuring that they continue to grow. The question is not so much whether they can be used, but whether community leaders can, in fact, take more responsibility for the programme in all its aspects.

Programmes to facilitate independent living

So far, this chapter has focused on programmes which help children to return to the care of their original family or other members of the extended family. But for many young people living in institutional care this will not be possible: attempts to trace families may be unsuccessful, or may never be attempted in a systematic way. Some children will find themselves rejected by their families, while others may simply feel alienated by a long period of separation. Some will have had such negative experiences of family life that to return would be unacceptable to both child and family.

It is widely recognised that many children leaving institutional care after a long period typically experience great difficulties in adjusting to an independent lifestyle in the community. Some of these difficulties were outlined at the beginning of this chapter, and the issue was examined in detail in Chapter 5. What sort of support is provided to young people to help them to leave institutional care and move into independent living? The answer for most institutions covered by SCF's research is 'little or nothing'. At worst, youngsters are simply turned out into the community without the vocational and life skills, emotional maturity and sense of personal identity and self-esteem needed to cope adequately in society.

But some interesting approaches to support do exist, and two sharply contrasting examples are given below. One appears to have been quite successful, the other much less so. Both demonstrate that the key to successful integration of institutionalised children into the community does not consist of special 'leaving care' programmes only.

In Sri Lanka, concern was expressed by the government and NGOs over many years about the situation of young people leaving child care institutions (especially after long periods) and facing great difficulties in adjusting both to independent life in the community and to the world of work. In response, SCF began a programme of aftercare hostels (Box 11.1).

Box 11.1   An aftercare hostel and vocational training programme

This programme began in 1985, and involved the opening of seven residential hostels to receive young people from a variety of government and voluntary sector residential homes and schools, including establishments for young offenders. In addition, two training centres were set up in order to equip young people with different vocational skills: when places were available, other young people from the local area were also accepted for training.

The hostels aimed to provide a homely and caring environment in which young people would have opportunities for personal growth, the development of self-confidence and independence, and the learning of life, vocational and social skills. Hostel staff assisted young people in finding suitable accommodation, and supported them after leaving the hostel.

The programme was not considered to be successful, and eventually the hostels (and later the vocational training centres) were closed. A comprehensive evaluation of the hostel programme conducted in 1989 identified a number of weaknesses in planning, management and co-ordination which had contributed to the difficulties encountered. It also revealed the very high cost of the programme in relation to its limited success – a key factor in the decision to discontinue the work. Before discussing some of the key issues involved in the demise of this programme, it is useful to cite another programme which assisted young people to become independent after a period in residential care.

In Angola, long years of civil war produced a situation in which State children's homes contained large numbers of teenagers whose families could not be traced. Many of these young people had psychologically damaging experiences connected with the war, yet little was being done to assist them in the institutions beyond meeting their immediate physical needs. Often they were angry, exhibited disturbed and aggressive behaviour, and had a sense of hopelessness regarding their future (Box 11.2).

Box 11.2   A house-building project for young people leaving care in Angola

This project began in Huambo, the Province with the largest institutional population, and offered teenagers the opportunity to build their own homes in the municipality of their choice. In conjunction with the local authorities and traditional chiefs, young people were provided with land on which they were assisted by experienced builders to construct their own homes, with building materials provided by SCF. Hence they acquired useful skills as well as gaining a home. They were also given basic household equipment.

In the space of about a year, more than fifty houses were built. A resumption of the war prevented further progress, but when (over a year later) it became possible to visit these young people again, it was discovered that they had survived the period of conflict extremely well when compared to those who had remained in the institutions. They had managed to establish small businesses, had maintained their houses, and, perhaps most significant of all, they were coping well with no external support.

In presenting these two contrasting examples, the aim is not simply to highlight their success or failure, but to uncover the key issues underlying both. Comparisons between the programmes are in any case difficult, since the situation in the two countries was dramatically different. In Sri Lanka, the programme was designed around the needs of young people who had experienced many years of institutional care; in Angola, the problem was one of traumatised young people having no prospect of return to their families, and feeling a sense of alienation and hopelessness.

The success of the project in Huambo (which, interestingly, was not mirrored in similar programmes in Luanda) seemed to be due primarily to the high investment which the young people were able to make in their own future, and the high degree of involvement in and commitment to the planning and building of their houses. By way of contrast, the aftercare hostel programme in Sri Lanka, though aiming to help young people to become independent and manage their own lives, worked against its aims by channelling teenagers into further residential experience. With the benefit of hindsight, this was clearly counter-productive. For reasons revealed by the evaluation, the hostels actually replicated some of those features of institutional living which had created the difficulties faced by young people on leaving the institution in the first place.

In some situations, hostel accommodation may be an appropriate means of enabling young people to manage the difficult transition from residential care to independent living, and to provide a more 'adult' ethos than is possible in a children's home. But, where the purpose of the hostel is to attempt the difficult task of undoing the damage done by long periods of care in unsatisfactory institutions, the appropriateness or feasibility of this strategy must be questioned. Unless those features of institutional care which create problems for young people when they come to leave are addressed, it is unlikely that hostels (however well-run) will be able to compensate.

The aim of institutional care should always be to provide children with skills and experiences which will enable them to become healthy, well-adjusted young adults able to take on adult roles and play a positive part in their community. If institutional care fails to do this, it is failing in its central purpose, and that is the issue which needs to be addressed directly. Adding on a further residential experience will always carry with it the danger of perpetuating the difficulties engendered by institutional care.

Conclusions

The key message to emerge from this discussion is simple: residential care – like the family – should provide an appropriate range of experiences which will enable the growing child to take her place in the adult world. This means finding an appropriate balance between meeting the emotional, physical and educational needs of children, as suggested in the discussion of 'good-enough' residential care in Chapter 6. In few, if any, cultures does the role of parent end when children reach the age of 16 or 18; it continues to be significant during the early adult years. In the same way, young people brought up in substitute care are likely to need some form of continuing help and support, and those who have accepted responsibility for the care of children also have a responsibility to continue an appropriate level of support after the formal period of care has ended.

One final issue to emerge from the evaluation of the aftercare hostel programme in Sri Lanka is worth noting: the rate of referral to the hostels was much lower than anticipated, and, when this was explored, it was found that the majority of the children were, in fact, being sent back to the care of their families. Why, then, had these young people remained for so long in substitute care? A more recent study showed that the reason for admission was not known to the institution for almost one-quarter of the sample![179] The report clearly highlights the need for gatekeeping policies to prevent the inappropriate admission and retention of children in institutions. It is therefore appropriate to conclude this chapter by re-emphasising the *central importance of gatekeeping policies and practices* highlighted in Chapter 4. The programmes reviewed in this chapter all aimed to return young people to a more normal lifestyle within the community. Some of these young people will have been unavoidably separated from their families, but many will have been separated because of the inappropriate admissions policies of institutions, often based on the mistaken belief that institutions can provide a better future for children than life in their own families.

12 Towards a policy framework for prevention

This chapter draws together the main themes which emerge from the discussion of approaches to prevention in Part II, and considers some of the broader policy issues involved in the promotion of preventive child care. In Chapter 8, a broad distinction was drawn between *developmental* and *responsive* approaches to prevention. Is prevention therefore a function of development, or of welfare? And which is the more appropriate approach?

Developmental approaches to prevention were defined as those which seek to influence the wide range of family and community circumstances which may ultimately lead to family breakdown. Responsive prevention, on the other hand, comprises a range of approaches which respond to specific problems (sometimes at a very late stage in their development), and which attempt to divert young people away from the care system. It was acknowledged, however, that there is no clear dividing line between the two approaches, and that some programmes may take a developmental approach and also provide a means of influencing the lives of families already experiencing serious difficulties.

Very often, developmental approaches are the favoured option of development agencies. Responsive approaches, on the other hand, may be viewed as the function of welfare agencies, where concern is with the individual rather than with broader development issues. Surely the developmental approach is to be preferred? Once again, the distinction is not as clear-cut as this. It is not a question of 'either ... or', since there may well be room for both approaches. Moreover, under the broad umbrella of responsive approaches, some will be more developmental in character. Not all responsive approaches can be described as 'welfarist'.

SCF's view is that *both* approaches may be appropriate. Governmental and non-governmental organisations should be concerned to promote the well-being of families and communities via a very wide range of programmes, all of which can be seen to contribute to the welfare of children by improving the economic, social and environmental conditions in which children grow up. In this sense, programmes as diverse as day care provision, food-security, adult literacy, water supply and income-generating programmes all serve to diminish the likelihood of family breakdown and the need for children to be admitted into institutional care. As suggested in Chapter 9, however, most such programmes do not have the prevention of the need for institutionalisation as a central or explicit objective.

On the other hand, there is also a clear need for responsive programmes. Development programmes never reach all potential beneficiaries, and it is often the most vulnerable who fail to benefit and who fall through the net of support structures. Peace and Hulme, for example, found that, in practice, income-generating programmes were very difficult to target to the poorest families.[180] Within broadly disadvantaged communities, there are always going to be exceptionally vulnerable individuals and families who, for a variety of reasons, are not going to become involved in community-development programmes, and may be especially vulnerable to some form of family breakdown. Some – but not all – such families will benefit from a more targeted approach which responds individually to their particular circumstances. If this individualised approach prevents the unnecessary separation of a child from the family and a potentially long period of time in an unsatisfactory institutional environment, then it is justified. The cost of such approaches may be relatively high, but, in relation to the much higher cost of many years of institutional care, may well be warranted.

On the other hand, it has to be recognised that even individualised preventive approaches will not always be effective, and that some children will continue to need alternative care arrangements. In some cases, children need to be protected from their own families by external intervention; in others, young people may make a conscious choice to leave the care of their families, for a wide variety of reasons.

An example of a national strategy for prevention

Few countries included in SCF's research have adopted anything approaching a coherent policy for supporting vulnerable families and preventing the unnecessary admission of children into institutional or other forms of substitute care. Mozambique and Uganda are two notable exceptions. Langa has compiled a fascinating history of the development of non-institutional care policies in Mozambique, a condensed version of which is given in Box 12.1.

Box 12.1   Mozambique's policy of non-institutional care

Despite being one of the world's poorest countries, and with large numbers of orphaned, abandoned and separated children arising from the combined effects of prolonged civil war, periodic droughts and widespread poverty, Mozambique has succeeded in promoting a policy of using institutional care only where this is necessary and consistent with the best interests of the individual child.

In part, the approach was facilitated by the enforced closure of many residential homes after the exodus of foreigners from the country on achieving independence in 1975. This was followed by a decision by the government to take the remaining residential homes into State control, and to limit the activities of organisations wishing to establish institutions.

Two factors were particularly significant in the development of a national policy – an early awareness of children's rights, as evidenced by the adoption of the Declaration of the Rights of the Mozambican Child in 1979, and an enlightened awareness of the potentially damaging effects of institutional care on children's development. Moreover, the particular difficulties facing the country led to a realisation that an institutional response could never meet the needs of the country's huge numbers of separated children, and certainly could not be afforded financially.

A series of seminars during the 1980s served to heighten awareness of the need to promote interdepartmental co-operation in seeking to avoid the unnecessary admission of children into institutions, and emphasised the responsibility of families and local communities to care for parentless children. The Organisation of Mozambican Women was given a central role in public education and in implementing the policy at grassroots level.

A range of preventive approaches were initiated, including the development of day care centres; the provision of milk for orphaned and abandoned infants; a family tracing programme, and, most important of all, the active promotion of community-based support for children in difficult circumstances. The key role of local activists and political structures was supported by the production of a simple illustrated manual and complementary posters covering the care of separated children. Careful gatekeeping measures piloted in one institution, coupled with the promotion of substitute family care, have succeeded in keeping admissions to a very low level, and in ensuring that children do not remain in institutional care permanently.

The policies being pursued in Mozambique are an attempt to replace the legacies of an institutional approach with a community-based approach to care, built on existing cultural traditions weakened by war, natural disasters and severe economic difficulties. Had it not been for a clear government philosophy of community-based child care, it seems highly likely that institutions would have burgeoned, and that an escalation of demand for residential care places would have further undermined family and community responsibility for the care of children.

Key issues in the development of preventive strategies

The following key points emerge from SCF's research as being particularly significant:

● States which are signatories to the UN Convention on the Rights of the Child have an obligation to provide preventive services to families: 'The family ... should be afforded the necessary protection and assistance so that it can fully assume its responsibilities within the community.'[182] It is not sufficient for governments to pay lip-service to children's rights while ignoring the plight of countless children who are vulnerable to family breakdown.

● The most fundamental measures which governments can take to prevent the unnecessary separation of children into institutional care are probably those which ensure that the basic needs of children and families are met. Poverty continues to be the main reason for institutionalisation in the developing world.

● The prevention of care only becomes a priority when the disadvantages of institutional care are perceived. Knowledge of child development and of the likely impact of separation and institutionalisation are essential before the value of prevention can be appreciated. While institutional care continues to be seen as an appropriate response to the problems associated with poverty, there will be little incentive to promote more appropriate alternatives.

● With this in mind, public education on the importance of the family, on children's needs and children's rights, is important in dissuading parents from seeking inappropriate, institutional solutions to their problems. People's organisations, local political structures, and community groups may have a particularly important role to play here. In Mozambique, for example, the Organisation of Mozambican Women plays a key role in raising people's consciousness of the needs and rights of children.[183]

● Changes in legislation may be required in order to prevent inappropriate admission of children into institutional care.[184]

● Preventive intervention strategies can be plotted on a continuum. At the 'early' end are strategies to prevent unwanted pregnancies: at the 'late' end are approaches designed to prevent the permanent institutionalisation of children. Within these two extremes are a range of approaches, described in this book as 'developmental' and 'responsive', which have an impact at different stages in the 'career' of a problem.

● No one approach is necessarily better than another: a pluralistic approach which incorporates both developmental and responsive approaches is likely to be most effective in minimising the numbers of children in institutional care.

● Prevention, in its broader sense, is not the sole prerogative of social welfare departments. Every government department, as well as NGOs and intergovernmental agencies, has a responsibility for ensuring that children are provided with the best possible environment for their growth and development. Social policies and programmes in the areas of health, housing, education, transport, employment, poverty alleviation, and so on, as well as social welfare, all have an important bearing on prevention. Effective prevention therefore requires effective intersectoral co-operation.

● The development of community day care facilities can be especially important in enriching the lives of children, in enabling parents to work, and in supporting families.

● One of the most significant preventive resources is the school. Writing of the UK, Parker describes the role of schools as providing largely unrecognised opportunities for contributing to the task of prevention, in the form of a safe environment and a wide spectrum of rewarding and challenging activities.[185]

● There is a strong argument that governments should be concerned about the activities of organisations providing institutional care, and should consider what legislative measures, and the means to enforce them, are necessary to prevent the unnecessary and inappropriate admission and retention of children in institutional care.

● Programmes which directly seek to avoid the need for institutional and other forms of substitute care need to be based on empirical evidence on the reasons for admission, and not on generalised statements or assumptions about the circumstances leading to admission to care.

● The relatively high costs of responsive, individualised approaches to prevention need to be set against the high costs of institutional care, and the heightened disadvantage experienced by so many institutionalised young people.

- The most appropriate responsive approaches to prevention will probably emphasise:

  - enabling families to retain control over their own lives by their participation in programmes and their opportunities, wherever possible, to exercise choice;
  - the importance of helping families to become self-sufficient, rather than relying on recurring welfare handouts;
  - involving the wider community in exercising responsibility for supporting vulnerable children and their families;
  - the use of methods which, in the particular context, are appropriate and affordable: approaches which, for example, rely on trained and paid social workers, especially in scattered rural communities, are unlikely to be either affordable or cost-effective;
  - building on people's strengths, rather than an exclusive focus on problems and pathology.

- Sponsorship programmes have potential for making an impact on those children and families at greatest risk of separation. However, this requires a more targeted approach which is rarely promoted as part of a non-institutional strategy.

- The prevention of long-term institutionalisation of individual children should receive high priority. Gatekeeping policies and practices, whose importance has been emphasised throughout this book, should help to ensure that children do not remain in residential care for longer than necessary. Family tracing and reunification programmes should be given high priority, and the preparation of young people for leaving care should be a central feature of residential living, not a set of discrete activities offered just before the youngster is about to leave.

All States who are signatories to the UN Convention on the Rights of the Child, and any organisations concerned with children's rights, must share a concern to promote ways of enabling vulnerable children to remain within their families and communities wherever this is possible and consistent with the best interests of the individual child. A great deal of lip-service is paid to the value of family life by governments who do little to support the most vulnerable families. As Damania illustrates by reference to India:

> on the one hand, government policy states that a family is the best place for a child to grow up in; on the other, the government provides more funds for starting institutional settings for child care and provides hardly any funds for promoting noninstitutional programmes.[186]

However, it must be recognised that family care will not always be possible. Moreover, some children need to be separated from their families for their own protection and well-being. For those children who *do* need to be apart from their families, the main form of care provided by governments and welfare agencies in the majority of developing countries continues to be institutional care – and often of a highly unsatisfactory quality. This need not be the case, and Part III therefore examines the potential for developing alternative approaches to substitute care.

Part III

Substitute family care

The child ... should grow up in a family environment, in an atmosphere of happiness, love and understanding.[187]

Introduction to Part III

In Western societies, the last fifty or so years have seen a major shift in policies and practices regarding children who are unable to live with their families. Before the Second World War, most children facing orphanhood, abandonment and family breakdown who were unable to live within their extended families lived in orphanages and other institutions. Institutions also provided for substantial numbers of young offenders whom it was thought needed to be removed from their families, and for large numbers of disabled children, at a time when special facilities were felt to be more appropriate than integrated, community-based provision.

A number of factors have led to a progressive reduction in the use of residential care for children in the West, ranging from the writings of Bowlby and others (who drew attention to the potentially damaging effects of institutional care on children, especially those in residential nurseries, as discussed in Chapter 1) to the high cost of residential forms of care. As residential child care has contracted, increasing emphasis has been placed on substitute family care for those children for whom return to their own families has not been possible or appropriate. In the UK today, residential care for children is seen almost exclusively as a short-term measure designed to achieve particular objectives, such as treatment in respect of emotional or conduct disorders, or preparation for independence, return home or placement in substitute family care.

In Western societies, a common distinction is made between adoption and fostering. Adoption is usually regarded as a type of family placement in which the rights and responsibilities of one or more parents are fully and irrevocably transferred to one or more adoptive parents. The intention is to provide a form of family care as close as possible to care within the child's biological family.

Fostering, on the other hand, is usually seen as a less permanent family placement which does not involve the transfer of parental rights and responsibilities, and in which the child maintains some sort of continuing link with the natural parents. Foster parents, unlike most adopters, normally receive an allowance for their care of the child, and the placing agency has a continuing responsibility for the placement.

Clearly, an important distinction between adoption and fostering lies in the motivation of the carers. Adopters usually want to extend their family by offering full membership to an unrelated child; foster parents, on the other hand, are more likely to be motivated by a sense of responsibility, a desire to help a child, and the rewards which this is thought to bring.

In practice, the distinction between adoption and fostering is not always clear-cut: for example, some foster placements have been regarded as permanent, while in some Western countries it has become possible, under certain circumstances, for adoptive parents to receive an allowance in respect of their adopted child. Moreover, adoption has come to be seen as not necessarily severing the links between the child and biological parents, though a permanent change in the child's legal status is an intrinsic feature of legal adoption.

This increasing emphasis on substitute family placements has required the deployment of highly skilled, specialist social workers, and there has been an increasing recognition of the skilled and difficult role of foster parents, and, in respect of older or 'special needs' children, of adopters. Some foster parents are now paid fees or a salary in addition to fostering allowances, and, under certain circumstances, adopters can also receive allowances, usually in relation to children who are 'hard to place'. These factors have created a situation in which substitute family care can no longer be described as an inexpensive option, though, in the light of the escalating costs of residential care, it continues to be a cost-effective as well as a professionally favoured one.

Despite the high level of resourcing of fostering in the UK, this type of care is not without its difficulties. In addition to its increasing cost, fostering also has a high breakdown rate: reviewing the evidence of the failure rate of long-term fostering, Berridge and Cleaver give an alarming overall figure of around 50 per cent.[188]

In most parts of the developing world the picture is quite different. On the one hand, the vast majority of children unable to live with their families are absorbed into the extended family and, in some cases, community networks, with various forms of traditional adoption and fostering existing in many parts of the world. On the other hand, in most developing countries, institutional care has continued to be the norm for children for whom the State or non-governmental organisations have taken responsibility: relatively few have attempted to develop programmes of adoption and fostering.

One significant difficulty in gaining public acceptability of substitute family care relates to cultural norms regarding the nature of family life. In cultures which traditionally have strong extended family systems, the boundary between members of the extended family is a permeable one which allows for mutual support and reciprocity, including the care of children. However, the boundary between the extended family and the outside world may be relatively impermeable, limiting the extent to which it is considered appropriate to care for a child who is outside the traditional group of clan or tribe.

Although the terms 'adoption' and 'fostering' are used throughout Part III, both terms carry a variety of meanings in different contexts. In Western societies, 'adoption' is normally associated with a change in legal status achieved through the making of a court order, but, in other cultures, traditional forms of adoption exist which do not confer a changed legal status.

It may be useful at this point to consider varieties of substitute family care in terms of the roles played by the child's natural parents and the substitute parents respectively. Goody suggests that there are five main parenting roles:

- bearing and begetting;
- endowment with civil and kinship status;
- nurturing;
- training;
- sponsorship into adulthood.[189]

While it is common in Western societies to find all five roles played by the child's biological parents, in many developing countries it is normal for a number of these roles to be shared with others: grandparents and older siblings, for example, may have a vital role to play in nurturing, while other relatives or unrelated adults often help with training.

Adoption (whether legal or *de facto*) can be regarded as an arrangement whereby all these roles (apart from the first) are delegated to the adoptive parents (who may well share some of them with other people in accordance with cultural norms). Fostering, on the other hand, implies the sharing of only some of these roles, usually on a time-limited basis. Thus, for example, traditional forms of fostering (often referred to as 'fosterage') of older children in West Africa may primarily be a means of sharing with another individual or family the responsibility for the child's training.

Adoption is normally seen as a permanent living arrangement for the child, conferring full membership of his adoptive family, or, in Goody's terminology, endowment with civil and kinship status. Fostering, on the other hand, is generally seen as a short-term arrangement, though this may drift into permanence. There is usually no intention to confer membership of the foster family or clan to which he belongs, and this may be the case even if the arrangement becomes a long-term one. The child's sense of identity will usually continue to stem primarily from his birth family and lineage.

In some situations, adoption and fostering are confused, and, where the two concepts are allowed to become blurred, this can create uncertainties, misunderstandings and insecurity for the child, the natural family and the carers. An example of this problem is given in Box 13.1.

In this book, the placement of a child within his extended family is not regarded as a form of substitute family care. In all the countries which have contributed to SCF's research, a traditional sense of responsibility exists for parentless children to be cared for within the extended family, though the nature of such obligations varies from one culture to another, particularly in the degree of closeness which exists between child and relative.

In some situations, relatives may need assistance in order to provide care for a parentless child: this was discussed in Part II, and is therefore not considered here.

13 Adoption

As already indicated, the distinction between adoption and fostering is not always clear and sharp. For the sake of clarity, the term 'adoption' is used here to describe situations in which a child is reared, on a permanent basis, by one or more adults to which she was not born: the parenting roles of endowment with civil and kinship status, nurturing, training and sponsorship into adulthood are all transferred to the adopter(s). This chapter is primarily concerned with adoption outside the extended family. The child is likely to feel a sense of belonging to her adoptive family, and ties with her birth parents would usually – but not necessarily – be broken.

Fostering, by contrast, applies to situations in which a child lives with a family into which she was not born, but without any expectation of permanent membership of her 'new' family, and with the probability that some contact with her birth parents will continue. Depending on the individual circumstances, the parenting roles of nurturing, training, and possibly sponsorship into adulthood, will be transferred to the foster parents.

It is not intrinsic to either type of arrangement that the placement be formalised by law, and, as will become clear, both forms of substitute care are widespread, but often will not involve the intervention of any sort of welfare agency.

Adoption in a worldwide and historical perspective

Forms of adoption are found as far back as the ancient civilisations of Babylon, China and Rome. In general, their primary aim was not to meet the needs of parentless children, but to provide an heir for the purposes of inheritance of property and the performance of ceremony. For example, the

Code of Hammurabi (in Babylon) covered a wide range of issues concerning adoption, including a detailed examination of issues regarding the relationship between the child and adoptive parents, the circumstances under which an adopted child may be reclaimed by the natural parents, and the complex issue of inheritance rights.[190] Under Roman law, adoption was only permitted by adopters who were beyond child-rearing age, and it existed to provide an heir for the childless. At the time of adoption, the person adopted had to be an adult. Roman law was typical of ancient civilisations in allowing adoption for the purposes of inheritance and religious observance: it had little to do with the emotional needs of either young childless couples or parentless children.

Traditional forms of Chinese adoption served two main, gender-based purposes: boys were adopted for the purposes of obtaining an heir, while girls were adopted in order for the family to obtain a *tongyangxi* – a future wife for a male child of the family.[191] This avoided the necessity of paying bride-price, and helped to ensure the future daughter-in-law's loyalty and integration into the family. It seems that girls were also adopted by childless couples in the belief that the adopted daughter would help enhance the mother's chances of conceiving a boy. Similarly, adoption is an ancient practice in Korea, motivated primarily by the need to ensure an appropriate and high-status male heir to continue the family lineage.[192]

It is also an ancient Chinese tradition for families to accept an unrelated girl into the family, as a maid. In times of hardship, it was a common practice to sell a daughter to a wealthier family. Wu has reviewed the considerable body of evidence that adopted girls, until comparatively recently, had a higher mortality rate than biological daughters.[193] He also suggests that the finding of Rin, that the youngest daughters of Chinese families in Taiwan tend to suffer from tension and aggression, is due to the fact that they would be vulnerable to being given up for adoption if the family were to face more difficult times.[194]

In medieval Europe, Christianity opposed the abandonment and sale of children, and monasteries found themselves offering care to unwanted and abandoned children. This was paralleled by what Boswell has described as 'the kindness of strangers' in rescuing abandoned and unwanted children and caring for them as their own.[195] But it was not until 1926 that the first Adoption Act provided a legal means of adopting children in the UK.

Indigenous forms of adoption have also evolved in many developing countries. In India, for example, customary laws were codified under the Hindu Adoption and Maintenance Act of 1956, although the practice of adoption in Hindu culture also stems from ancient times. Once again, its prime purpose was to continue the family lineage, to provide for the inheritance of property, and to satisfy religious obligations – the most notable being the requirement of a son to perform the last rites of his father.

The legal situation of adoption in India is considered in some detail in *The Development of Adoption in India: A Case Study.*[196] Indian law only permits adoption by Hindus, and does not allow adoption if the applicants already have a child of the same gender. It is worth noting that this Act seems to place more emphasis on the needs of parents rather than those of children: there is no emphasis on the need to pursue the best interests of the child.

In Sri Lanka, customary adoption was used both for the purposes of instituting an heir and to provide parental care for unwanted children or for children whose natural parents were too poor to care for them. Interestingly, Sri Lanka's Adoption Ordinance of 1941 allowed adopted children to continue to inherit from their birth family, though in all other respects the adoption law severs all the rights of birth parents. Prior to the enacting of this ordinance, it was common practice for adopters to be given gifts at the time of adoption, though the ordinance prohibited the receiving of any kind of reward in consideration of the adoption, unless sanctioned by the courts.

In Vietnam, traditional forms of adoption fall into two main categories: first, the adoption of very young children, usually by childless couples, who, in every respect, care for the child as their own. Such children are generally well cared for. Second, there are families who take in a child out of charity, and who will expect the child to work and be grateful. Such children are not always treated as part of the family: clearly, some accept their role and adapt to it, others do not, rebel and are unhappy. Either form of adoption can involve relatives or non-relatives, but full acceptance into the family by non-relatives seems not to be very common – although childless couples wanting a child may be a notable exception. There is no history of adoption law in Vietnam, though there are now moves to enact adoption legislation: at present, *de facto* adoption placements can be registered with the People's Committees as a means of formalising the process.

In most African cultures, the idea of adoption is quite alien, though, in many countries, adoption legislation based on Western models was introduced, usually in the late colonial period. In most African societies, children are considered to be the responsibility – and even the property – of the clan, not of the child's parents. The upbringing of the child is very much a shared responsibility. Kenya provides an example of this, Colton writing that:

> before the arrival of Europeans here there was no need for adoption because the problems of homeless children did not exist. In fact, there was no word for adoption in the vernaculars or in Kiswahili. If the child lost a parent or parents he was automatically taken in by the most immediate relatives since in most tribal customs children were regarded as a responsibility of the clan as a whole.[197]

Not only was legal adoption seen as unnecessary in Kenyan society, it was also inconceivable (as in many African societies) that a parent could sign away a child of their own flesh and blood. It is not unusual to come across instances in Africa where a parent has signed a consent to Western-style adoption but has completely failed to understand that legal adoption involves an irrevocable severance of contact between the child and the birth family. As one East African father put it when an application was being made for his child to be adopted: 'How can I give my child away, who is my own blood?'[198] Although adoption legislation was introduced in Kenya in the early 1930s, only 26 children were legally adopted during the first 30 years of its enactment, the vast majority of adoptions being conducted in accordance with traditional practices.

Experience in Uganda demonstrates the dilemma involved in attempts to introduce *de facto* adoption into a society in which the notion of caring for an unrelated child has not found widespread acceptance. A childless widow who felt unable to share the fact of adoption with either the child or with her kinsmen and neighbours expressed the difficulties as follows:

> If I tell anybody about it, this girl may be harassed by my relatives. I fear they will call her names that imply she is a rootless outsider who has no say in important family matters. Yet she is my only child and I want to leave everything of mine to her.[199]

Brazil is another country where formal, Western-style adoption laws co-exist with informal forms of indigenous adoption. The latter typically involve a childless couple or person(s) wishing to adopt simply taking in an unwanted or rejected child and registering her birth as though born to the adoptive family. The practice is, strictly speaking, illegal. Intermediaries (such as hospital staff) are frequently involved, and it is widely believed that money frequently changes hands in these transactions. It is estimated that 90 per cent of adoptions in Brazil take this form. Writing about traditional forms of adoption in South America generally, Johnson suggests that children adopted according to traditional practices are likely to be treated differently from other children in the family: misbehaviour is likely to be less tolerated, and the adopted child will probably have to work longer hours than other children in the family.[200]

In the Philippines, adoption legislation dates back to 1923, but informal adoption existed long before this. Various factors have motivated people – usually the wealthier classes – to take in children who are destitute, illegitimate or abandoned. Reasons include the need for domestic assistance or the desire to have someone to care for them in their old age; religious piety may also be a reason. It was also customary for couples with children to give a child to relatives who were unable to have children of their own.[201] Since the introduction of adoption laws, the majority of cases have been either inter-country adoptions or adoption within the extended family.

Islam prohibits adoption by virtue of a stipulation in the Koran.[202] In Islamic societies, *Kafalah* is a form of family care which does not involve a change in kinship status, but does allow an unrelated child, or a child of unknown parentage, to receive care, education and inheritance, and to have legal protection. However, some Islamic societies have enacted adoption legislation (for example, Tunisia, Egypt and Syria), though in some cases this is mainly for the benefit of non-Islamic citizens.

Traditional adoption: Some key points

From this brief review of some traditional forms of adoption, a number of key points emerge as being of most significance: it must, however, be borne in mind that information about the many different forms of traditional adoption is far from complete.

● In most traditional societies, children whose parents are unable to provide care for them are absorbed into extended family systems as a matter of course. Such arrangements are unlikely to be labelled 'adoption', and most are regulated by custom rather than statute.

● Forms of traditional adoption of a child from outside the extended family network are less common, though there are some indications that in some cultures it is a more widespread practice than the 'received wisdom' would suggest. The earlier quotation from a Ugandan widow is an illustration of the tension between prevailing cultural norms and the individual desire to adopt on the part of people who are prepared to contravene such norms in order to acquire a child for adoption from outside the extended family.

● Most forms of traditional adoption are essentially private arrangements between the adults involved. Most do not involve any government or other welfare agency, and there will usually be no formalising of the situation through the courts, though in some cases there may be a system whereby village chiefs or leaders have a role to play in registering the child's changed status.

● Traditional forms of adoption have evolved to serve a variety of needs: these include providing children for childless (or sonless) families, as well as ensuring continuation of the family line and serving religious and ceremonial purposes. The need to provide families for abandoned or orphaned children has usually been a secondary consideration, and, if traditional forms of adoption are to meet the needs of such children, the concept may need to be changed and developed.

● In many forms of traditional adoption, the needs of parents, rather than those of children, seem to be paramount. Few legal frameworks, where they exist, are based on the principle that the child's interests are the paramount consideration. Even fewer permit adoption without parental consent except in the case of verified abandonment.

● Where legal adoption exists, the legislation may reflect traditional practice – as in India – and place limited emphasis on the needs and rights of the child. Alternatively, it may be little more than an import of Western legislation, and, in many countries, may have limited use except in adoption by foreigners.

● In some countries, indigenous forms of adoption co-exist side by side with formal, legal adoption. Growing urbanisation and the declining capacity of the extended family to provide care for parentless children, together with the growth of inter-country adoption, are the main factors which have prompted the development of agency-based, child-centred adoption – modelled on Western practice.

● Children placed for adoption according to custom will not necessarily be treated in the same way as children born to the family. Adopted children will not necessarily be accepted as full members of the family – they may be 'kept' rather than 'cared for'. The pattern varies with different cultures and different circumstances, but in many cultures it would be considered acceptable to treat unrelated children differently from children born to the family.

Adoption programmes for separated children

One of the most striking findings from SCF's research is the following paradox: on the one hand, there are large numbers of children being maintained under highly unsatisfactory institutional conditions, often with little or no contact with their families. It is precisely these children who are most likely to be damaged by the experience of long-term institutional care, and who are most likely both to be available for adoption and to be considered 'adoptable'. On the other hand, few of these children are considered for adoption. Why is this, when adoption is frequently perceived in the West not only as offering the best possible quality of secure family life, but as probably the most cost-effective option?

As already indicated, not all countries have a framework of adoption law and an agency-based adoption service. In many of those which do, the legal framework has been developed primarily around the needs of foreign adopters, rather than as a response to the needs of parentless children for whom adoptive homes might be sought within their own country. In some countries where adoption programmes have been developed for parentless children, they are of such poor quality that it is questionable whether they meet the children's needs for care and protection. Nevertheless, in some countries it is possible to find agency-based programmes which have sought to place parentless children in permanent substitute family care, and which do so in a way which pursues the interests and rights of children.

The rest of this chapter looks at some of the constraints and obstacles to the development of adoption programmes, drawing on two countries which offer examples of unsatisfactory practice, and at the opportunities for promoting adoption for parentless children, drawing particularly on evidence from India.

The adoption of parentless children: Problems and constraints

In Uganda, a local Church-based NGO which provides residential care facilities for children has been placing children in substitute family care for many years. Although described by the agency as a fostering scheme, it is more akin to a form of *de facto* adoption, and hence falls within the working definition of adoption suggested earlier. In legal terms, 'fostering' is seen as a step towards legal adoption, but, in the large majority of cases, no application for adoption is made. However, the intention of the programme is permanent placement, but the majority of children are not accorded any new legal status, and hence may experience problems in such areas as the inheritance of property (Box 13.1).

Box 13.1   A *de facto* adoption programme in Uganda

Children in residential care are selected for placement on the basis that relatives cannot be traced and that no family claims are made on the child. There is no advertising or promotion of adoption, but prospective adopters contact the home directly, are shown a selection of available children, and are invited to choose a child. Visits to the family are then made by a District Probation Officer, a report is written, and the child is handed over: in some cases this is now done through the Magistrates' Court, though in many cases there is no legal formality. It appears that children are selected for placement according to the preference of the adopter, rather than the assessed needs of the child. The assessment of the families is cursory in nature, and there is no special preparation of the child. No

continued

Box 13.1 continued

arrangements are made for regular post-placement follow-up, though some adopters bring the children back for medical check-ups and, on occasions in the past, they have received some limited material assistance.

A sample of 23 children were chosen for a follow-up study: of these, only 10 could be located, and of these 10, there were serious concerns about the well-being of the children in 3 cases (including one child who had been sexually abused, and two who appeared to have been seriously neglected).

It appears that, in most cases, the adopters claim that the child has been born to them, and conceal (from the child, the extended family and the community) the fact that the child was obtained from a residential institution.

Writing about two similar schemes in Uganda, the Uganda Foster Care and Adoption Association provide information on the almost complete lack of supervision and follow-up of children placed in families, and conclude:

> these rather ugly statistics depict the extent to which children can be abused in the absence of a well-planned fostering programme. Foster parents themselves don't seem to understand the usually temporary nature of fostering. It appears most of them undertake fostering when actually they mean to adopt the children. Some parents, after getting used to the children, take it for granted that the children are theirs. They never come up to obtain adoption committal.[203]

The cost of legal representation is one major factor which has deterred carers from applying to adopt a child who had been placed for 'fostering' when there was no possibility of the child returning to her own family. Adoption applications can only be made in the High Court, and the high cost of legal representation puts such action beyond the means of many families.

In Brazil, a country with a particularly large number of children living in institutions, there are now moves to promote the concept of adoption of parentless children by families within the country. There are many difficulties, however, chief among them being an adoption system which continues to discriminate against local adopters (Box 13.2).

Box 13.2   Adoption in Brazil

In Brazil, although adoption laws exist, in practice they are often seen as ineffective in facilitating the adoption of abandoned and orphaned children within the country. One reason for this is that a great deal of power and discretion is placed in the hands of the Juvenile Court, which leads to a situation in which there is frequently a great deal of conflict between adoption agencies and the courts; one writer refers to:

continued

Box 13.2 continued

the arbitrariness of adoption procedures and the lack of organisation and understanding between adoption agencies and juvenile courts. Each depends on the other for swifter and more efficient action, but in practice it is almost as though they were antagonistic.[204]

There is a legal stipulation that overseas adoption should be considered for children who cannot be adopted by Brazilian adopters, but some courts tend to ignore this, and, in practice, the legal system greatly favours adopters from overseas.

As yet there are few adoption agencies committed to promoting the concept of adoption within Brazil for children who would otherwise be consigned to spending their childhood in unsatisfactory institutional care.[205]

From this and other evidence collected by SCF, the following key problems emerge:

● Individuals and organisations providing residential care are frequently trapped in an institutional frame of reference, and see it as outside the scope of their mandate to consider non-residential placements. Their concern, usually, is to provide residential care, not to facilitate the child's placement in the most appropriate environment for her growth and development.

● Although childlessness is an ubiquitous phenomenon in all countries, this does not automatically create a large 'pool' of potential adopters. There are several reasons for this: different cultures sanction different ways of coping with childlessness (a term which, in some societies, will refer either to the absence of children, or the absence of sons), including the taking of an additional wife, or divorce and remarriage. The sense of shame which childlessness carries in many cultures may also hinder the open acceptance of childlessness (and the failure it is seen to imply) which may form an important first step toward family-building through agency-based adoption.

● In many cultures, the idea of providing parental care for an unrelated child is widely perceived to be unacceptable, if not abhorrent. This is amply illustrated by the Thai saying: 'Bringing up children of others is like having food chewed by others.'[206] However, as described below, assumptions about the unacceptability of non-family care, if unchallenged, can act as powerful disincentives to the promotion and development of adoption services.

● Particular beliefs and customs may place restrictions on the matching of children to potential adopters: gender, racial background, religion, colour, caste or social status and family background may be significant factors in determining the 'adoptability' of children by particular families and in particular situations. Children of unknown parentage may be particularly difficult to place in some cultures. In others (such as Sri Lanka), importance will be attached to the child's horoscope. Once again, however, experience suggests that these potential barriers to adoption of unrelated children may not be as serious as might be assumed.

● The lack of coherent and child-focused adoption legislation has greatly hindered the development of an adoption service. In India, for example, there is no unified adoption law: the Hindu Adoption Ordinance of 1956 only permits legal adoption by Hindus, and, as already indicated, does not provide a firm legal foundation for a child-centred adoption service. In this context, it is therefore encouraging to learn that adoption has nevertheless been successfully promoted.

A particular difficulty is that many young children destined to spend a substantial part of their childhood in institutional care are not legally available for adoption. Many do have parents, but enjoy little or no contact with them, yet the parents are not willing to relinquish them for adoption. Legislation which enables courts to dispense with the consent of parents is extremely uncommon outside Western countries, though Angola is an interesting exception, where parents can lose their rights if they are deemed to have abandoned their child for a period of a year or more.

● In countries where an adequate framework of adoption law does exist, judicial procedures and bureaucratic obstacles can greatly hinder the development of adoption (see Box 13.2).

● The absence of effective adoption programmes for parentless children in developing countries also reflects the lack of social work expertise in this specialised aspect of social work practice. Although a number of NGOs have promoted inter-country adoption, few have become actively involved in developing intra-country adoption.

● The lack of an overall and coherent framework of policy for the development of adoption as one of a range of options for the care of children who cannot be returned to the care of their own families is also important.

● Finally, a number of difficult practice issues need to be addressed in the development of adoption services. One of these concerns the importance of openness to the fact of adoption, and the importance of adopted children being told of their history, to which there is considerable resistance in some cultures (for example, India, as demonstrated in the case study referred to in Box 13.4). This underlines the need for prospective adopters to receive educational input, and not just assessment, by social workers skilled in the complex issues involved in adoption. In India, the provision of peer-support for adopters and adoptees was also seen as appropriate.

The adoption of parentless children: Opportunities and progress

This list of constraints to the development of adoption may suggest that, in many cultures, great difficulties will be experienced in promoting the concept and practice of adoption. However, none of these constraints should be seen as insurmountable. Potential does exist for developing permanent substitute family care outside the child's extended family network for children whose families are unable, for whatever reason, to resume their care. They involve seeking opportunities to develop and extend traditional forms of substitute care, drawing on Western experience in order to evolve forms of care which are child-centred, culture-sensitive and affordable.

First, however, it is necessary to consider the potential place of adoption as an alternative to institutional care in the developing world. What categories of children should be considered as eligible for adoption, and what are the likely characteristics of the people likely to seek to adopt them?

Adoption services are not to be seen as an instant solution to the problems of children living in institutions, and at best will only cater for a small minority of institutionalised children. In general, however, the following groups of children may be able to benefit from adoption:

- young children who have been abandoned, where attempts to find their parents have been made and have failed;
- young children who have been orphaned, where alternative carers within the extended family system are not available;
- children who are the result of unwanted pregnancies, especially among unmarried women, and particularly in those societies in which unwed motherhood confers a sense of shame, and in which resources to support such children are very limited;
- children separated from their families, where return to the family is neither possible nor desirable, and where informed parental consent to adoption can be obtained: examples include children seriously abused within the family and children whose parents have rejected them;
- there may be another group of children separated from their families for reasons which include long-term mental illness on the part of the parent, and long-term imprisonment, where informed consent has not been obtained, but where there is legal provision for dispensing with parental consent.

There is evidence in many Third World countries that significant numbers of young children in institutions could be placed for adoption. As already indicated, children placed in institutions as infants and who have no family contact are most likely to experience serious psychological damage if they spend prolonged periods in institutional care, yet it is precisely these children who are most likely to be adoptable. The situation in Brazil illustrates this point (Box 13.3).

Box 13.3   Lost opportunities for adoption in Brazil

In Brazil there is evidence that a far greater percentage of children being brought up in institutions could be placed for adoption. Rizzini states:

> there is a greater number of children who live in total abandonment than is officially recognised ... Many children abandoned in their first year spend several months or even years in care awaiting the process of selection before they can be considered for inclusion in a family adoption programme. When this happens, often it is already too late. Older children have greater adaptation difficulties and the period they spend in care hinders their development in every sense, turning them into 'problem' children with far fewer chances of being adopted.[207]

Clearly, adoption can only be developed as a service for parentless children in situations in which potential adopters can be identified. What kind of people wish to adopt? In Western countries, the large majority of adopters are couples who are unable to have children of their own by the normal biological means. But, in developing countries, attitudes to childlessness and infertility may seriously hinder the acceptability of adoption as an alternative route to family-making. It is therefore important to examine the issue of childlessness before analysing the characteristics of people who are likely to seek to adopt.

Childlessness in many cultures carries a powerful stigma, and confers a profound sense of shame. In Jamaica, for example, childless women are referred to disparagingly as 'mules'. Writing of African cultures, Agiobu-Kemmer concludes that:

> among various ethnic groups in Africa, which cut across national boundaries, the greatest misfortune that can befall a man or woman is to be childless. No matter how rich and successful the individual may be, life is miserable and unfulfilled without children. Children are the 'essence and sap of life'. According to a Yoruba folk song, they are considered to be 'clothing and adornment' for their parents. Anyone who does not have children has nothing to cover his shame and nakedness.[208]

In many African cultures, the traditional response to childlessness is for the man to take an additional wife, or to divorce his wife and remarry. Infertility will normally be seen as the woman's 'fault'. In the Buganda language, for example, the word for 'infertile' literally means 'infertile woman': the possibility of male infertility is not entertained. In some cultures, it is expected that a family with children will give one or more to a relative who has none.

However, recent trends in many developing countries are eroding these traditional responses to childlessness. Fortunately, if paradoxically, the circumstances which contribute to the phenomenon of child abandonment may also create a situation where adoption becomes more acceptable. Urbanisation, the rise of the nuclear family, and economic constraints may all conspire to create a situation in which childless couples may be more responsive to the idea of adoption, rather than seeking an alternative marriage partner, or seeking a child from a relative who already has several children.

Experience in India suggests that, in general, adopters fall into the following categories:

- childless couples who see adoption as a means of creating a family;
- couples with children born of the marriage who wish to extend their family but who cannot, or who do not wish to have additional children of the marriage;
- couples wishing to adopt as an expression of their concern for parentless children.

Very often in programmes in countries in which adoption has yet to gain widespread acceptance, prospective adopters tend to be middle-class urban families, though, as indicated in *The Development of Adoption in India: A Case Study*,[209] attempts are now being made to promote the concept among people in rural areas.

What lessons can be learned from the experience of attempting to promote adoption as a service for parentless children? This section draws heavily on the case study referred to above (Box 13.4).

Box 13.4   The development of adoption in India: The work of the Indian Association for the Promotion of Adoption (IAPA)

The IAPA is an organisation committed to the promotion and advocacy of adoption within India, and to the creation of the necessary social and legal conditions for securing the child's welfare. It is also actively involved in the

continued

Box 13.4 continued

placement of children for adoption.

By means of tenacious and multi-method promotional and educational approaches, it has succeeded in making great progress in increasing the acceptability of non-relative adoption in a culture where birth antecedents, caste and community affiliations, and gender preferences are accorded high importance.

Despite the lack of unified adoption legislation, an unevenly developed social work profession and generally low level of social welfare resources, the IAPA has worked closely with government, other organisations concerned with child welfare, and the judiciary to help to achieve the required social and legal conditions for the acceptance of adoption. It has also achieved a measure of influence over national policies and programmes.

The following factors emerge from SCF's research as significant in developing adoption services in developing countries:

● The development of adoption services needs to be based on a comprehensive understanding of local culture: a thorough grasp of cultural beliefs and norms in relation to the following issues is essential before adoption services can be planned:

- attitudes to childlessness: explanations of infertility; social attitudes (for example, shame, social stigma) towards childlessness;
- existing practices in respect of *de facto* adoption;
- cultural norms in respect of caring for unrelated children: the importance of blood-ties; norms in respect of the way in which unrelated children are treated in comparison with children born to the family: attitudes to unknown – or what is perceived as unsatisfactory – parentage;
- gender preferences;
- attitudes to issues of race, tribe, clan, caste, colour or social class;
- norms in respect of the inheritance of property.

Experience in various parts of the world suggests that a variety of cultural norms and beliefs will impinge on the development of adoption, but that:

● Public education campaigns can be a potent means of promoting the acceptability of adopting unrelated children despite apparent cultural contra-indications. Creative and imaginative use of radio and television, newspaper articles and so on can be effective in influencing public opinion, but public education campaigns are only likely to achieve results over long time-scales, hence the need for persistence and tenacity.

● The development of adoption services will benefit from a supportive legal framework. Ideally, adoption laws need to be comprehensive, intelligible, child-centred, and to enable adoption agencies (whether government or voluntary) to carry out a professional service. It is, however, noteworthy that adoption has been successfully promoted in India, despite the lack of a uniform and coherent child adoption law, and despite the difficulties involved in persuading the authorities to declare abandoned children available for adoption.

● Adoption procedures need to be intelligible, inexpensive and accessible: they should not operate in a way which discriminates in favour of overseas or wealthy and articulate adopters.

● Adoption services should be integrated with other child care services to ensure that adoption meets the needs of children already requiring homes, and to avoid creating a new 'market', as has happened in some countries where the demands for babies from couples overseas have encouraged parents to relinquish their children for adoption.

● Adoption agencies need staff of high professional calibre. Adoption work is generally regarded as a specialised branch of social work, requiring sophisticated skills in areas such as assessment, education, counselling and group work, as well as skills in marketing and publicity. It also requires staff of high integrity, especially if they are operating in countries where abuses occur (for example, child trafficking associated with inter-country adoption).

The adoption of 'hard to place' children

Practice in many Western countries has now exploded the myth that only white-skinned, healthy newborn infants can be placed for adoption, and a great many adoption agencies are now placing adolescents, children with disabilities and children from racial minority groups for adoption. In many developing countries, while the majority of children considered difficult to place are being placed for adoption with overseas families, a number of agencies are pioneering programmes to place them for adoption within their own society. In Brazil, Terre des Hommes has been active in promoting the adoption of children considered hard to place on account of age and skin colour within the country. In Thailand, Christian Outreach have begun work on a pioneering programme to place institutionalised children with various forms of disability in adoptive families or with their own birth families.

Promoting adoption: Concluding comments

The available evidence suggests that residential care is most damaging for the following groups of children:

- children admitted to large and impersonal institutions as young infants;
- children who spend substantial periods in institutions;
- children living in institutions who have little or no contact with their parents or other members of their extended families.

It is in this context that adoption should be viewed as an important part of any strategy of moving away from an excessive reliance on residential care as a means of caring for children unable to live with their families. Although only a minority of children living in institutions will be considered to be eligible for adoption, it is precisely those children who are most likely to be damaged by institutional care for whom adoption can be considered most readily.

In Western societies, the adoption of children by non-relatives evolved as part of the response to the social problems created by migration, industrialisation and urbanisation in the latter half of the nineteenth century and the beginning of the twentieth. Many developing countries are now experiencing similar disruptions to family life, for broadly similar reasons. While each country will need to develop its own particular response to the needs of parentless children, it seems likely that some form of adoption is likely to be an appropriate and cost-effective option in attempting to link the needs of parentless children with those of families wishing to care for them.

Experience in India and elsewhere suggests that agency-promoted adoption is most likely to develop initially in urban environments, reflecting the incidence of nuclear families, greater access to the mass media, and a generally higher level of education. Adoption has almost always been much slower to develop in rural areas. It is noteworthy, however, that most of the children requiring adoptive families (abandoned children, unwanted, illegitimate children, and orphaned children having no relatives willing and able to care for them) are also primarily products of urban environments.

The development of adoption programmes in some countries will be extremely difficult: perceived cultural barriers to the idea of caring for unrelated children, the lack of a coherent legal and social policy framework, and the unavailability of skilled social workers may all be impediments to the promotion of child-centred forms of adoption. Experience suggests, however, that none of these should be seen as an insurmountable barrier. Any attempt to introduce adoption programmes must, however, be based on a thorough appraisal of the constraints and opportunities which such programmes may provide for parentless children to be given the benefits of a secure and permanent family life. This is a much better – and cheaper – alternative to a childhood spent in an institution.

14 Fostering

As already indicated, 'fostering' is defined here as an arrangement whereby a child lives with an unrelated family, usually on a temporary basis, without any implication that his birth parents lose their parental rights or responsibilities. It usually involves transferring to the foster parents the parenting roles of nurturing, training, and possibly sponsorship into adulthood.[210] The term 'fostering' is, however, used in a variety of ways in different countries. Some use the word as a generic term for any kind of substitute family placement: others use it more specifically for agency-arranged placements of children within extended family systems. The word is also used – very inappropriately – to describe sponsored children, and thereby gives a wholly false and misleading impression of the relationship between the sponsor and the child.

It is important to remember that, in virtually all countries of the South, it is common to find children living with families other than their own, usually but not always within the extended family system. In most non-Western societies, the rearing of children is not seen as the responsibility solely of the child's parents, and many people within the extended family system will share this responsibility. It is not, therefore, surprising to find various forms of indigenous fostering in which responsibility for children's care, socialisation and education are shared, on a more extended basis, by various people within the family network. In most societies, there is an obligation within the extended family, and sometimes within the local community, to accept responsibility for the care of children who are temporarily unable to live with their own immediate family. This would not normally be labelled 'fostering', and the arrangement would be negotiated informally between the adults involved without the intervention of State or other welfare agencies.

Formal, agency-operated fostering schemes exist only in a small minority of the countries covered by SCF's research. A few countries now have well-developed fostering programmes modelled along the lines of Western practice (see, for example, *The Development of Fostering in Hong Kong: A Case Study*[211]), and this chapter looks in brief at a number of other fostering schemes, mostly initiated in response to specific local circumstances.

Some traditional forms of fostering

Foster care has a long tradition in India, and is represented in Hindu scripture and mythology. There is a long-established custom, known as the *Gurukul* system, for students to live with their teachers – sometimes for the entire period of their formal education. With the development of schools in India, this custom declined, though it continues to be common for children to be boarded-out with relatives for the purposes of education where appropriate schooling is not available close to the family home. Boarding schools and hostels attached to day schools also continue to provide accommodation for children unable to travel to school on a daily basis.

West Africa provides some interesting examples of fostering arrangements (sometimes referred to in the literature as 'fosterage' or 'minding'). In Sierra Leone, it is extremely common for children to be raised by adults other than their biological parents – relatives, friends, neighbours or patrons. Young children from the age of weaning until about 6 years old are frequently sent to 'grannies' – older women, often living in rural areas, and not necessarily related to the child by birth. The practice is seen to benefit the biological parent (for example, by spreading the burden of a large family, or by early resumption of post-natal fertility by the cessation of breast-feeding). It also benefits the foster mother, partly because children contribute their labour, and also through the obligation on the part of the birth parents to provide material support to the foster mother. Fostering may also create a pattern of obligation on the part of the growing child towards the foster mother which may, for example, be particularly significant in her old age. There are also perceived advantages to the child, in terms of the 'granny's' experience in raising children, her attentiveness to his needs, and the amount of time and affection she can offer. But there may also be some disadvantages for the child, which are elaborated below.

Fostering is also a widespread practice in respect of older children. After the age of about 6 years, it is more usual for children to be sent to the care of younger adults, often in the urban areas, for education or training. The aim may be for children from rural areas to gain access to educational provision, and/or because of the perceived benefits of living with a person of higher educational – and possibly social – standing than the child's own parents.

In a fascinating article, Bledsoe explains how patterns of fostering in Sierra

Leone, though ostensibly used as a means of enhancing the education and training of the child who is fostered with a teacher or other person of higher status than the family, also fulfil a significant purpose in facilitating social mobility and securing patronage for the family.[212] Fostered children frequently come in for harsh treatment, and are expected to contribute substantially to the household economy of the foster home (often more so than other children in the family). This is usually tolerated by the child's own parents, partly because of the social benefits accruing from fostering, and partly because of the value placed within local culture on hardship as a route to success in life.

One significant fact to emerge from the research of Bledsoe and her colleagues is that fostered children may be significantly more likely than children living with their own mothers both to be nutritionally disadvantaged and less likely to gain access to hospital when ill.[213] The research suggests that fostered children tend to have less food, and less protein-rich food, than other children in the household. Moreover, girls are more vulnerable in this respect than boys. Fostered children are also more likely to be denied food as a punishment, with more serious consequences for girls than boys, because of their limited capacity to seek food from alternative sources.

Within West Africa there are many different variations on the practice of fostering. One interesting example provided by Goody is the use of children as pawns – as security against a loan.[214] Another widespread practice is the fostering of older girl children to act as household maids.

It is worth adding that Goody reports on research undertaken to assess the psychological effects of various forms of fostering on children in Gonja society, and concludes that, using the criteria of 'success' for men, and 'marital stability' for women, fostered children seem to be slightly more advantaged than non-fostered children. One reason for this may well be the high value placed on fostering within wider society. This is an interesting contrast to the potential for short-term disadvantage indicated in the work of Bledsoe,[215] though, clearly, the criteria used to measure impact are not gender-neutral.

Although various approaches to fostering in West Africa have evolved primarily as a means of sharing parenting tasks, with the child's natural parents continuing to be actively involved in the child's care, it nevertheless appears that particular social circumstances may make it likely that a child will be fostered out: for example, the children of single mothers, or children whose mothers receive no support from their husbands, are particularly likely to be fostered out at an early age.[216]

Fostering appears to be common in many parts of Sub-Saharan Africa, though it appears that in West Africa it is a particularly widespread phenomenon which has been studied most extensively by anthropologists.

In Mozambique there are strong traditions of children being cared for within the extended family. As in many African societies, the payment of bride-price (principally in the southern part of Mozambique) seems significant in establishing the father's family's right to children of the marriage, and also their obligation to care for them.[217] However, what is particularly interesting in the findings of research undertaken as part of an evaluation of the SCF Family Tracing Programme in Mozambique is the willingness of families from outside the extended family to provide care for unaccompanied children. Three rather surprising findings are particularly significant: first, the sense of responsibility (as opposed to a traditional obligation) felt by substitute carers as women and mothers, as illustrated by the following testimony:

> I could never leave a child who had no one to take care of her. I wasn't obliged to take these children. There's no difference between them and my own children. I feel ashamed when they don't have clothes and shoes.[218]

A second significant finding from this research was the lack of evidence that children in substitute care are treated differently from other children in the household. Third, the sense of responsibility felt towards unrelated children seemed relatively unaffected by the widespread incidence of poverty. Quotations from other women illustrate the surprising extent to which responsibility towards children in the community transcended the families' material circumstances:

> It would be enough to see that the child had no one. I would have to take care of her as my own.

> I'd like to take care of more [children] even with the problem of drought and hunger.[219]

It seems likely that this sense of community responsibility towards children is primarily a rural phenomenon, and that, in the more urban areas, the sense of community solidarity which exists in villages is weaker, and there are more concerns about children in substitute families being more open to abuse or exploitation. It may also, at least in part, reflect the impact of the war in Mozambique, which may have served to enhance a sense of community solidarity.

From the available evidence on patterns of traditional fostering, the following points seem to be particularly significant:

● In most traditional societies, child-rearing is not to be seen as the sole task of the child's biological parents, but rather as a range of tasks which may be shared among members of the extended family and community.

Different societies have evolved different practices with regard to the sharing of child-rearing tasks, and it is not uncommon to find traditions whereby children spend considerable periods living with families other than their immediate biological family, usually for the purposes of discipline, education and training, or securing patronage for the child's parents. Such arrangements would be seen by those involved as adding new relationships to the child's social world, not as replacing the child's biological parents. In general, the child would continue to derive his sense of identity from his own family and lineage.

● Although most traditional forms of fostering have evolved as ways of delegating certain parenting tasks on a non-permanent basis to other people, they have sometimes also been used to provide family care for children who are unable, either temporarily or permanently, to live with their own families.

● As already noted in Chapter 9, children who are unable to live with their own family, for whatever reason, are, in most societies, absorbed within the wider family system – and sometimes within the community system – unquestioningly, whether on a permanent or short-term basis. This would not normally be labelled as either 'fostering' or 'adoption', and would not usually involve any intervention on the part of welfare agencies.

● In rural areas, there is more likely to be a sense of community responsibility for separated children than in cities. The Mozambique study has provided evidence of significant numbers of placements of separated children with unrelated families, arranged spontaneously within village communities, despite strong traditions within this society of children being the responsibility of the extended family. The situation in urban areas appears quite different, with greater fears of children being exploited or abused.

● It is considered quite acceptable in some cultures for fostered children to be treated differently from other children living in the same household: access to food, forms of punishment and expectations of the child's contribution to the household economy are all areas in which the child may be disadvantaged *vis-à-vis* other children in the same household, and girls may be more disadvantaged in these areas than boys. The child's natural parents would not necessarily find this fact surprising or unacceptable. However, as evidenced by the Mozambique study, concerns about differential treatment of unrelated children may not always be well-founded.[220]

Fostering programmes for separated children

Chapter 13 concluded that effective adoption programmes are lacking in most parts of the developing world. It is clear from SCF's research that the concept of fostering is even less familiar, and that approaches to fostering vary greatly in scope and scale, target group of children, primary objectives, and organisational framework. Although it is difficult to categorise these approaches neatly and precisely, three main categories of fostering can be identified:

1 Informal fostering arrangements resulting from attempts by community leaders, volunteers and social workers to facilitate the placement of parentless children within their own communities. In such situations, fostering may mean little more than the mobilisation of existing community responsibility for separated children.
2 Small-scale, situation-specific programmes designed as immediate, non-institutional responses to the needs of particular groups of children. Although the intention may not be for the programme to become a permanent fostering scheme, the children involved are likely to need long-term support.
3 Larger-scale fostering programmes which are planned as ongoing schemes designed to meet the needs of children drawn from a wider range of circumstances, which require long-term funding and formal organisational structures. These programmes are usually modelled on Western foster care, and require a substantial investment not only of skilled human resources, but also in promotional and public education campaigns to secure the acceptance of the idea of fostering and to facilitate the recruitment of foster parents.

1   Informal fostering arrangements made by community leaders, volunteers and social workers

This approach is an extension of traditional fostering, with community leaders (possibly with a formal responsibility for child welfare), volunteers or social workers acting in a facilitative role. Two examples serve to illustrate this approach, the first from Lesotho (Box 14.1).

Box 14.1   Fostering as part of a community-based strategy for children

The Lesotho Save the Children Fund has recently shifted its primary emphasis from the provision of residential care to the development of non-institutional,

continued

Box 14.1 continued

family- and community-based approaches. As part of this new approach, their social workers are attempting to find imaginative solutions to child care problems on a case-by-case basis. This may, for example, involve recruiting foster parents within the child's own community, or finding a member of the local community to move into the family home of the children in order to care for them in their own home environment. Where appropriate, short-term or long-term material help is being sought, sometimes through sponsorships, to provide whatever level of assistance is required. Community leaders are involved in the selection of potential carers and in the supervision and monitoring of the placements.

A second example comes from the *The Role of the Substitute Families in Mozambique: A Case Study.*[221] Significant numbers of parentless (though not necessarily orphaned) children in Mozambique have been spontaneously absorbed within the extended family and community systems, but sometimes the arrangement of substitute care has required a facilitation role from local officials and volunteers (Box 14.2).

Box 14.2   Substitute family care in Mozambique

In situations in which parentless children have not been spontaneously absorbed within extended family and community systems, volunteers from the Organisation of Mozambican Women and local officials play a vital role in making positive efforts to identify families willing to care for such children.

This would not be described as a formal fostering programme – rather it involves the facilitation and support of substitute family placements, which are possible because of the sense of community responsibility for the welfare of separated children.

No regular allowances are paid, though steps are sometimes taken to ensure that the family benefits from general community distributions, and sometimes kits, including items such as seeds and tools. Items of domestic equipment are also given to encourage family self-sufficiency.

Although it has been found that poverty may deter people from accepting an unrelated child into the family, the evaluation of SCF's Family Tracing Programme has revealed that not one of the 43 substitute families interviewed had considered ceasing to care for the child because of the lack of material resources.

The indications are that children in substitute families did not feel poorly treated in relation to other children in the household, despite the additional demands placed on the family by the material and other needs of the child.

These two approaches depend upon an existing sense of responsibility within the community, and differ from the spontaneous arrangements made by the community itself only in requiring some sort of facilitation role in terms of arranging the placement and, in some cases, negotiating support and monitoring of the placement.

2   Small-scale, situation-specific fostering programmes

In this approach, a social welfare agency (government or NGO) establishes a
fostering programme in response to the needs of a particular group of
children. The intention is not usually to set up a rolling fostering programme
which will continue to arrange placements for children, though the
individual children involved in the programme may need some form of long-
term support. Three examples suffice to illustrate this approach to fostering.

In Uganda, there is no tradition of children living with unrelated families,
but the legal framework has made provision for fostering since the
Approved School Act of 1954. However, this Act is seen as a Western
'import', and its provision for fostering was rarely used until comparatively
recently. Box 14.3 contains a brief account of a small-scale fostering
programme initiated by SCF in response to the needs of a group of children
who were found to be unaccompanied following the Ugandan civil war.

Box 14.3   A fostering programme in Uganda

SCF started a fostering programme after the war of 1980–1986, placing
approximately 25 children aged 2–14 years who were orphaned, separated or
abandoned. Different organisations had found the children in transit camps and
brought them to a house in Kampala. Some had medical or nutritional problems
and were transferred to children's homes for immediate care.

SCF contacted people who were thought to be interested in providing care.
Most were low-income families. An application form was filled in, with court
procedures usually completed after placement. Information was gathered from
villages, and the prospective foster parents were assessed by social workers in
order to screen out people with inappropriate motivations. After placement they
were initially visited regularly, and, though the foster parents were not paid
allowances, they did receive some material assistance in kind, plus payment for
the child's medical treatment and school fees.

The placements were not intended as a long-term arrangement, though the
majority proved to be so in the absence of better alternatives. Some children
were returned to the care of relatives once they had been traced, though, in
some cases, foster parents resisted this. A small number of placements were
disrupted by behavioural or economic problems.

Generally, the feedback on the scheme was positive, though the necessary
longer-term follow-up work has not been undertaken adequately. This scheme
was very modest in scale, and was prompted by the immediate circumstances of
a particular group of unaccompanied children, rather than the desire to establish
an ongoing fostering scheme. It was, however, one factor in the subsequent
establishment of the Uganda Foster Care and Adoption Association, which is
committed to promoting both types of substitute family care.

Another example of a small-scale fostering scheme, born out of special circumstances and prompted by the particular problems of providing adequate care for very young children in large government institutions, is now being planned in Angola (Box 14.4).

Box 14.4   A fostering programme in Angola

The civil war in Angola created a substantial problem of children separated from their families, and, while a family tracing programme run jointly by the government and SCF has successfully reunited substantial numbers with their families, particular concern was expressed about the plight of very young children in institutions, among whom the mortality rate was very high. Although Angolan law covers adoption, there is no legal provision for fostering.

Despite this, fostering is now being promoted, and the intention is for young children to be placed mainly with women who have professional experience in caring for children in residential, day care or educational settings. Thorough assessment of the foster parents will be undertaken; where necessary, their houses will be enlarged to provide room for additional children, and, though no regular allowances are to be paid, material assistance will be provided according to need. The service is to be operated from government children's homes, and residential staff will provide support to and monitoring of the placements.

A further example of an imaginative approach to fostering is the 'community-based foster home' promoted particularly by Redd Barna in Africa.[222] It is something of a hybrid between a foster home and a small family-group residential home. It has been developed both as a form of permanent substitute family care and as a shorter-term arrangement for children while steps are being taken to resettle them with their own families. Community-based foster homes have been found to be particularly appropriate for unaccompanied children who have already spent a long period living in groups (for example, in transit camps), and may be particularly appropriate for adolescents who want to remain together, but in a non-institutional environment. The programme is summarised in Box 14.5.

Box 14.5   The community-based foster home

This is a model of alternative care for unaccompanied children which has been promoted in various countries in Africa. Essentially, the model consists of establishing a small group of children under the care of foster parents (usually a widow or married couple) who are respected members of their own community. It is used as a means of keeping sibling groups together and maintaining children's membership of their own communities.

continued

Box 14.5 continued

The group normally comprises between two and seven children, who live together in as normal a 'family' environment as possible. Emphasis is placed on integration with the local community, including attendance at local schools, and it is anticipated that a considerable degree of support from the local community will be given. The 'family' follows the same life-cycle as a 'normal' family, with children remaining as long as they wish.

The characteristics, recruitment procedures and methods of supporting foster parents vary. In some situations, a salary is offered, but the preferred means of support is via provision of a home and the materials necessary to enable the 'family' to achieve self-sufficiency – land, agricultural implements, animals, household equipment, or a grant to set up a small business, along with the material necessities to get the 'family' established.

It is generally anticipated that support and counselling from the appropriate government department or project staff will be required at least for the first two years.

---

3   Larger-scale, ongoing fostering programmes

The third category of fostering programme is the approach most often encountered in the West – the attempt by a government or voluntary agency to initiate an ongoing fostering programme which will usually include promotional and marketing activities as well as the professional tasks of recruiting, assessing and approving prospective foster parents, preparing and placing children, and supporting and monitoring placements.

In some instances, some of these activities are absent, possibly with extremely serious consequences for the children concerned. For example, in one of the programmes studied by SCF in South-East Asia, fostering has been developed not so much because it is perceived to be preferable to institutional care, but as an 'overspill' facility which is used by some State institutions when they are full.[223] Children are simply sent to families in the outlying villages when there is no vacancy in the institution. Foster parents are apparently not assessed for the task, and receive no education or training: they are paid a sizeable allowance, but receive no ongoing monitoring or supervision. In a cultural context in which the care of unrelated children is a relatively unfamiliar phenomenon, it seems likely that this arrangement will not consistently meet the needs of children.

By way of contrast, the fostering programme in Hong Kong represents a much more professional approach.[224] From its earliest roots in a small-scale experimental programme pioneered by a voluntary organisation in the late 1960s, the work has slowly evolved into a government-funded programme which aims to provide for about *one-quarter* of all children in care by 1995.

However, the development of fostering in Hong Kong has faced many problems and constraints, and these are summarised in Box 14.6.

Box 14.6   A fostering programme in Hong Kong

The development of fostering in Hong Kong can be seen as an attempt to introduce an essentially Western concept of foster care into a Chinese society undergoing rapid economic and social change. Although they have strong traditions of caring for other people's children, Chinese societies see the idea of caring for *unrelated* children as quite unfamiliar. It has not been uncommon in Chinese society for children to be taken into families for the purpose of household service, and adopted children would not be treated in the same way as children born in the family. An additional problem is that fostering has sometimes been equated with child-minding, which, in Hong Kong, generally involves physical care rather than the full range of parenting tasks. This has led to a degree of neglect of some foster children's nurturing needs.

The programme has been developed by a group of NGOs in co-operation with the government Department of Social Welfare. It has benefited from a supportive framework of legislation and social policy, and plans are now in hand for the expansion of fostering to reach approximately one-quarter of all children in care in Hong Kong.

Many problems have been experienced, including objections on the part of natural parents, difficulties in recruiting foster parents and in securing their participation in training, increasing costs (despite the modest level of foster parent allowances) and, most significantly, problems in co-ordinating the planned use of foster care with the activities of social workers working with the child's family.

However, despite these difficulties, the Hong Kong experience is that fostering has gradually become more acceptable as a viable, but not inexpensive, alternative to institutional care. With increased resources and more imaginative publicity, the prospects for further development are good.

One of the difficulties in the Hong Kong approach revealed by SCF's research is that, though ostensibly catering for children aged up to 8 years who were likely to be able to return to their own families, in practice, many placements were of unclear purpose and indeterminate duration. Not surprisingly, therefore, some became permanent. In turn, this created difficulties in relation to contact between some foster children and their parents. This highlights the need for fostering to be part of a carefully planned range of approaches for children, requiring careful assessment of children and their families, and purposeful work with both in order to achieve the required changes.

A similar conclusion emerged from the following case study of fostering programmes in India. There have been a number of experiments with fostering in India, and, though some of these have undoubtedly proved to be successful and have been sustained, others have been discontinued. Unlike Hong Kong, fostering in India was developed in rather a piecemeal way, without the commitment of government to developing a coherent fostering service (Box 14.7).

Box 14.7   Fostering programmes in India

In India, the government in Delhi first attempted to promote a fostering scheme in 1965. Various states decided to implement fostering schemes, each one responsible for enacting its own legislation, and using NGOs to implement the programmes. Many of these schemes proved unsuccessful, however, and were discontinued.

The main problems have been in the areas of recruiting foster carers with appropriate motivation and adequate housing; securing adequate and long-term funding; working within a legislative framework which, in some states, proved to be highly restrictive; difficulties faced by social workers in undertaking planned and purposeful work with families to prevent placements 'drifting' into permanent care, and problems of 'matching' children and foster carers around issues of caste, religion, colour and language.

However, a few child welfare agencies have pursued fostering tenaciously with a reasonable degree of success, and the lessons learned from their more positive experience are incorporated in the section later in this chapter, entitled 'Issues relating to the development of larger-scale fostering programmes'.

What conclusions can be drawn, then, from SCF's research on fostering?

General issues relating to fostering

● The acceptability of a child being cared for by unrelated adults varies greatly between cultures. It is clear that in some cultures there is a danger that foster children are treated less well than other children in the household. On the other hand (as with adoption), negative attitudes to caring for unrelated children can and do change, and such cultural attitudes need not necessarily be an insurmountable barrier to the development of fostering.

● Some of the successfully established fostering programmes are found in cultures in which the perceived barriers to the idea of caring for unrelated children are strong. This is the case both with large-scale fostering programmes (as in some states in India, and in Hong Kong) and also with the more *ad hoc* fostering programmes. In respect of the former, public education and promotional campaigns have been effective in changing attitudes, and it is clear that the development of fostering programmes does depend heavily on the willingness of the agency involved to commit considerable resources and imagination to the task of public education and promotion. This is likely to require an investment which may only reap dividends in the long term.

● Children living with unrelated carers may be prone to abuse in some cultures. In this context it is interesting to note that, in Western societies, there is a higher incidence of abuse towards children by foster parents than by natural parents, especially in the case of sexual abuse.[225]

● In some cultures, it is socially acceptable for unrelated children to be treated differently from other children within the family – for example, in respect of contributing their labour. It is therefore of paramount importance to understand cultural norms in respect of the care of unrelated children: understanding the motivation of foster parents will also be a key issue. It is important to note that the existence of some forms of what would be considered abuse in Western societies may not be perceived as such within other cultures, and therefore will not necessarily lead to a breakdown of the fostering placement.

● Fostering tends to drift into a form of permanent care more akin to *de facto* adoption, and, where this happens, the children can be left in an ambiguous legal and social situation, failing to receive the kind of support and assistance they require. The 'fostering' programme in Uganda described in Chapter 13 illustrates some of the difficulties involved where the distinction between adoption and fostering is blurred.

In general, SCF's research shows that, though adoption need not imply a formal change in the child's legal status, it is important for the child, the carers and the natural parents that the *intention* of the placement is clear, especially with regard to its anticipated duration. If the intention is for permanent care, all parties will benefit if this is declared overtly, whether or not legal adoption takes place. Where the intention is for the placement to be non-permanent, it is important that all parties understand this, and that the necessary steps are taken to work towards the child's return home, if possible, within a defined time-frame. Where circumstances change, and what was intended as a non-permanent placement should appropriately become long-term, all parties will benefit from an overt acknowledgement that the circumstances, and the intention of the placement, have changed.

Particular difficulties may be experienced when children in long-term foster care find that their entitlement to inherit property from their foster parents is ambiguous and possibly challenged by other relatives or members of the community. As already indicated, fostering may not imply either the endowment of civil and kinship status or sponsorship into adulthood.

In some situations, it is not possible to plan the duration of the placement, as with children separated from their families during armed conflict or refugee movements. In these situations, the lack of clarity about the duration of the placement is unavoidable. In such situations, some uncertainties are inevitable, but again all parties will benefit from open discussion which acknowledges the uncertainty, and attempts to define and redefine the options available to the child as the situation changes.

Issues relating to informal and small-scale, situation-specific fostering

● Perhaps surprisingly, the evidence reviewed by SCF's research suggests that informal and small-scale, situation-specific fostering can achieve an unexpectedly high level of success, though it must be emphasised that, in some instances, the lack of consistent long-term follow-up may mean that some difficulties with these approaches have not yet come to light. One possible reason for the success of such schemes is that they tend to place children with families within their existing social networks, and hence build on existing attachments and responsibilities. Moreover, children fostered under these circumstances are in contact with other members of the community who have an investment in ensuring the child's well-being. A second possible reason is that very often it is based on existing community coping strategies, and, in particular, may capitalise on a sense of community solidarity which may result from difficult circumstances, such as war or famine.

● However, experience tends to suggest that small-scale fostering programmes designed around specific situations do not always succeed in providing the kind of long-term follow-up and support that is needed. What is intended as an immediate response to a particular problem with unaccompanied children may have long-term consequences which need to be predicted and provided for. For example, not only does support to such placements and monitoring of them tend to decay over time, but work to trace the child's family and achieve reunification where appropriate may be neglected.

● Although labelled as 'fostering', many informal schemes are actually more akin to a form of *de facto* adoption. However, very often they do not provide the child or foster parents with the security which stems either from a change in legal status or from the clearly stated intention of permanence.

● An important safeguard to the fostered child, in the absence of effective professional support, is the sanctioning of the placement by the community. Involving community leaders in the selection of the family and in the support and monitoring of the placement is likely to reduce significantly the risk that the child will be inadequately cared for. In her book on child abuse, Korbin identifies a key indicator of a child's vulnerability to abuse as the 'embeddedness' of the child's care within kin and community networks – a network of concerned individuals may reduce the likelihood of abuse and neglect.[226] In areas (notably in urban environments) where community structures are weak, this is likely to be difficult, but it is also in urban areas that professional support and monitoring may be more achievable.

● A key issue in any type of fostering is the motivation of the foster parents. The problem is how to assess that motivation: in more formal fostering programmes, a comprehensive assessment of the prospective foster parents is undertaken, but, in less formal schemes, it may well be that people such as community leaders will be able to offer useful comments on the motivation of a family which is offering to care for an unrelated child.

● The economic circumstances of the foster family are probably one of the most important predictors of a successful outcome. Bearing in mind the possibility, in many cultures, of foster children being subject to discrimination in terms of food, other material benefits and demands on their labour, it seems likely that poverty on the part of the foster family will significantly increase the danger of differential treatment or abuse. On the other hand, experience in Mozambique suggests that children in unrelated substitute families fared well despite widespread poverty.

● It may therefore be necessary to find some means of assisting the foster family materially. The payment of fostering allowances is not necessarily the most appropriate means of offering assistance, and there is some scope for developing other means of supporting foster families through the provision of grants or loans aimed at facilitating the whole family's economic self-reliance. This was the intention behind the community-based foster home cited in Box 14.5, despite the difficulties experienced in implementing the approach.

Issues relating to the development of larger-scale fostering programmes

● Children may face a higher risk of neglect, abuse or exploitation when cared for by unrelated adults. This risk may be minimised when the community has a sense of responsibility for the care of the child, but this is less likely in urban environments, where larger-scale fostering programmes are more likely to be developed. While a thorough appraisal of cultural attitudes is clearly required, a willingness to engage in a process of creative innovation, while at the same time acknowledging and guarding against the potential for abuse and neglect of children, is likely to be a crucial ingredient in a successful fostering programme.

● Fostering has become well-established in the West as a cost-effective and appropriate method of care for the majority of children separated from their families on a non-permanent basis. However, the evidence reviewed here suggests that the situation in developing countries is extremely complex, and that promoting fostering is much more difficult than it may at first appear. Fostering programmes in India and Hong Kong illustrate what can be achieved through carefully planned, tenaciously promoted and adequately funded programmes, in cultures in which the idea of caring for unrelated children is not widely accepted. On the other hand, the difficulties involved are considerable, and the successful promotion of fostering may require a very long-term commitment of resources.

● Fostering is not necessarily cheaper than residential care. Although fostering in Western countries has, in part, been developed because of its lower cost in relation to residential forms of care, this is not necessarily the case in developing countries. Two issues seem to be particularly significant here. First, while the allowances paid to foster parents may be very modest, fostering requires a high calibre of social work staff to assess children's needs and to plan their care, to recruit and assess prospective foster parents, to match children and foster parents, and to prepare them for placement and support them during it. When the costs of maintaining the necessary team of social workers and support systems are included, fostering may no longer be such a cost-effective option. Second, while it is undoubtedly true that good-quality residential care is expensive, poor residential care may well be cheaper than the real cost of a good fostering programme.

● Clarity of purpose in planning care is vitally important. In most cases, fostering schemes ostensibly do not aim to provide permanent substitute family care for the child. Fostering is usually seen as a short-term arrangement for a child while particular problems within the family are being resolved. But experience suggests that, unless planned and purposeful work is undertaken to resolve the problems which created the need for the child's placement in care, fostering tends to drift into permanence, but without offering the child the security of knowing where his future lies. In few of the countries covered by SCF's research was any systematic work undertaken to enable the child's long-term future to be secured. While it might be argued that indeterminate fostering may be more satisfactory than indeterminate residential care, the surrounding uncertainty may create difficulties and insecurity for the child, the foster parents and the child's own parents.

● As a general rule, successful fostering schemes are likely to be most effective in situations in which there is a well-developed welfare system (whether governmental or non-governmental), characterised by:

- skilled staff who are able to undertake purposeful work with children and families, and who have access to a range of care resources which are used in a planned (rather than a reactive) manner;
- adequate long-term funding.

● Fostering is sometimes used, inappropriately, as a short-term response to a long-term problem. Unlike in the West, where care (whether in foster homes or residential care) is offered in response to specific problems to which solutions are actively being sought, most children enter the care system in developing countries because of long-term problems. Chronic poverty is almost always an underlying cause, often coupled with marital breakdown or other long-term problems such as mental illness or imprisonment on the part of one of the parents. In such situations, children, if they really need alternative care, are likely to need it on a long-term basis, which the fostering programmes reviewed by this research do not aim to provide. Where the need is for a short-term and finite period of care, this is more likely to be available within wider family or community networks.

Therefore, short-term fostering, if it is required, is only likely to be successful if complemented by measures to address the issues which led to the need for the child to be separated. It is difficult to find examples of this happening effectively in the developing world.

● The recruitment of suitably motivated families is a problem for fostering programmes in all parts of the world. It is likely to be a particularly serious problem in countries where the idea of fostering is not well established, and, as with promoting the idea of adoption, requires tenacious publicity. It is interesting to note that one of the characteristics of the more successful fostering schemes is the availability of a 'pool' of families within which to recruit – for example, Church organisations which have used their own networks as a recruiting ground, or, in the case of Hong Kong, a group of European families. Recruitment will be affected by such issues as housing shortages and/or overcrowding, and employment opportunities, especially for women.

● Although some successful fostering schemes have been developed outside a country's legal framework, a supportive framework of law and legal practice is clearly an important factor. Agencies which operate fostering schemes are likely to face issues such as statutory funding of fostering, and the legal status of foster parents *vis-à-vis* that of natural parents. In Uganda, for example, the availability of appropriate court orders provided foster parents with a measure of legal security, though they will not ensure the children's right to inherit property from their foster parents. In some states in India, however, legislation has been more of a constraint than a support.

● Fostering is most likely to develop as an appropriate option if there is a coherent government policy linking fostering, adoption, residential care and preventive strategies in order to facilitate a discriminating and well-targeted use of fostering. In addition, a framework of agency co-ordination is also important.

● Foster care is prone to failure, and therefore requires effective back-up services. Even in Western countries which invest substantial sums of money into developing a highly professional fostering service, the failure rate is high.[227] While little information is available on foster home breakdown in developing countries, Western experience suggests that effective fostering schemes require good-quality residential care, both to prepare children for family placements and to help them to deal with the consequences of foster home failure.[228]

● Fostering may not be as acceptable to the child's parents as residential care. In the case of orphaned, abandoned or lost children, there are no parents who need to consent to fostering, but, where the parents are known, they may be unwilling to agree to fostering. Fostering highlights the natural parent's inadequacies and creates a situation of rivalry for the child's affections and loyalty. Parental consent was one of the most significant limiting factors in the development of fostering in Hong Kong.

● Formal fostering programmes are unlikely to be viable unless foster parents are given adequate material support. Material assistance comes in many forms: Western approaches (paying a regular fostering allowance in cash) may not be the most appropriate means of supporting foster carers, and may carry with them the danger of the foster child being perceived as a privileged member of the family. An approach being promoted by the Uganda Foster Care and Adoption Association is to make grants or loans to foster families to facilitate the capacity of the family as a whole to achieve economic self-reliance. In Hong Kong, the differential between fostering allowances and average wages was seen as a serious impediment to recruiting foster parents.

● The development of fostering programmes requires a long-term commitment of funds, which many NGOs are unwilling or unable to make. At a time when so many Third World governments facing enormous financial constraints are giving social welfare programmes reduced priority, it is clearly going to be difficult to find both the initial investment required to launch a fostering programme and the long-term revenue commitment which fostering schemes require.

One possible strategy, which has been little exploited to date, is to link fostering programmes, whether run by governments or NGOs, to sponsorship schemes as a source of funding. Sponsoring an orphaned or separated child would probably have considerable 'donor-appeal' and could provide the long-term funding required, though, as was discussed in Part II, not all agencies find the idea of individual sponsorship ideologically acceptable.

● Fostering benefits from a high degree of community involvement. Most fostering programmes have been devised around Western models, with recruitment, matching, placement, support and monitoring being provided by social workers. On the one hand, it is clear that fostering in any cultural environment (including Western societies) carries a risk of the child being neglected or abused: on the other, it is a mistake to believe that the various tasks involved in fostering can only be carried out by social workers. There are many ways in which community leaders, people's organisations, schoolteachers and others can be involved, for example in identifying potential foster homes and in monitoring and supporting foster families.

Fostering and 'special needs' children

It is often assumed that attitudes towards the care of unrelated children, coupled with attitudes towards physical and intellectual disability, effectively preclude the possibility of placing children with disabilities in foster homes in many cultures. In Hong Kong, however, SCF piloted a programme of fostering for children with a moderate learning disability. It was found that recruiting Chinese families to foster these children was less of a problem than had been anticipated, though it called for a different recruitment strategy, an increased workload for social workers, and enhanced fostering allowances.

It is difficult to generalise from this one modest programme, which, like the more general fostering programme in Hong Kong, had the advantage of access to considerable financial and material resources. It does, however, suggest that assumptions about the 'fosterability'of 'special needs' children should be questioned, and that experiments in placing children with disabilities in foster care should be encouraged.

Concluding comments

In many Western societies, fostering is now used extensively to provide care for children unable to live with their own families and who cannot be placed for adoption. The increasing trend away from residential forms of care towards fostering has been motivated both by an acknowledgement of the disadvantages of residential care in comparison with substitute family care and of the relatively lower cost of fostering.

The experiences reviewed in SCF's research reveal some encouraging signs. In less formal approaches to fostering which build on community support, positive outcomes for children have been achieved, despite some obvious limitations. In any case, it may well be in the best interests of children that they should face the potential difficulties which fostering may involve, rather than be consigned to a childhood spent in an unsatisfactory institutional environment. A number of factors emerge as significant in predicting the successful outcome of these more informal fostering placements. Chief among these are:

- the economic security of the family;
- the sanctioning of the placement by the local community;
- an assessment of the motivation of the foster parents.

These indicators have not been rigorously tested, however, and more research is required in order to gain a fuller understanding of the factors which facilitate the successful placement of children with unrelated families.

However, Western-style fostering programmes in the developing world experience many more difficulties, and it is clear that the 'better and cheaper than residential care' argument cannot be readily applied. Chief among these difficulties is the necessity of locating fostering programmes within an effective social welfare structure which offers planned and purposeful work with both children and their families, in order to prevent the uncertainties and ambiguities of unplanned, drifting placements which have been clearly demonstrated to be so damaging to children in Western societies. This requirement may make fostering a more expensive option than residential care, and, in many developing countries, it is questionable whether the kind of social welfare structures which fostering programmes require are either affordable or appropriate.

There is also good reason to question the appropriateness of formal fostering programmes to the needs of children in developing countries. In this book, the term 'fostering' is used to indicate a mainly non-permanent form of care. In practice, however, it frequently drifts into indeterminate and long-term care, in the absence of child care planning. But most of the children who need substitute care in the developing world are the victims of chronic and long-term problems, with poverty almost always an underlying factor.

Children requiring permanent family care should, wherever possible, be placed for adoption, whether legal or *de facto*, and thereby be provided with the sense of permanence and family identity that adoption is more likely to confer. If, on the other hand, the problems which create a need for substitute care are intrinsically short-term, then fostering may be appropriate. But, in such situations, it is more likely that care can be provided within the extended family network, and, if not, that residential care might be a more practical and achievable option than an elaborate and expensive fostering programme.

There may, however, be some scope for developing more formal fostering programmes without attempting to replicate the social welfare structures which are generally associated with them. The various tasks associated with the implementation of fostering programmes should not be seen as the exclusive preserve of professional social workers: community leaders, people's organisations, women's associations, schoolteachers and others may also play a role in identifying families (where possible, within the child's own community), assessing their suitability and arranging, supporting and monitoring the placement. Welfare organisations which are prepared to loosen professional control over these activities may feel that they are exposing a child to potential risks – but these are probably no greater than the risks to children's lives resulting from allowing them to languish in unsatisfactory institutional care.

The principal place for Western-style fostering programmes is in urban environments in well-resourced countries, such as Hong Kong, in which the capacity of extended family and community systems to support separated children has been seriously weakened, and in which there exist the social welfare structures and the skilled human resources necessary to support a professional fostering service. Experience suggests that the development of such programmes will be slow and difficult: on the other hand, it has been demonstrated in Hong Kong and in some states in India that perseverance and optimism have enabled good-quality fostering programmes to be developed.

15 Inter-country adoption: Solution or problem?

Inter-country adoption is a highly emotive issue which elicits strong reactions, both for and against. In this debate, empirical evidence often appears less significant than ideological arguments, such as exploitation of the South by the North, or philosophical objections to trans-racial or trans-cultural placement. This chapter attempts to take a more objective look at the subject.

The term 'inter-country adoption' describes arrangements which involve children leaving the country where they have been living in order to be placed with a family in another country. In the majority of cases, this involves 'trans-cultural' adoption (the placement of a child with a family in a cultural environment different from that of her birth family). In many cases it is also 'trans-racial' adoption – the placement of a child with a family of a different racial origin. However, this is not an inevitable feature of inter-country adoption. For example, most children placed for adoption overseas from Jamaica and Hong Kong are placed with families from a similar racial background, though usually living in a different cultural environment.

In this chapter, the term 'sending countries' is used to describe countries from which children are placed overseas for adoption; 'receiving countries' are those to which children are moved for the purpose of adoption. The term 'adoptive family' is used to describe people who adopt children: in most instances, adopters are married couples, but the term does not exclude the adoption of children by single people or non-married couples. This chapter confines itself to the adoption of children by one or more adults who are not related to the child.

Inter-country adoption: A brief history

There is nothing new in the idea of children being raised by unrelated families in a foreign country. Myths and legends give many examples – from Moses and possibly Joseph in the Old Testament to one of the many myths about Oedipus – the latter being particularly interesting because of his search for identity, something which characterises so many cases of adopted children.[229]

Inter-country adoption of unaccompanied children first began on a large scale after the end of the Second World War, when significant numbers of children orphaned or separated from their parents in Europe (and, to a lesser extent, Japan and China) were placed overseas for adoption, mainly in the USA. It was, however, the Korean, and subsequently the Vietnam, Wars which drew attention to the situation of large numbers of children who were either orphaned by war or abandoned or given up as an indirect effect of civil war and its economic and social consequences for families. Inter-country adoption during this period can be categorised largely as a humanitarian response from Western nations, most notably the USA, on the part of people wishing to find a tangible way of expressing their concern for people affected by war; national guilt may also have played a part.

However, from the 1970s onwards, the nature of the response from receiving countries changed. The availability of young children for adoption within most Western countries declined due to the combined effects of increasing access to contraception and abortion, the greater acceptability of single parents, and the increased resources available to them. Gradually, inter-country adoption became motivated less by humanitarian concerns and more by the demands of families unable to adopt within their own country, for whom developing countries offered a potential supply of children. The shift of emphasis from 'families for children' to 'children for families' is highly significant, with the language of 'supply and demand' turning inter-country adoption into a complex and highly controversial issue.

From the 1970s on, inter-country adoption became less of an *ad hoc* phenomenon, with organisations beginning to arrange adoption placements on a much larger scale than hitherto. This change began in Korea and Vietnam, and, by the mid-1970s, adoption of children from other Asian countries and Latin America by families in the USA, Europe and Scandinavia was widespread. Significantly, and despite the high incidence of child welfare problems, few African countries have become involved as important sending countries. This appears to reflect the relative 'attractiveness' of Asian and Latin American children to the European and North American 'market'.

More recently, revelations of the plight of children in institutions in post-Ceausescu Romania led to a great deal of activity and publicity in respect of inter-country adoption. It is highly significant that, while the initial spate of adoptions were of children from institutions, large numbers of children were subsequently adopted directly from their birth families. This reflected difficult economic and social circumstances, rather than orphanhood or abandonment, and also the willingness of parents to give up their children – sometimes encouraged by financial incentives.

Currently, there is a great deal of variation in the sending countries, with many changing their laws to facilitate or to curtail inter-country adoption. The general trend, however, appears to be in the direction of fewer placements. It was estimated in 1987 that approximately 15,000–20,000 children were being adopted from the Third World annually,[230] but this figure has probably declined since.

Concerns about inter-country adoption began to be expressed as early as the 1950s, and in the 1970s and 1980s there was a growing awareness of the nature and scale of the abuses that were taking place, including the sale and trafficking of children for adoption. In 1964, the Hague Conference on Private International Law drew up a Convention on Inter-country Adoption to provide international regulation, but it was signed by very few countries, and hence has had little impact. In 1986 the Declaration on Social and Legal Principles Relating to Adoption and Foster Placement of Children Nationally and Internationally was adopted by the UN Assembly. This declaration is in the form of a set of recommendations rather than a treaty, and sets out a number of clear principles, including that of the child's best interests and the priority for children to be cared for by their own parents.

The UN Convention on the Rights of the Child re-affirmed the principle that 'the child's best interests shall be the paramount consideration'.[231] It also required States Parties to ensure that adoption is authorised by competent authorities, and that safeguards are included (for example, that no improper financial gain is involved). However, the same Article of the convention requires States Parties to:

> recognise that inter-country adoption may be considered as an alternative means of child's care, if the child cannot be placed in a foster or an adoptive family or cannot in any suitable manner be cared for in the child's country of origin.

While this implies that other means should be explored for caring for children within their own country, it is unfortunate that the wording of this Article appears to support the *principle* of inter-country adoption, with no emphasis placed on the need actively to promote inter-country alternatives where these do not already exist.

After the adoption by the UN General Assembly of the Convention on the

Rights of the Child, the brief for inter-country adoption was given to the Hague Conference on Private International Law. The decision that the Hague Conference should focus on inter-country adoption was prompted by a dramatic increase in what had become a worldwide phenomenon, and the complex human and legal problems to which this gave rise. At the conference's Sixteenth Session in 1988 it was decided to prepare a 'convention on adoption of children coming from abroad', and their Secretary-General was requested to seek the co-operation of the non-member States which were particularly involved in the sending of children for adoption in other countries. The intention was to go beyond a traditional convention to the establishment of substantive principles and a legal framework for co-operation between the authorities in sending and receiving countries. The Hague Conference produced an extremely informative background report on inter-country adoption,[232] and on 29 May 1993 the Hague Convention on Inter-country Adoption was adopted by 63 States. The main provisions of the Hague Convention are discussed later in this chapter.

Adoption law and practice: A global perspective

In Chapter 9, adoption was considered in its worldwide context. Some of the key issues to emerge from that discussion are significant to any consideration of inter-country adoption:

- Many traditional forms of adoption have evolved to meet the needs of adopters, rather than children.
- Even today, not all legislative frameworks governing adoption are entirely child-centred, or emphasise the needs and rights of children.
- In some cultures, any mechanism which permanently severs the ties between children and parents is considered inconceivable. From this it follows that it is difficult for parents in some cultures to give informed consent to adoption.

Almost by definition, inter-country adoption involves conflicting views about the meaning and effects of adoption. Although many developing countries do have adoption laws, in many cases these may be seen as 'colonial imports', and may be of little use in practice, especially in former UK colonies. This is particularly the case in Africa, where Western concepts of adoption may be regarded as completely alien.

Three further issues need to be highlighted. First, as already indicated, inter-country adoption may involve children who have not experienced separation or family breakdown. Instead, they sometimes form a new 'market' of children living with their families, whose parents can be induced to part with them. In contrast, parentless children living in institutions may sometimes be excluded from consideration for adoption, either at home or overseas.

Second, in virtually all developing countries there are strong traditions of orphaned and abandoned children being cared for within the extended family and community systems. The erosion of these social systems (for example, as a result of rapid urbanisation) has rarely been matched by the development of an appropriate welfare system by governments or non-governmental organisations. Consequently, when children find themselves without family carers, there is unlikely to be an appropriate range of other alternatives available within the country. Inter-country adoption may therefore be seen as a first option, rather than as a last resort. Moreover, in some countries, the legislative and procedural framework may actually favour inter-country rather than intra-country adoption.

Finally, the majority of children living in institutions in developing countries are neither abandoned nor fully orphaned, with most having at least some continuing links with their own families. But, when skilled social workers are lacking, thorough assessment and planning for the future of separated children is rarely available. Hence, while some children with no prospect of family reunion will remain indefinitely in institutional care, others who do have families may be sent for adoption overseas.

Inter-country adoption: The evidence about outcome

The arguments against inter-country adoption fall into two main groups. First, most inter-country adoptions involve placing children with a family from a different racial and cultural background, with the potential that children will grow up with a confused sense of personal and racial identity. Geographical distance makes it difficult for children to retain meaningful links with their cultural origins and develop an understanding of them. For these reasons, such placements are unlikely to meet the child's needs fully. Such arguments are not entirely supported by the empirical evidence.

The second argument concerns the way in which inter-country adoption is conducted: the evidence about abuses of children's rights and other forms of malpractice is reviewed later in this chapter. First, what is the evidence on the outcome of inter-country adoptions?

Although there is now a sizeable body of research evidence on the outcomes of inter-country adoption, few studies have been undertaken in the UK – one important exception being Bagley and Young's study of 100 adults who were adopted in the UK, mainly as very young children from

Hong Kong.[233] In other Western countries, inter-country adoption is undertaken by agencies specialising in this form of work, unlike in the UK, where most placements are arranged privately or through third parties (and are therefore, strictly speaking, illegal). It is reasonable to assume that placements arranged through a competent agency are more likely to be successful, on account of the likelihood of a thorough and careful assessment and preparation of the adopters, work with the natural parents, preparation of the child, matching of the child to the family, and post-placement support.

It is widely recognised that many children placed for adoption overseas do present immediate and short-term problems, including health, language and behaviour problems, but that these difficulties are often dealt with satisfactorily. Studies into the longer-term outcome of adoption have to face considerable methodological issues. For example, how can adopted children be identified? This is a particular problem in countries like the UK, where most inter-country adoptions are arranged privately.

How is 'success' to be measured? The most useful research evidence comes from studies which examine the incidence of unfavourable outcomes (such as the breakdown of a placement, and problem behaviour) together with the views of older children and adults who have been adopted from overseas, and the perceptions of adopters who have seen their adopted children grow into adolescence or adulthood.

Some studies claim very high success rates for inter-country adoption – as high as 95 per cent.[234] However, they should be viewed with caution for several reasons: first, sampling methods may mean that unsuccessful adoptions are under-represented; second, some studies examine the experience of younger adopted children, but there is good reason to believe that many of the difficulties associated with identity formation, especially in respect of racial and cultural identity, tend to emerge only in adolescence and early adulthood.

In their review of research into inter-country adoption, Thoburn and Charles offer the following summary:

> the majority of children (around 80%) do well-enough although issues of racial, cultural and personal identity are likely to be problematic for a substantial minority, and their educational performance is likely to be below that of other (mainly middle-class) adoptees and non-adopted children. Being older at placement, having a history of trauma or physical ill health increase the risk of emotional problems. As with British adoptees, problems are most likely to show themselves in adolescence, and are likely in a minority of cases to be severe and extremely difficult for families and professionals to handle. An unknown proportion of these 80 per cent or so who are generally satisfied by the adoption experience will nevertheless have problems around the issue of identity which may last throughout their lives.[235]

Interestingly, there is some evidence that families who already have children from their marriage and then adopt are likely to face an enhanced risk of problems, especially if the adopted child is close in age to another child in the family. On the other hand, there is also evidence that adopters with established parenting skills are the most effective in managing difficulties which emerge with children from other countries.

The greater vulnerability of older children who are adopted from overseas is highly significant. The older the child is at placement, the greater will be the degree of cultural adaptation required.[236] Older children are also likely to have a history which may include, for example, neglect within the family, large numbers of changes of 'home', and poor-quality institutional care. Some 'unlearning' of survival skills may be needed, along with a changed perception of the role of adults in their lives.

There is a worrying trend in a number of sending countries to place younger children within the country, and to seek inter-country adoption for older children, and those with particular difficulties, such as physical disability.[237] Although a trend towards the placement of older children for adoption can also be seen in most Western countries, a reasonable degree of success is achieved on the basis of extremely high standards of professional social work, which are rarely possible in the sending countries. The research evidence on inter-country adoption suggests that it is older children especially who face an enhanced risk of an unsuccessful outcome. Moreover, the *consequences* of breakdown are extremely severe for children placed outside their own country. Returning to their original country may not be possible, and the prospects of admission into residential care in a country and culture which may still feel alien is a frightening prospect for a child experiencing rejection.

A particularly interesting study by Dalen and Saetersdal found that, while their sample of inter-country adoptees adjusted well during childhood, as the children reached adulthood they found they were not fully accepted in society.[238] In reviewing the research evidence into inter-country adoption, Triseliotis concludes:

> on the evidence so far, we could in fact hypothesise that during childhood the quality of parenting may be the most important factor in building self-esteem and a positive self-concept. But as the adopted person – especially black and ethnic children – moves away from parental protectiveness towards adulthood, then community attitudes assume much greater importance, and if hostile and rejecting can prove devastating to the self.[239]

Overall, the research evidence on the outcome of inter-country adoption is reasonably encouraging, suggesting a success rate broadly similar to that of intra-country adoption, though with some 'identity' issues tending to emerge in adolescence and early adulthood. This is a surprising finding when the particular complexities of inter-country adoption are taken into consideration. One possible – and partial – explanation is that families who adopt children of a noticeably different physical appearance are unlikely to deny or minimise the reality of adoption: this would seem consistent with Kirk's thesis that a key to successful adoption lies in the open acknowledgement and acceptance of the 'differentness' facing both adopted children and adopters.[240] It certainly seems likely that adopters who live in an area which accepts people from different racial and cultural backgrounds, and who are able to take active steps to enable children to understand and identify with their origins, are most likely to help the child to adjust psychologically and socially.

One particular difficulty which is likely to face children who are adopted from overseas is that information about their origins will be difficult for them to find. Adoption laws and practices in many sending countries do not allow for access to records by adopted persons. On the other hand, some organisations concerned with inter-country adoption do now facilitate the visits of adoptive parents and their children to discover and explore the child's cultural origins.

Unacceptable practices

Thus, the evidence on the outcome of inter-country adoptions is not sufficient cause, of itself, to regard inter-country adoption as unacceptable. However, closer examination of some of the practices currently involved does raise considerable doubts.

Much of the drive for inter-country adoption in recent years has come from prospective adopters, not from professionals seeking adoption placements for children. There is a very real danger that adoptions will reflect the needs of adults, and not those of children. Identifying and quantifying the incidence of abuse and malpractice in inter-country adoption is, by the very nature of the problem, difficult. The following analysis draws on the literature on inter-country adoption, together with evidence derived from SCF's own experience in the field. The unacceptable practices prevalent in inter-country adoption can be summarised as follows:

● Mothers in some countries are encouraged to relinquish their children, sometimes for financial gain. There is considerable evidence of children literally being bought and sold for the purposes of adoption: various documents submitted to the UN Secretary-General for ECOSOC's Commission on Human Rights offer a good deal of evidence that international child trafficking does occur, for purposes which include inter-country adoption as well as sexual exploitation and cheap labour. Defence for Children International have been particularly involved in assembling such evidence.[241] There is also growing evidence, largely of an anecdotal nature, that children relinquished by their families for inter-country adoption are being trafficked for the purposes of organ transplants.[242]

● There is evidence in some countries of the existence of 'baby farms', in which pregnant girls are kept until the birth of their babies, which are then placed for adoption in a way that gives their mothers a limited element of choice.

● Consent to adoption is not always freely given, and the nature of legal adoption under Western laws is not always fully understood. 'Middlemen' are frequently involved, and, while some may be genuinely trying to pursue the child's best interests, there is no doubt that others are seeking personal gain.

● It is not unusual for abandonment to be seen as a reason for children to be placed for adoption, even though the parent's intention may not have been to abandon the child permanently. It is a mistake to regard abandonment, or placement in an institution, as necessarily indicative of a permanent rejection of the child. Rather, for many families it may be a survival mechanism which the family uses, as a last resort, when facing impossible problems of poverty and environmental stress.

● Parents frequently do not receive adequate counselling on the meaning and effect of adoption and on alternative ways of providing care for the child. This is not surprising in view of the lack of skilled social workers in many sending countries.

● The lack of realistic and appropriate alternatives in cases where the child's family is unable to provide for her needs frequently leads to a situation in which inter-country adoption is considered as the only viable alternative to institutional care, rather than because it meets the child's needs adequately.

● Documents and judicial evidence are sometimes falsified: 'proxy mothers' have been known to be used to give 'parental' consent in respect of children who were not theirs. The bribing of officials is not uncommon in many countries.

● Even reputable international organisations are known to engage in quite unacceptable practices in the field of inter-country adoption. One example, drawn from a country in which SCF is working, concerns an international organisation which matches older children (up to the age of 12 years) with families 'on paper', and then arranges placement without the child being carefully introduced to the adopters within her own familiar environment. The first meeting between a 12-year-old and her 'new' family might therefore be in a completely unfamiliar cultural environment, where a foreign language is spoken and there are no trusted adults available in whom she might be able to confide. The trend towards older and 'hard to place' children being considered for inter-country adoption is now evidenced in countries such as Thailand, Hong Kong and Brazil, and, in this context, such practices should be regarded with considerable concern.

● The practice of inter-country adoption in *countries in crisis* should be approached with particular care. Although the mass media are frequently active in drawing the world's attention to the numbers of children affected by war, famine or political upheaval, it is precisely in such crises that the ill-considered movement of children may be especially inappropriate. Although much publicity may be given to children who appear to be unaccompanied – for example, as a result of sudden mass movements of people – such children are more likely to have become separated from their families accidentally than to have been abandoned or orphaned. It is precisely under these circumstances that it may be most difficult to trace the child's parents – hence it may be impossible to establish that a child has been abandoned or orphaned, or, alternatively, that a valid and informed consent to adoption can be obtained. Moreover, at times of national crisis, the government may be in a particularly weak position to exercise control over organisations wishing to arrange for children to be adopted.

● Finally, inter-country adoption is often associated with lower standards of practice in respect of the qualities expected of adopters than is the case involving domestic adoption in Western countries. It is not unusual for couples who have been deemed ineligible to adopt in the UK to succeed in adopting a child from abroad.

The Hague Convention: The principal provisions

The conclusion of five years of work by the Hague Conference in completing the Hague Convention marks a significant turning point in the history of inter-country adoption, which hopefully will lead to an elimination of many of the abuses outlined above. Article 4 of the Hague Convention requires that the State of origin must ensure that the child is adoptable, that other alternatives have been considered, that an inter-country adoption is in the individual child's interests, and that the necessary consents have been freely given. Article 5 gives the receiving State the responsibility to determine that the prospective adopters are eligible and suitable to adopt, that they have received appropriate counselling, and that the child will be authorised to enter and permanently reside in the country.

The Hague Convention provides for the creation of central authorities in contracting States to co-operate with each other over inter-country adoption; they must accept certain responsibilities in respect of particular adoptions, though these duties can be delegated to accredited bodies (usually adoption agencies). The Hague Convention sets out a range of procedures regarding, for example, the compiling of reports, the obtaining of consents, the placement process and arrangements for the child's transfer. Although it is primarily the responsibility of the State of origin to make the placement decision, the receiving State has a veto, and there are certain circumstances in which either State can halt the proceedings.

The prohibition of improper financial or other gain is very much to be welcomed. However, the principal weakness of the Hague Convention is that, as a result of pressure from the USA, independent intermediaries, such as doctors and lawyers, can continue to be involved in the making of arrangements for inter-country adoptions, despite the widespread abuses in which such intermediaries have been involved. This controversial decision appears to conflict with the UN Convention on the Rights of the Child, which requires that 'the placement of the child in another country is carried out by competent authorities or organs',[243] though this is open to a range of interpretations.

However, individual States, if they so choose, can insist on agency adoptions, and, though the involvement of adoption agencies is no guarantee against malpractice, it is likely to offer greater safeguards than placements arranged by lawyers whose principal interest is not the welfare of children.

The Hague Convention marks a large step forward in regularising the conduct of inter-country adoption: just how far it will go in ending the widespread abuses which occur remains to be seen. Both receiving and sending countries now need to amend their legislation, but what priority developing countries will give this task remains to be seen. More crucial still is the need for sending countries to develop their child care services further, so that effective local alternatives to inter-country adoption are made available.

Alternatives to inter-country adoption

In countries which have a well-developed welfare system, there are likely to be a number of alternatives to inter-country adoption. These may include support to the child's current carers, placement within the wider family (possibly with some material assistance), adoption within the country, placement with foster parents, and a variety of different types of residential care.

However, in many sending countries, the combined effects of poverty and urbanisation have frequently eroded the capacity of extended family and community networks to provide care for orphaned and abandoned children. Moreover, the lack of social welfare staff within the relevant government department and NGOs may mean that placement options for separated children within the wider family are not explored. Most countries lack a range of resources for separated children – there may be no State provision for supporting children within their own families; intra-country adoption may be limited by factors such as lack of welfare structures, high cost and bureaucratic difficulties; and fostering programmes may not be available at all, leaving institutional care as the only possible alternative. The presence of inter-country adoption as one of the few options available may act as a disincentive for government to take responsibility for the development of a proper range of alternatives for separated children. This creates a vicious circle, in which inter-country adoption continues to be justified as the principal alternative to institutional care.

In deciding on the most appropriate placement for a child for whom no family-based alternatives exist, the costs and benefits of inter-country adoption may have to be balanced against those of whatever forms of residential care are available. In this context, and for some children, inter-country adoption may offer the only realistic opportunity of living in a nurturing environment which can meet their emotional and social needs. What then needs to be done is to ensure that effective standards are introduced to make sure that inter-country adoption is conducted in an acceptable manner.

Minimum standards of practice in inter-country adoption

In situations where there is no satisfactory means of meeting the needs of children within their culture and country, the following conditions must be met if inter-country adoption is to be a satisfactory option:

● The placement of the child for adoption should be motivated by the needs of the child; the needs of prospective adopters should always be a secondary consideration.

● Arrangements for the placement should be made by competent adoption agencies (governmental or non-governmental) in both sending and receiving countries. Staff with an appropriate level of expertise in adoption need to be involved at each stage in the adoption process. Adoption through private intermediaries is quite unacceptable.

● No payment, either in cash or in kind, should be involved with the exception of legitimate legal costs and adoption agency expenses.

● There should have been a thorough and exhaustive consideration of all possible intra-country options, and parents should be fully involved in exploring these options. There must be a clear and considered view that the particular placement being considered is the most appropriate means of meeting the needs of the child.

● Informed consent to adoption must be freely given by the child's parents: this must be based on a full understanding of what adoption under Western law means, and must not involve material benefit to the parents.

● In the case of children whose parents' address is unknown, active and thorough steps must be taken to trace their parents and other potential carers before they are deemed to have been abandoned.

● Particular care must be taken in selecting adoptive parents for older children, and in the crucial processes of matching child and family, preparing the child for placement, and introducing the child to the family.

● Particular caution needs to be exercised in placing children for adoption overseas from countries experiencing armed conflict, political upheaval or natural disaster. In such situations, it may be impossible to trace parents, and it may be particularly difficult to uphold good standards of practice.

● There is no justification for lower standards being applied to inter-country adoption in receiving countries. The same requirements of prospective adopters, and the same standards of practice, should be applied as in intra-country adoption.

Conclusions

Although this chapter has highlighted the negative aspects of inter-country adoption, it would be wrong to dismiss practice in this area as universally unsatisfactory. Despite the abuses and malpractices which exist, there are organisations which conduct inter-country adoption in a competent and responsible manner. Inter-country adoption may, for some children, offer the only realistic prospect of family life, in situations where there is no short-term prospect of appropriate intra-country options being provided.

If the Hague Convention is ratified by sending as well as receiving countries, and if the central authorities take effective action to eliminate abuses and to uphold high standards of practice, then, for some children, inter-country adoption will offer the best, and possibly the only, hope for a secure future in a family setting.

However, the reality in most developing countries is that neither the political will nor the resources are likely to be available to implement the requirements of the Hague Convention. There is clearly an important role for NGOs to advocate for change and to assist governments to undertake the necessary developments in legislation, policies, practices and procedures.

But inter-country adoption can never be more than an expensive solution to the needs of a very small number of children who are living in the developing world and who cannot be cared for within their own extended family and community networks. Whatever steps are taken to improve the *practice* of inter-country adoption, *as a strategy* it fails to address the most important issues facing separated children in the developing world. It does nothing to respond to the root causes of homelessness among children, or to respond to the need to facilitate the development of appropriate resources and policies to enable children to be brought up in a family environment wherever possible, and within the context of their own community and culture. Indeed, SCF's research has concluded that, in some countries, inter-country adoption has effectively served to make matters worse by diverting attention and scarce resources away from programmes which may be striving to find more appropriate local solutions to the many problems facing children and families in the poorest countries of the world.

16 Conclusions: An agenda for change

One of the most obvious, but nevertheless striking, findings of SCF's research has been that, in many developing countries, institutionalisation continues to be the automatic and exclusive response by governments and other agencies towards children who are deemed unable to live with their families. Many of these countries are signatories to the UN Convention on the Rights of the Child, despite the Convention's clear admonition that the family is 'the natural environment for the growth and well-being of all its members and particularly children'.[244] Institutions fail to address the causes of deprivation and poverty; they deal only with the symptoms, but, in so doing, many unwittingly ensure that deprivation continues into the next generation by failing to equip young people to play their part in society as adults and as parents.

It is extremely difficult to estimate the numbers of children in institutional care, though the figure of 6–8 million worldwide given by Defence for Children International may be a conservative estimate.[245] What is clear is that, in relation to the total numbers of children living in circumstances such as extreme poverty or otherwise unsatisfactory living conditions, the numbers are small. Children in institutions do, however, represent some of the world's most disadvantaged children, and it is significant that, in some countries, government approaches to them typify and symbolise broader attitudes towards the more vulnerable sections of their societies.

With regards to future trends, some causes of orphanhood are declining (such as the loss of parents as a result of epidemics of infectious diseases other than HIV/AIDS), but others are on the increase. These include:

- rapid urbanisation, often associated with the erosion of the capacity of extended family and community systems to provide back-up care for children in difficult situations;

221

- forced migration through wars and famines, leading to the separation of children from their families, whether accidental or deliberate;
- changing conditions in the labour market – for example, more families with both parents working; increasing employment opportunities in the informal sector, with more children working and potentially living on the streets;
- increasing numbers of single-parent families (generally fatherless), and, in particular, an increase in teenage pregnancies;
- most significantly of all, increasing poverty in large parts of the developing world;
- finally, though many infectious diseases have declined, the dramatic impact of HIV/AIDS is increasing, not only causing the death of large numbers of parents, but also having a significant impact on those sections of the population who might otherwise be considered as alternative carers for orphans.

Economic and social changes such as these add weight to the urgent need for governments and NGOs to review their policies and approaches towards the care of separated children. Moreover, economic decline and the effects of structural adjustment policies in many countries are likely to mean a declining expenditure on social welfare provision, and underline further the need to promote affordable and cost-effective approaches.

What, then, are the principal conclusions to emerge from SCF's research? What changes need to be made by governments, NGOs and donors if the prospects for vulnerable children are to be significantly enhanced?

1   The need to begin with a clear assessment of the problem

- Most institutions resemble a medical prescription which has been made without a preceding diagnosis. Many organisations which provide institutional care seem to assume that the 'answer' to the problems of vulnerable children is residential care, but the 'question' is neither posed nor explored. SCF's research has revealed a significant number of organisations which are committed to providing institutional care, regardless of objectively assessed need. One of the worst offenders is a large international NGO which, in effect, exports an Austrian model of care regardless of its appropriateness to the circumstances and culture of the local situation, and, in some cases, regardless of the perception of the relevant government authorities concerning its need or relevance.

- At the level of the individual institution, *gatekeeping* is frequently lacking in respect of individual children who are referred for care. Very often, assessment and planning consist of nothing more than the decision to admit, or not admit. No consideration is given to gaining a full understanding of the child's needs, circumstances and personal resources, or to the potential range of options, which might, for example, include supporting the child with her own family, seeking a home within the extended family, or finding some means of placing the child with an unrelated family.

2   The need for government responsibility for vulnerable children

● Very often, the political will simply does not exist to move away from institutional responses, and this seems to be the case particularly in countries which have already achieved significant economic growth. Mozambique and Uganda, by way of contrast, stand out as two countries which have made a real and systematic attempt to influence the circumstances of children and families in the most difficult of circumstances. They have promoted non-institutional approaches despite huge resource constraints and the difficulties caused by many years of civil war.

● What is needed is a framework of law and social policy to facilitate the support of vulnerable families; to ensure that children are not unnecessarily separated from their families; to enable the development of non-institutional responses, and to restrict the activities of organisations whose practices are unsatisfactory. Those governments which have chosen to sign the UN Convention on the Rights of the Child have *a clear obligation* to take such action.

3   The need for systematic approaches to prevention

● Prevention *is* better than cure, or rather *care*. There is an urgent need for governments, donors and NGOs to consider carefully what steps can be taken to reach significant numbers of families facing extreme hardship in order to prevent the need for children to be separated into residential care. Part II of this book considered a wide range of different approaches to prevention, broadly categorised as 'developmental' or 'responsive'. Governments and NGOs which argue that they cannot afford to support the large numbers of children and families facing desperate situations need to be reminded that they certainly cannot afford either the material or the human costs of an institutional response, especially if the numbers of children requiring care increase rapidly.

● It has been suggested in this book that most children in institutional care can probably be supported in their own families, at much lower cost. No single approach can be prescribed: but a preventive strategy requires co-ordinated government and NGO action at many levels and in many areas – ranging from family planning to health care; from associations of the parents of children with disabilities to family centres; from mother-and-baby homes for single parents to vocational training for young offenders. Perhaps the most fundamental measures are:

1   to ensure that the food-security and other basic survival needs of families are adequately met;
2   to provide pre-school provision and primary education for children.

These are vital in supporting families, enriching the lives of children, and as a means of enabling the next generation of parents to provide a better future for their offspring.

4   The need for non-institutional forms of care

● Another central recommendation of SCF's research is the urgent need to explore non-institutional options for children who cannot be supported within their own families. Once again, no one solution is advocated. Rather, the aim should be to promote a pluralistic approach which seeks to experiment with and promote a range of substitute family placements. Governments and non-governmental agencies must help families and communities to accept responsibility for caring for children. Old taboos about the acceptability of caring for unrelated children must be challenged, and new thinking needs to be promoted. Part III concluded that the development of adoption and fostering presents both challenges and opportunities. The challenges consist particularly in recruiting adoptive and foster parents, and in carefully defining the objectives and intended duration of placements in order to provide children with a clear sense of identity and permanence. The promotion of substitute family care requires tenacity and persistence, a long-term investment of human and material resources, changes in legislation and policy, and the introduction of new practices. The rewards, however, will be reaped by children for whom the gift of a family is an infinitely better alternative to a childhood spent in an institution.

5   The need for new approaches to residential care

● SCF's research programme does not argue for rejecting the idea of residential care in principle. Rather, it advocates a move away from a residential care approach which does little more than meet the physical needs of children to one which responds to the whole range of children's needs. Particular emphasis needs to be placed on children's basic need to be loved and cared about, to feel a sense of belonging, and to develop a strong personal identity – in other words, a shift in emphasis from *roofs* to *roots*. Chapter 6 provided a framework for the development of residential care practice which is 'good-enough' to meet the full range of children's needs. It was argued that this does not necessarily require a large investment of material resources, but, rather, an understanding of the needs of 'the whole child', and significant changes in values and approaches.

6   The need to listen to children

● One of the reassuring findings of this study has been the remarkable resilience of children. It has been heartening to find some children who, rather than allowing themselves to be passive victims of unsatisfactory institutional care, have taken active steps to help to shape and change their experience. In some instances, children have managed to make institutions 'good-enough' by creating, within their peer-group structures, an atmosphere of affection, acceptance and solidarity which has gone some way to compensate for what otherwise would be a deeply depriving experience. But the resilience shown by some should never be an excuse for failing to provide vulnerable children with the best that society can offer them.

● Organisations concerned with child care need to find ways of empowering children and enabling them to articulate their needs and opinions. Children can be extraordinarily resourceful. Not only do they have a right to express their views:[246] when given responsibilities, children have demonstrated that, far from being merely the passive recipients of care, they can actively contribute to the process of developing and enhancing their environment.

7   The need to change the perceptions and priorities of donors

● One of the principal recommendations of this research is addressed to donors. Institutional responses are described by Swift as 'rescue programmes', which are often 'confused acts of power by individuals who wish to exercise benevolence in a social structure that is not benevolent'.[247] All too often, institutional responses are prescribed and supported without an understanding of the problem, and with no attempt to find more appropriate and cost-effective means of supporting vulnerable children, many of whom need never have been separated from their families. Donors need to be encouraged to look beyond the immediate and visible appeal of children's homes to consider whether more appropriate and more sustainable strategies for helping disadvantaged children and their families can be promoted.

Some of the most progressive policies, most enlightened institutions and most effective work in promoting community-based alternatives are found in some of the world's poorest countries. This is partly a consequence of 'making a virtue out of necessity', but it is clear that the main issue involved in developing more appropriate approaches is not the need for more resources, but rather a proper understanding of children's needs; a value orientation that sees children as subjects with rights, rather than as objects of charity; a real desire to listen to what they themselves have to say about their needs and aspirations, and the political will to translate those values and understandings into practical measures that will meet the needs of children and their families more effectively.

As Patrick Worth puts it, himself a former resident of an institution:

An institution is not a place. An institution is the way people think.[248]

Notes

1 UN Convention on the Rights of the Child, 1989, Article 3.
2 Defence for Children International (DCI), 1985, *Children in Institutions*, Geneva, DCI.
3 Winnicott D W, 1965, *The Maturational Process and the Facilitative Environment*, New York, International Universities Press.
4 Bowlby J, 1951, *Maternal Care and Mental Health*, Geneva, World Health Organisation.
5 Rutter M, 1981, *Maternal Deprivation Reassessed* (2nd edn), London, Penguin.
6 Erikson E, 1950, *Childhood and Society*, Harmondsworth, Penguin.
7 Erikson E, op. cit., pp. 239ff.
8 McGurk H, Caplan M, Hennessy E and Moss P, 1993, 'Controversy, Theory and Social Context in Contemporary Day Care Research', in *Fourth Annual Research Review of the Journal of Child Psychology and Psychiatry*, January.
9 Salter Ainsworth M D, Bell S M and Stayton D J, 1974, 'Infant–mother Attachment and Social Development: "Socialisation" as a Product of Reciprocal Responsiveness to Signals', in Richards M (ed.), *The Integration of a Child into a Social World*, London, Cambridge University Press.
10 LeVine R A, 1974, *Parental Goals: A Cross-Cultural View*, Bureau of Educational Research, University of Nairobi.
11 Erikson E, op. cit., p. 254.
12 Rutter M, op. cit.
13 See, for example, Ainsworth M D and Bell S M, 1969, 'Some Contemporary Patterns of Mother–infant Interaction in the Feeding Situation', in Ambrose A (ed.), *Stimulation in Early Infancy*, New York, Academic Press.
14 Robertson J and Robertson J, 1967 and 1968, *Young Children in Brief*

Separation – 1, Kate, 2, Jane and 3, John, Tavistock Child Development Research Unit.

15   See, for example, Robertson J and Bowlby J, 1952, 'Responses of Young Children to Separation from their Mothers', in *Courrier (Centre Internationale de l'Enfance),* Vol. 2, pp. 131–42.

16   Weisner T S and Gallimore R, 1977, 'My Brother's Keeper: Child and Sibling Caretaking', *Current Anthropology,* Vol. 18, No. 2, p. 176.

17   Bowlby J, 1946, *Forty-four Juvenile Thieves: Their characters and home-life,* London, Baillère, Tindall and Cox.

18   See, for example, Ainsworth M D, 1962, 'The Effects of Maternal Deprivation: A review of the findings and controversy in the context of research strategy', in *Deprivation of Maternal Care: A Reassessment of its Effects,* Geneva, World Health Organisation.

19   Bowlby J, 1979, *The Making and Breaking of Affectional Bonds,* London, Tavistock Publications, p. 125.

20   Werner E E, 1979, *Cross-Cultural Child Development: A View from Planet Earth,* California, Brooks/Cole, p. 247.

21   LeVine S and LeVine R, 1983, 'Child Abuse and Neglect in Sub-Saharan Africa', in Korbin J E (ed.), *Child Abuse and Neglect: Cross-Cultural Perspectives,* Berkeley and Los Angeles, University of California Press.

22   Rohner R, 1975, *They Love Me, They Love Me Not,* Yale, HRAF Press, pp. 166–8.

23   See, for example, Boswell J, 1988, *The Kindness of Strangers,* New York, Pantheon Books.

24   An example is Uganda – see Parry-Williams J, 1992, *Legal Reform and Children's Rights in Uganda – Some Critical Issues,* mimeograph, Kampala, SCF (UK), p. 4.

25   Charnley H, Mausse M and Sitoi M, 1993, *The Role of Substitute Families in Mozambique: A Case Study,* London, SCF.

26   Much of the information here was gained from SCF researchers' discussions with a group of former 'inmates' in Rio de Janeiro, but their picture of institutional life is also borne out by Altoé S, 1990, *Infâncias Perdidas* ('Lost Childhood'), Rio de Janeiro, Xenon. She also confirms that, in the seven FUNABEM institutions studied, the majority of children had both parents living.

27   Vietnamese Association of Social Workers, 1974, *A Study on the Conditions of Civilian War Orphans Living in Home Settings in Phu Yen Province,* Saigon, Research and Training Centre for Social Development.

28   See, for example, Chutikil S, Punpeng T, and Xuto N, 1987, *Children in Especially Difficult Situations (Thailand),* Bangkok, National Youth Bureau/The Office of the Prime Minister, p. 96.

29   Charnley H et al., op. cit.

30   Vietnamese Association of Social Workers, op. cit., p. 39.

31 Simms F A, 1986, *An Evaluation of Children's Institutions in the Kingdom of Lesotho, and Consideration of Alternatives*, Maseru, Government of Lesotho with UNICEF and SCF.

32 UN Convention on the Rights of the Child, 1989, Articles 3, 9, 13 and 19.

33 Espert S F, 1989, *An Institutional Opening and Humanisation*, Bogotá, UNICEF.

34 Wijetunge S, 1991, *A Study of Children's Homes to Investigate the Needs of Children in Institutional Settings*, Colombo, Redd Barna.

35 Ibid.

36 'Can I go home with you?', *Viva*, July 1975, Nairobi.

37 Freire F (ed.), 1991, *Abandano e Adoção* ('Abandonment and Adoption'), Curitiba, Terre des Hommes.

38 Rizzini I, 1985, 'A Internação de Crianças em Estabelecimentos de Menores: Alternativa ou Incentivo ao Abanandono?' ('The Placement of Children in Children's Homes: Alternative or Incentive to Abandonment?'), in Rizzini I (ed.), *O Menor em Debate*, Rio de Janeiro, University of Santa Ursula.

39 Simms F A, op. cit., pp. 35–8.

40 Tolfree D, 1994, *Residential Centre for Unaccompanied Refugee Children in Mogadishu: A Case Study*, London, SCF.

41 Ponnappa S, 1989, *Development Experiences of Guild*, New Delhi, Foster Parents Plan International.

42 Altoé S, op. cit.

43 Rizzini I, 1984, 'Instituições Para Menores: A Quem Serve?' ('Institutions for Children: Whom do they Serve?'), *ESPAÇO Cadernos de Cultura, Informe Científico*, No. 10, December.

44 Ibid., translation from p. 122.

45 Simms F A, op. cit., pp. 121ff, offers an interesting cost analysis of institutional care with community-based care and rehabilitation.

46 Simms F A, op. cit., pp. 47–8.

47 Dammann P, 1992, 'Glasnost's Children', *The Guardian*, 6 March.

48 See Kelly M, 1994, *Over-run by Aid: A Case Study of Western Interventions in the Institutions of Romania*, London, SCF.

49 DCI, 1985, op. cit., claim that 'children are incarcerated with adults, to some degree and under varying conditions, in virtually all countries, regardless of the latter's political, socio-economic or other characteristics'.

50 Personal communication to SCF researcher.

51 'The Dark Side of Masaka Cult Revealed', *The New Vision*, 23 October 1991; a most extreme example comes from Uganda, where the government had to close an extremely unsatisfactory institution run by an extreme sect. About 140 children were living in appalling physical conditions, and were receiving no formal education. Many of the

children were alleged to have been illegally abducted or enticed into the home. The article gives a detailed account of the home and the operation to close it.

52 DCI, op. cit., p. 9.

53 Parsons T, 1960, *Structure and Process in Modern Societies*, Glencoe, Ill., Free Press, p. 56.

54 The term 'institution' here is used to describe a particular type of organisation – a residential home – and not in the formal sense of sets of social and cultural norms and roles.

55 Etzioni A, 1964, *Modern Organisations*, Englewood Cliffs, NJ, Prentice-Hall.

56 The government strategy for promoting non-institutional forms of care is discussed in more detail in Parry-Williams J, 1993, *Legal Reform in Uganda as Part of a Strategy for Promoting Community-Based Care: A Case Study*, London, SCF.

57 Wooden K, 1976, *Weeping in the Playtime of Others: America's Incarcerated Children*, New York, McGraw-Hill, p. 70.

58 Rowe J and Lambert L, 1973, *Children Who Wait*, London, Association of British Adoption Agencies.

59 Ponnappa S, op. cit., gives further information on the interesting history of this enlightened children's home.

60 Quoted in Luppi C A, 1987, *Malditos Frutos do Nosse Ventre* ('Cursed Fruits of Our Womb'), São Paulo, Icone Editora.

61 UN Convention on the Rights of the Child, 1989, Article 9.

62 Millham S, Bullock R, Hosie K and Haak M, 1986, *Lost in Care: the Problems of Maintaining Links between Children in Care and their Families*, Aldershot, Gower.

63 Simms F A, op. cit., pp. 31 and 48.

64 Personal communication to SCF researcher in Lesotho.

65 Wijetunge S, op. cit., p. 156.

66 Espert S F, op. cit., p. 57.

67 Rizzini I, 1985, op. cit.

68 Personal communication to SCF researcher.

69 Ponnappa S, op. cit., p. 40.

70 Pinchbeck I and Hewitt M, 1969, *Children in English Society*, London, Routledge and Kegan Paul.

71 Personal experience of the author.

72 Goffman E, 1961, *Asylums: Essays on the Social Situation of Mental Patients and Other Inmates*, Harmondsworth, Anchor Books.

73 See Miller E J and Gwynne G V, 1972, *A Life Apart: A Pilot Study of Residential Institutions for the Physically Handicapped and the Young Chronic Sick*, London, Tavistock Publications.

74 See, for example, their article entitled 'The Institution as an

Environment for Development', in Richards M (ed.), 1974, *The Integration of a Child into a Social World*, London, Cambridge University Press.

75 Ibid.

76 Tolfree D, 1994, *Residential Centre for Unaccompanied Refugee Children in Mogadishu: A Case Study*, London, SCF.

77 Naidu U S, 1986, *Causes of Deprivation of Family Care of Institutionalized Children*, Bombay, TATA Institute of Social Sciences.

78 Quoted from a report on residential homes in an East African country.

79 Quoted in Espert S F, op. cit., pp. 53 and 35–6.

80 Personal observation by SCF researcher, South-East Asia.

81 Tolfree D, 1994, *A Babies' Home in Africa: A Case Study*, London, SCF.

82 This statement of philosophy relates to the Seva Samajam Boys' Home, and is set out in Ponnappa S, op. cit., p. 40.

83 King R D, Raynes N V and Tizard J, 1971, *Patterns of Residential Care: Sociological Studies in Institutions for Handicapped Children*, London, Routledge and Kegan Paul.

84 Tizard J, Sinclair I and Clarke R V G (eds), 1975, 'Quality of Residential Care for Retarded Children', in *Varieties of Residential Experience*, London, Routledge and Kegan Paul.

85 Tizard B, Cooperman O, Joseph A and Tizard J, 1972, 'Environmental Effects on Language Development: A Study of Young Children in Long-stay Residential Nurseries', *Child Development*, Vol. 43, pp. 337–58.

86 Tizard B, 'Varieties of Residential Nursery Experience', in Tizard J, Sinclair I and Clarke R V G (eds), op. cit., p. 117.

87 This is taken from Tolfree D, 1994, *A Babies' Home in Africa: A Case Study*, London, SCF.

88 Erikson E, op. cit.

89 Newson J and Newson E, 1976, *Seven Years Old in the Home Environment*, London, Allen and Unwin.

90 See, for example, UNICEF, 1991, *Children in Institutions in Central and Eastern Europe*, Innocenti Essay No. 3, Florence, UNICEF.

91 Personal observation by SCF researcher.

92 Wooden K, op. cit., pp. 108 ff.

93 UN Convention on the Rights of the Child, 1989, Article 31.

94 Extract from observation notes arising from a visit to a government remand home in East Africa.

95 Goffman E, op. cit.

96 Personal communication to SCF researcher.

97 LeVine R A, op. cit.

98 An example is given on page 69.

99 Wolins M (ed.), 1974, *Successful Group Care: Explorations in the Powerful*

Environment, Chicago, Aldine Publishing.

100 Bronfenbrenner U, 1974, 'Reaction to Social Pressure from Adults Versus Peers among Soviet Day School and Boarding School Pupils in the Perspective of an American Sample', in Wolins M, op. cit.

101 Tolfree D, 1994, *Residential Centre for Unaccompanied Refugee Children in Mogadishu: A Case Study*, London, SCF.

102 Polsky H W, 1962, *Cottage Six: The Social System of Delinquent Boys in Residential Treatment*, New York, Russell Sage.

103 Millham S, Bullock R and Cherrett P, 1975, *After Grace – Teeth*, London, Human Context Books.

104 Wongchai Y et al., 1992, *Final Report on Achievement Factors for Life Adjustment Skills of Children: A Comparative Study of Ex-residents of the DPW Institutional Child Care and Children in Families*, Bangkok, SCF.

105 From a focus group discussion conducted by SCF researcher.

106 Simms F A, op. cit., p. 48.

107 Personal experience by SCF researcher during visit to Lesotho.

108 Ponnappa S, op. cit.

109 Personal communication to SCF researcher.

110 Wongchai Y et al., op. cit.

111 UN Convention on the Rights of the Child, 1989, Article 19.

112 DCI, op. cit.; quotations are from pp. 29 and 11.

113 The G Allan Roeher Institute, 1989, *Vulnerable: Sexual Abuse and People with an Intellectual Handicap*, Ontario, G Allan Roeher Institute, p. 11.

114 Quoted from confidential SCF file material.

115 Muhumuza J, 1993, *Resettling Children from Institutions with Family and Relatives*, Kampala, SCF and Government of Uganda.

116 Winnicott D W, op. cit.

117 UN Convention on the Rights of the Child, 1989, Article 9.

118 UN Convention on the Rights of the Child, 1989, Article 12.

119 UN Convention on the Rights of the Child, 1989, Article 3.

120 For an interesting comparative analysis of the costs of residential care and various forms of community-based support to children and families, see Simms F A, op. cit., pp. 121ff.

121 See, for example, Tutt N, 1974, *Care or Custody: Community Homes and the Treatment of Delinquency*, London, Darton, Longman and Todd; although now dated, this book offers a useful summary of the reasons why residential treatment is largely ineffective.

122 Berridge D, 1985, *Children's Homes*, Oxford, Basil Blackwell.

123 Tolfree D, 1994, *Common Room and Transit Home for Street Children in Nepal: A Case Study*, London, SCF.

124 Rogers E and Floyd Shoemaker F, 1971, *Communication of Innovations: A Cross-Cultural Approach* (2nd edn), New York, The Free Press.

125 Smale G G, 1993, *Managing Change through Innovation*, London,

National Institute for Social Work, p. 27 (pre-publication draft).

126 Potter W, 1994, *Training Strategies for Residential Child Care: A Comparative Case Study*, London, SCF, p. 26.

127 Potter W, op. cit.

128 Rogers E and Floyd Shoemaker F, op. cit., p. 110.

129 Part of this is derived from Parry-Williams J, 1993, written up as a case study under the title *Legal Reform in Uganda as Part of a Strategy for Promoting Community-Based Care: A Case Study*, London, SCF.

130 Potter W, op. cit.; this programme is one of the training strategies reviewed by Potter in his *Comparative Case Study*.

131 Gälldin Åberg B, 1992, *Process of Change: Altering the Practice of Care in a Children's Home in the Middle East*, Stockholm, Rädda Barnen.

132 Rogers E and Floyd Shoemaker F, op. cit.

133 Smale G G, op. cit.

134 Potter W, op. cit.

135 Beckhard R and Pritchard W, 1992, *Changing the Essence: The Art of Creating and Leading Fundamental Change in Organisations*, San Francisco, Jossey-Bass.

136 Potter W, op. cit.

137 Tolfree D, 1994, *A Babies' Home in Africa: A Case Study*, London, SCF.

138 In accordance with the UN Convention on the Rights of the Child, 1989, Article 12.

139 Kelly M, 1994, op. cit.

140 Quoted in Smale G G, op. cit.

141 Smale G G, op. cit., p. 14.

142 From the Preamble to the UN Convention on the Rights of the Child, 1989.

143 Heywood J, 1965, *Children in Care* (2nd edn), London, Routledge and Kegan Paul, and Holman B, 1988, *Putting Families First*, Basingstoke, Macmillan.

144 Quoted from Heywood J, op. cit., p. 53.

145 See Holman B, 1988, *Putting Families First*, Basingstoke, Macmillan.

146 Beveridge J, 1954, *Beveridge and His Plan*, London, Hodder and Stoughton, p. 106.

147 Children Act of 1989, Section 17.

148 Holman B, op. cit.

149 See discussion in Chapter 3.

150 This distinction is suggested in Holman B, op. cit., pp. 119–20.

151 Dunn L L, 1993, *Parenting Education in Jamaica: A Case Study*, London, SCF.

152 The benefits of pre-school programmes in the West have long been acknowledged. For example, in a large-scale study in the UK of the effectiveness of pre-school provision, it was found that children who

had attended playgroups or nursery schools showed enhanced achievement at ages 5 and 10, and that socially disadvantaged children benefited more than those from more privileged backgrounds – see Osborn A F and Milbank J E, 1987, *The Effects of Early Education*, Oxford, Clarendon Press. The importance of promoting early childhood care and development in the Third World is cogently argued in Myers R, 1992, *The Twelve who Survive*, London and New York, Routledge.

153   Rizzini I et al., 1984, op. cit.

154   Montagu J (ed.), 1992, *Children at Crisis Point*, pp. 106ff, London, SCF, gives a brief description of one such programme.

155   *Social Welfare into the 1990s and Beyond*, 1991, White Paper, Government of Hong Kong.

156   Taylor M, 1994, *A Family Resource Centre in Hong Kong: A Case Study*, London, SCF.

157   Holman B, op. cit., p. 219.

158   Dunn A, Hunter S, Nabongo C and Ssekiwanuka J, 1991, *Enumeration and Needs Assessment of Orphans in Uganda*, Kampala, SCF.

159   Kasule S, Kaboggaza J and Roys C, 1994, *The Child Social Care Project, Rakai: A Case Study*, London, SCF.

160   Simão J and Charnley H, 1994, *Non-Institutional Care in Inhambane Province, Mozambique: A Case Study*, London, SCF.

161   This programme was discussed in some detail in Chapter 7 (Case Example 2).

162   Peace G and Hulme D, 1993, *Children and Income Generating Programmes*, Working Paper No. 6, London, SCF, p. 7.

163   Boothby N, 1993, 'Reuniting Unaccompanied Children and Families in Mozambique: An Effort to Link Networks of Community Volunteers to a National Programme', *Journal of Social Development in Africa*, Vol. 8, No. 2.

164   For a critique of child sponsorships, see 'Letters to a God', and 'Why you should not Sponsor a Child', *New Internationalist*, No. 194, April 1989.

165   A summary of some of these research findings can be found in an unpublished report by Associate Prof. Vasikasin W et al., 1991, entitled 'Progress Report of "A Study of Models and Practices to Decrease Mothers in Abandoning their Babies" Project'.

166   Tharincharoen S, 1993, *The Ban Sai Samphan Shelter for Single Mothers and Babies: A Case Study*, London, SCF.

167   For a fuller discussion of the problems and needs of street children, see Ennew J, 1994, *A Guide to Programmes with Street and Working Children*, SCF Development Manual No. 4.

168   See, for example, Bond T W, 1992, *Street Children in Ho Chi Minh City*, Ho Chi Minh City, Terre des Hommes.

169   Bond T W, op. cit., is again a good example.

170   Personal communication to SCF researcher.

171   For a full description of this programme, see Tolfree D, 1994, *Common Room and Transit Home for Street Children in Nepal: A Case Study*, London, SCF.

172   Chandy N, 1988, 'Assistance Offered to Children in their Home Countries: Perspectives on Child Care in India', in *Support of Children in Need and Intercountry Adoption*, Frankfurt, International Social Service.

173   Bonnerjea L, 1994, *Family Tracing: A Good Practice Guide*, London, SCF.

174   Interview with a child in Uganda during SCF's research.

175   See, for example, Tolfree D, 1991, *Refugee Children in Malawi*, London, International Save the Children Alliance.

176   Quoted in Bonnerjea L, op. cit., p. 42.

177   See, for example, Richman N, 1993, *Communicating with Children: Helping Children in Distress*, SCF Development Manual No. 2; Bonnerjea L, op. cit.; Ressler E M, Boothby N and Steinbock D J, 1988, *Unaccompanied Children: Care and Protection in Wars, Natural Disasters, and Refugee Movements*, New York and Oxford, Oxford University Press. UNHCR, 1985, *Guidelines on Interviewing Minors*, Geneva, United Nations High Commission for Refugees; and Ennew J, op. cit.

178   See Tolfree D, 1994, *Common Room and Transit Home for Street Children in Nepal: A Case Study*, London, SCF.

179   SCF (UK), 1994, *Study into Reasons for Admissions into Residential Care*, Colombo, SCF (pre-publication draft).

180   Peace G and Hulme D, op. cit., pp. 22ff.

181   Langa J, 1994, *The History of the Policy of Non-institutionalisation in Mozambique*, London, SCF.

182   From the Preamble to the UN Convention on the Rights of the Child, 1989.

183   See Langa J, op. cit., p. 11.

184   Parry-Williams J, 1993, op. cit.

185   Parker R A (ed.), 1980, *Caring for Separated Children*, London, Macmillan.

186   Damania D, 1989, 'Observations on the Child Welfare Scene in India', *Child Welfare*, Vol. 68, No. 2, March/April, p. 144.

187   From the Preamble to the UN Convention on the Rights of the Child, 1989.

188   Berridge D and Cleaver H, 1987, *Foster Home Breakdown*, Oxford, Blackwell.

189   Goody E, 1982, *Parenthood and Social Reproduction – Fostering and Occupational Roles in West Africa*, London, Cambridge University Press.

190   Fawzi A/Mageed, 1988, *Adoption of Children – With special reference to the procedure of refugee child adoption in Sudan*, University of Juba.

191   See Johnson K, 1993, 'Chinese Orphanages: Saving China's Abandoned Girls', *Australian Journal of Chinese Affairs*, No. 30, July.

192   See Byung Hoon Chun, 1988, 'Difficulties and Prospects in Increasing the Rate of In-country Adoptions in Korea', in *Support of Children in Need and Intercountry Adoption*, Frankfurt, International Social Service.

193   Wu, David Y H, 1981, 'Child Abuse in Taiwan', in Korbin J E (ed.), *Child Abuse and Neglect: Cross-cultural Perspectives*, Berkeley and Los Angeles, University of California Press.

194   Rin H, Caudhill W and Lin T Y (eds), 1969, 'Sibling Rank, Culture and Mental Disorders', in *Mental Health Research in Asia and the Pacific*, Honolulu, East–West Center Press.

195   Boswell J, 1988, op. cit.

196   Bharat S, 1993, *The Development of Adoption in India: A Case Study*, London, SCF.

197   Quoted in Sprung Miller B, 1980, 'The Child without a Family of His Own: A Review of Currently Recorded Activities and Programmes for Children with Special Needs', in UN Department of International Economic and Social Affairs, *Adoption and Foster Placement of Children: Report of an Expert Group Meeting on Adoption and Foster Placement of Children, Geneva, 11–15 December 1978*, New York, UN.

198   Quoted in Sprung Miller B, op. cit., p. 32.

199   Quoted in Tuhaise C, 1993, paper on *Child Fostering in Uganda: A Solution or an Additional Problem? Lessons for Developing Countries*, presented at the 8th International Foster Care Conference, Dublin.

200   See Johnson O R, 1981, 'The Socioeconomic Context of Child Abuse and Neglect in Native South America', in Korbin J E (ed.), op. cit.

201   Balanon L G, 1989, 'Foreign Adoption in the Philippines: Issues and Opportunities', *Child Welfare*, Vol. 68, No. 2, March/April.

202   Sura XXXIII, verse 5, which requires believers to 'call them by the names of their fathers ... But if you know not their father's name, call them your brothers in faith, or your Maulas.'

203   Uganda Foster Care and Adoption Association, 1991, *A Comprehensive Report on Visits to Child Care Institutions and Foster Families with the Aim of Studying the Practice of Fostering in Uganda*, Kampala, UFCAA, p. 18.

204   Loosely translated from Luppi C A, op. cit.

205   A notable exception is to be found in the work of an interdisciplinary team in Porto Alegre, which arranges both inter-country adoption and domestic adoption placements, and is documented in 'Intercountry Adoption of Brazilian Children – A Report of the Work of an Interdisciplinary Team in Porto Alegre, Brazil', in *Support of Children in Need of Intercountry Adoption*, Frankfurt, International Social Service, 1988.

206   Quoted in Hoksbergen RAC (ed.), 1986, *Adoption in Worldwide Perspective*, Lisse, Swets and Zeitlinger.

207 Luppi C A, op. cit.
208 Quoted from *Child Survival and Child Development in Africa*, 1991, paper given at the seminar, 'Child Development in Africa: Building on People's Strengths', held in Maseru, Lesotho, 25–30 November, organised by the Bernard van Leer Foundation in co-operation with the Ministry of Education, Lesotho, p. 5.
209 Bharat S, op. cit.
210 See Goody E, op. cit.
211 Quok C-S, 1993, *The Development of Fostering in Hong Kong: A Case Study*, London, SCF.
212 'No Success without Struggle: Social Mobility and Hardship for Foster Children in Sierra Leone', 1990, *Man* (new series), Vol. 25, pp. 70–88.
213 See Bledsoe C H, Ewbank D C and Isiugo-Ananihe U C, 1988, 'The Effect of Child Fostering on Feeding Practices and Access to Health Services in Rural Sierra Leone', Vol. 27, *Social Science and Medicine*, No. 6, pp. 627–38.
214 Goody E, 1982, *Parenthood and Social Reproduction – Fostering and Occupational Roles in West Africa*, London, Cambridge University Press.
215 Bledsoe C H et al., op. cit.
216 See Bledsoe, C H et al., op. cit.
217 Charnley H, Mausse M and Sitoi M, 1993, *The Role of Substitute Families in Mozambique: A Case Study*, London, SCF.
218 Ibid., p. 12.
219 Ibid., p. 16.
220 Ibid., p. 17.
221 Ibid.
222 Jareg E, undated, *The Community Based Foster Home: A Model*, Oslo, Redd Barna.
223 It is interesting that some of the early developments of fostering in countries such as the USA at the beginning of the twentieth century also had this 'overflow' function – see Trotzkey E L, 'Institutional Care and Placing-out', in Wolins M (ed.), op. cit.
224 Quok, C-S, op. cit.
225 Rean McFadden E, of East Michigan University, has given figures, derived from the USA, of maltreatment by foster parents compared with natural parents: the incidence of maltreatment by foster parents was given as 8 per thousand, compared with 3 per thousand for natural parents. These alarming statistics do, however, have to be set against the background of many foster children being at higher risk of being abused because of their previous experiences: unpublished paper, 'The Vulnerable Child in Foster Care', presented at the Annual International Foster Care Conference in Michigan, USA, 1989.
226 Korbin J E (ed.), op. cit.

227   See, for example, the Dartington study of a cohort of 450 children in care, which found that, in a group of children who had remained in care for at least two years, no less that 40 per cent had witnessed a breakdown of a placement: Millham S, Bullock R, Hosie K and Haak M, 1986, *Lost in Care*, Aldershot, Gower. For a useful summary of the research evidence on foster home breakdown, see Berridge D and Cleaver H, 1987, *Foster Home Breakdown*, Oxford, Blackwell.

228   A useful discussion of the interdependence of residential care and fostering can be found in Berridge D, 1985, *Children's Homes*, Oxford, Blackwell.

229   See Graves R, 1960, (Rev. edn), *The Greek Myths*, Vol. 2, Harmondsworth, Penguin.

230   Hoksbergen RAC et al., 1987, *Adopted Children at Home and At School*, Lisse, Swets and Zeitlinger.

231   UN Convention on the Rights of the Child, 1989, Article 21.

232   Van Loon J H A, 1990, *Report on Intercountry Adoption*, The Hague, Permanent Bureau of the Conference.

233   Bagley C and Young L, 'The Long-term Adjustment and Identity of a Sample of Inter-country Adopted Children', *International Journal of Social Work*, No. 4, pp. 16–22.

234   Thoburn J and Charles M, 1992, 'A Review of Research which is Relevant to Inter-country Adoption', in *Inter-departmental Review of Adoption Law: Background Paper No. 3, Inter-country Adoption*, London, Department of Health, Welsh Office and Scottish Office, p. 13.

235   Ibid.

236   For a fuller discussion of the issues of cultural adjustment, see Tolfree D, 1978, 'Problems of Inter-country Adoption', *Social Work Today*, Vol. 10, No. 13, 21 November.

237   This is now the stated policy of a number of governments, for example, those of Thailand and Hong Kong.

238   'Transracial Adoption in Norway', *Adoption and Fostering*, Vol. 11, No. 4, 1987, pp. 41–6.

239   'Inter-Country Adoption: A Brief Overview of the Research Evidence', *Adoption and Fostering*, Vol. 15, No. 4, 1991, p. 51.

240   Kirk D H, 1964, *Shared Fate: A Theory of Adoption and Mental Health*, New York, Free Press of Glencoe.

241   See, for example, DCI, 1989, *Protecting Children's Rights in International Adoption*, Geneva, DCI.

242   Fawzi A/Mageed, op. cit.

243   UN Convention on the Rights of the Child, 1989, Article 22(e).

244   From the Preamble to the UN Convention on the Rights of the Child, 1989.

245   DCI, 1985, op. cit.

246 UN Convention on the Rights of the Child, 1989, Article 12.
247 Swift A, 1989, 'Victims of Rescue', *New Internationalist*, No. 194, April, p. 14.
248 Worth P, 1989, 'My Life Story: From Oppression to Advocacy', *Archtype*, December.

Case studies commissioned by SCF

These case studies have been prepared as part of SCF's research, and published by SCF (UK), Overseas Information and Research, 17 Grove Lane, London SE5 8RD.

1 *The Development of Adoption in India* (1993) by Shalini Bharat
2 *The Role of Substitute Families in Mozambique* (1993) by Helen Charnley, Miguel Mausse and Monica Sitoi
3 *Parenting Education in Jamaica* (1993) by Leith L Dunn
4 *The Child Social Care Project, Rakai* (1994) by Sam Kasule and James Kaboggaza with Chris Roys
5 *The History of the Policy of Non-Institutionalisation in Mozambique* (1993) by Josefa Langa
6 *Legal Reform in Uganda as Part of a Strategy for Promoting Community-Based Care* (1993) by John Parry-Williams
7 *Training Strategies for Residential Child Care: A Comparative Case Study* (1994) by William Potter
8 *The Development of Fostering in Hong Kong* (1993) by Quok Chi-Sum
9 *Non-Institutional Care in Inhambane Province, Mozambique* (1994) by Joana Simão and Helen Charnley
10 *A Family Resource Centre in Hong Kong* (1994) by Marrolin Taylor
11 *The Ban Sai Samphan Shelter for Single Mothers and their Babies* (1993) by Supaporn Tharincharoen
12 *Common Room and Transit Home for Street Children in Nepal* (1994) by David Tolfree
13 *A Babies' Home in Africa* (1994) by David Tolfree
14 *Residential Centre for Unaccompanied Refugee Children in Mogadishu* (1994) by David Tolfree

Index

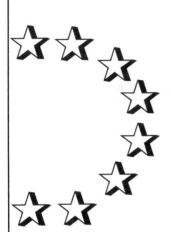

The Art and Science of Child Care

Research, policy and practice
in the European Union

edited by
MATTHEW COLTON,
WALTER HELLINCKX,
POL GHESQUIÈRE &
MARGARET WILLIAMS

This is the first volume in an international series on child care designed
to explore the field of child care from a wide variety of national and
professional perspectives. The book focuses on the existing gaps
between research, policy and practice, describing why the gaps exist
and what can be done - and already has been done - to close them.
Nineteen experienced authors from six European countries have
pooled their talents to bring to the reader a selection of important
advances in research and practice, with a focus upon the application
of these advances to policy. The underlying theme in every chapter is
integration between the human creativity which we call "art" and the
logical, expanding cycle of observation, inference and verification
which is the heart of science. The plan of the book takes us from the
general to the particular, beginning with a discussion of childhood
itself and moving on through an exploration of the ways in which
research, policy and practice might be linked to specific studies in
which they have been linked.

1995   288 pages   1 85742 285 6   £32.50
Price subject to change without notification

arena

Contested Adoptions

Research, law, policy and practice

Edited by
Murray Ryburn

This is the first book to consider the law and research and its
application in relation to contested adoption proceedings.. It examines
issues of policy and practice including such matters as attachment,
separation and assessment, and the role of the guardian ad litem. It
locates contested adoptions within the wider framework of the Children
Act 1989 and, perhaps most importantly, it includes contribution from
those with personal experience of contested adoptions. It is a book
which will be invaluable to all those who work in the adoption field,
including social work practitioners, guardians ad litem, and barristers
and solicitors practising family law, as well as social work students and
teachers on DipSW courses.

Murray Ryburn is Director of Social Work Courses at the University
of Birmingham.

1994   232 pages   Hbk   1 85742 187 6   £32.00
Pbk   1 85742 188 4   £16.95

Price subject to change without notification

WORKING TOGETHER IN

Child Protection

An exploration of the multi-disciplinary task and system

MICHAEL MURPHY

This book is a resource for all practitioners, students, managers and trainers who work in the child protection field. It explores the detailed working arrangements of one child protection system and examines the roles and perspectives of the agencies and practitioners who make up that system. It uses examples that are drawn from current practice to outline crucial arguments in the text. It suggests that multi-disciplinary child protection work is both complex and difficult, claiming that a series of structural blockages exist to effective joint working, in particular that we all harbour an ignorance of the perspective and reality of the other agencies and practitioners within the system.

The work goes on to propose a number of measures to be taken by practitioner, agency and government departments that will promote multi-disciplinary working at all levels, suggesting that good multi-disciplinary communication, co-operation and action is synonymous with good child protection work.

The child protection system in England and Wales is used as a case study, but comparisons are drawn with child protection systems in other parts of the world. It is argued that the key concepts and conventions of effective multi-disciplinary child protection work are constant and go beyond the boundaries of single systems.

Michael Murphy is co-ordinator on a Multi-disciplinary Child Protection Resource project.

1995   224 pages   Hbk   1 85742 197 3   £35.00
Pbk   1 85742 198 1   £14.95

Price subject to change without notification

arena

Child Care in the EC

A country-specific guide to foster and residential care

edited by M J COLTON & W HELLINCKX

"This book will be a valuable resource on our small European library shelf."
Community Care

Despite the current uncertainty about the future development of the European Community (EC), there is increasing recognition among child welfare administrators, researchers, practitioners and students across the EC that much can be learned from the policies and practices of other member states.

This book offers a systematic description of residential and foster care in each of the constituent countries of the EC. In addition, a concise account of the research on residential and foster care undertaken in each country is presented. The book is, therefore, unique in that it represents the first coherent account of policy, practice and research in the field of residential and foster care in all the countries of the EC.

M J Colton is Lecturer in Applied Social Studies, University College of Swansea, and is a member of the Executive Committee of the European Scientific Association on Residential and Foster Care for Children and Adolescents (EUSARF). **W Hellinckx** is Professor at the Section of Orthopedagogics, Faculty of Psychology and Educational Sciences, University of Leuven, Belgium, and is President of EUSARF.

1993   272 pages
Hbk   1 85742 178 7   £32.50   Pbk   1 85742 179 5   £14.95

Price subject to change without notification

Advocacy
Skills

A HANDBOOK FOR
HUMAN SERVICE PROFESSIONALS

Neil Bateman

Advocacy is a skill used by many people in human service organisations. Social workers, community medical staff and advice workers are a few who will use such skills. Advocacy is used to overcome obstacles and to secure tangible results for customers – extra money, better services and housing. Neil Bateman's book sets out a model for effective professional practice, and outlines a number of approaches to advocacy.

This is a seminal work; no other book has been published in the UK which explains how advocacy skills can be used and developed. Advocacy is becoming part of the everyday work of many people. Advocacy Skills will be a valuable handbook for anyone concerned with the rights of others.

Neil Bateman is currently a Principal Officer with Suffolk County Council, an adviser to the Association of County Councils and a visiting lecturer at the University of East Anglia.

1995   **176 pages**   **1 85742 200 7**   **£14.95**

Price subject to change without notification

arena

GROUPWORK

3rd Edition
Allan Brown

"If required to recommend just one book on working with groups, this would always be the choice" **Community Care**

"Allan Brown's book has made its mark by its overall balanced view, its accessible style, and, let us spell it out: at a price that front line low paid workers can afford. It offers up-to-date groupwork knowledge relevant to the harsh reality of front line practice. Third time round; it does it again with increased breadth." **British Journal of Social Work**

This highly successful book on groupwork practice, first published in 1979, has become a standard introductory text on most social work training courses. It is very popular with social workers, whatever their agency setting, and is also used by health visitors, youth workers and the voluntary sector.

This enlarged and revised third edition includes two new additional chapters. The first of these addresses the issue of groupwork in day and residential centres where special kinds of group skills are required in addition to those already well established for fieldwork groups. The second new chapter attempts to understand the significance of race and gender in groupwork and to begin to develop a framework for anti-discriminatory practice.

Allan Brown is Senior Lecturer in Social Work at Bristol University.

1992   239 pages   1 85742 087 X   £8.99

Price subject to change without notification

Assessing Needs AND Planning Care IN Social Work

Brian Taylor and Toni Devine

"...written clearly, is free of jargon and contains a wealth of information and thoughtful discussion. The theoretical content is skillfully related to examples of practice and I felt I was being gently lead through concepts which were sometimes complex and profound." **June Neill, Researcher, National Institute for Social Work**

"The authors have achieved a consolidation of current social work theory and practice concisely." **Community Care**

The focus of this book is on the development of the skills required at each stage of the social work process: assessment, care planning, implementation and evaluation. Throughout the book a balance is maintained between the focus on client involvement, and the role of the social worker in an agency. The latter part of the book addresses practical issues in developing new approaches to assessment and care planning: primary workers, individual support and managing change.

Brian J. Taylor, Assistant Principal Social Worker (Training), Northern Health and Social Services Board, Northern Ireland, and **Toni Devine**, formerly Lecturer in Social Care, North West Institute of Further and Higher Education, Londonderry.

1993   144 pages

Pbk   1 85742 144 2   £12.95   Hbk   1 85742 139 6   £28.00

Price subject to change without notification

arena

LIVING WITH DRUGS

THIRD EDITION

MICHAEL GOSSOP

"Living with Drugs *is perhaps the best book currently available on the subject"* **TIMES LITERARY SUPPLEMENT**

"Dr Michael Gossop is in a good position to discuss the problem, working on the Drug Dependence Clinical Research and Treatment Unit at Maudsley Hospital in London. His book Living with Drugs *gives an historical perspective of drug taking, and discusses the common drugs in use today from tea, coffee, alcohol and tobacco through cannabis and LSD to 'hard' drugs like heroin. He develops his theme that the total effect of drug taking is an interaction between the drug and the personality and expectations of the user. He develops his theme that the total effect of drug taking is an interaction between the drug and the personality and expectations of the user. He also attempts to give a more accurate picture of drug addiction ... and outlines ways in which the control of drugs may actually promote the effects they seek to prevent ... It is an enjoyable book, well written, richly illustrated from published reports and official documents, easy to read, and giving a balanced perspective."* **BRITISH MEDICAL JOURNAL**

"Dr Gossop's avowed intention is to correct the most common misconceptions about drugs and drug taking. In particular, he sets out to get rid of medical tunnel vision and replace it with a broader psychological and social perspective. He achieves this effortlessly and very successfully ... Dr Gossop presents his views clearly and unambiguously with a wealth of anecdotal and scientific information on every page."
BRITISH JOURNAL OF ADDICTION

1993   224 pages   1 85742 121 3   £9.99

Price subject to change without notification

arena